SELECTED PAPERS FROM THE FIFTH WORLD CONGRESS OF
CENTRAL AND EAST EUROPEAN STUDIES, WARSAW, 1995

Edited for the International Council for Central and East European
Studies by Ronald J. Hill, Professor of Comparative Government, Trinity
College, University of Dublin, Ireland

Titles in the series include:

Sue Bridger (*editor*)
WOMEN AND POLITICAL CHANGE
Perspectives from East-Central Europe

John Dunn (*editor*)
LANGUAGE AND SOCIETY IN POST-COMMUNIST EUROPE

William E. Ferry and Roger E. Kanet (*editors*)
POST-COMMUNIST STATES IN THE WORLD COMMUNITY

Graeme Gill (*editor*)
ELITES AND LEADERSHIP IN RUSSIAN POLITICS

Paul G. Hare (*editor*)
SYSTEMIC CHANGE IN POST-COMMUNIST ECONOMIES

Mark S. Johnson (*editor*)
EDUCATION IN TRANSITION

Anthony Kemp-Welch (*editor*)
STALINISM IN POLAND, 1944–56

Stanislav J. Kirschbaum (*editor*)
HISTORICAL REFLECTIONS ON CENTRAL EUROPE

Carol S. Leonard (*editor*)
THE MICROECONOMICS OF POST-COMMUNIST CHANGE

Kevin McDermott and John Morison (*editors*)
POLITICS AND SOCIETY UNDER THE BOLSHEVIKS

John Morison (*editor*)
ETHNIC AND NATIONAL ISSUES IN RUSSIAN AND EAST
EUROPEAN HISTORY

Judith Pallot (*editor*)
TRANSFORMING PEASANTS
Society, State and the Peasantry, 1861–1930

Richard Sakwa (*editor*)
THE EXPERIENCE OF DEMOCRATIZATION IN EASTERN
EUROPE

Barry P. Scherr and Karen L. Ryan-Hayes (*editors*)
TWENTIETH-CENTURY RUSSIAN LITERATURE

Ray Taras (*editor*)
NATIONAL IDENTITIES AND ETHNIC MINORITIES IN EASTERN
EUROPE

Ian D. Thatcher (*editor*)
REGIME AND SOCIETY IN TWENTIETH-CENTURY RUSSIA

International Congress of Central and East European Studies
Series Standing Order ISBN 0–333–71195–5
(*outside North America only*)

You can receive future titles in this series as they are published by placing a standing order.
Please contact your bookseller or, in case of difficulty, write to us at the address below with
your name and address, the title of the series and the ISBN quoted above.

Customer Services Department, Macmillan Distribution Ltd
Houndmills, Basingstoke, Hampshire RG21 6XS, England

National Identities and Ethnic Minorities in Eastern Europe

Selected Papers from the Fifth World Congress of Central and East European Studies, Warsaw, 1995

Edited by

Ray Taras
Professor in Political Science
Tulane University
New Orleans

First published in Great Britain 1998 by
MACMILLAN PRESS LTD
Houndmills, Basingstoke, Hampshire RG21 6XS and London
Companies and representatives throughout the world

A catalogue record for this book is available from the British Library.

ISBN 0–333–69553–4

First published in the United States of America 1998 by
ST. MARTIN'S PRESS, INC.,
Scholarly and Reference Division,
175 Fifth Avenue, New York, N.Y. 10010

ISBN 0–312–21346–8

Library of Congress Cataloging-in-Publication Data
World Congress of Central and East European Studies (5th : 1995 :
Warsaw, Poland)
National identities and ethnic minorities in Eastern Europe :
selected papers from the Fifth World Congress of Central and East
European studies / edited by Ray Taras.
  p.   cm.
Includes bibliographical references and index.
ISBN 0–312–21346–8 (cloth)
1. Ethnicity—Europe, Eastern—Congresses. 2. Nationalism–
–Europe, Eastern—Congresses. 3. Minorities—Europe, Eastern–
–Congresses. 4. Europe, Eastern—Politics and government—1989–
I. Taras, Ray, 1946– . II. Title.
DJK26.W67 1995
305.8'00947—dc21   97–44223
                                                              CIP

This book is printed on paper suitable for recycling and made from fully managed and
sustained forest sources.

10   9   8   7   6   5   4   3   2   1
07   06   05   04   03   02   01   00   99   98

Printed and bound in Great Britain by Antony Rowe Ltd, Chippenham, Wiltshire

Contents

vi   *Contents*

General Editor's Introduction

It is a great pleasure for me to introduce these volumes of papers that originated in the Fifth World Congress of Central and East European Studies, held in Warsaw in the week 6–11 August 1995, under the auspices of the International Council for Central and East European Studies and of the Institute of Philosophy and Sociology and the Institute of Political Studies of the Polish Academy of Sciences.

In the period since the previous world Congress, held in Harrogate, England, in July 1990, that part of the world that is the focus of Slavists' special attention had undergone the completion of changes that were already in train but the outcome of which was still uncertain. Moreover, given the inevitable time-lag between the conception of a major scholarly event and its occurrence, the major concerns at the beginning of the decade were not yet those of charting and analysing the transition from communist rule to some other form of political, economic and social entity and the impact of this on the societies and cultures of Russia, the Soviet Union and the countries loosely referred to as 'Eastern Europe': far less ambitious expectations were still the order of the day. Even though Poland had led the way in abandoning communist rule, shortly followed by all the other countries in 'Eastern Europe', it took some considerable imagination and conviction for the Executive Committee of the International Council to take the bold decision to hold the 1995 Congress in Eastern Europe, a decision that evoked a very positive response from our colleagues in Warsaw.

The different international climate immediately made itself felt, as scholars from the region were able to attend in large numbers a conference organised by a body that had been almost exclusively 'Western' in its previous experience. No longer were they specially invited guests (who on previous occasions had sometimes been denied exit visas to attend such Congresses), and it was a moving experience for me, as General Editor of the Congress proceedings, to receive letters and other communications by fax and e-mail from countries that in 1990 had no separate existence, or from provincial cities in the heart of post-Soviet Russia. Moreover, the opening of archives and the opportunities for new kinds of research, by scholars based in the countries concerned and by those entering from outside, meant that by 1995 there was much new information available, and scholars from the two 'sides' inevitably had much to say to one another.

The traditions in which the different groups had been trained meant that the styles of scholarship were not totally compatible, and there is a learning process in train that is likely to continue for some years. However, both the Congress itself and, more especially, the collaborative ventures such as this series of volumes containing selected papers, give opportunities for professional colleagues from around the world to make their own contributions to the new (and sometimes old) scholarly debates in ways that were hitherto impossible.

While not every paper that was presented or offered for publication was considered suitable for inclusion in the various thematic volumes, and individual editors sometimes had to make difficult choices and disappoint some authors, the endeavour as a whole must itself be seen as part of the global process of learning about the Slavic, Eurasian and Central and East European world: its peoples, its languages, its literature and cultural life, its history, politics, societies, economies, and its links with the rest of the world. Interest in the region is likely to grow, with new opportunities for contacts at various levels, and these volumes will, I am certain, serve both to educate and to inspire scholars and students anxious to understand.

It is very pleasant indeed to acknowledge once again the association of the Congress and the International Council with Macmillan, who will be publishing these volumes in the United Kingdom, and particularly the highly professional support and the keen personal interest of Tim Farmiloe for the whole project. If I may add a personal note, I should like to express my gratitude to John Morison and the Executive Committee of the International Council for charging me with the function of General Editor; to the editors of individual volumes, to whom fell the difficult tasks of assessment and selection followed by the tedium of editorial preparation; to my wife, Ethna, for her assistance in keeping track of several hundred typescripts, letters, faxes and e-mail messages; and to the many scholars who have patiently (and sometimes not so patiently – such are the pressures of modern academic life!) contributed to this complex international publishing venture. The collapse of communist rule has contributed sharply to globalisation, and the creation of this series of volumes has placed me at the hub of a world-wide enterprise, with editors on several continents and authors located in many countries of the world. It has provided me with a new kind of learning process for which I am humbly grateful.

Trinity College, Dublin RONALD J. HILL

Notes on the Contributors

Małgorzata Budyta-Budzyńska is at the Institute for Political Studies, the Polish Academy of Sciences, Warsaw, where she is completing her doctoral dissertation on the transformation of nationalism and ethnicity in Central Europe in the 1930s; she has published several journal articles on the subject.

Pamela Johnston Conover is professor of political science at the University of North Carolina; she has published extensively on the subject of political identities.

Rajat Ganguly was educated in India and the United States and has taught political science at the University of Southern Mississippi. He is the author of *Understanding Ethnic conflict: The International Dimension* (Longman, 1998).

Barbara E. Hicks is assistant professor of political science at the University of North Carolina; she specialises in East European politics and is the author of *Environmental Politics in Poland: A Social Movement Between Regime and Opposition* (Columbia University Press, 1996).

Ed Jocelyn received his doctorate in the Department of Modern Languages at the University of Bradford.

Iwona Kabzińska is at the Institute of Archeology and Ethnography, Polish Academy of Sciences, Warsaw.

Z. Anthony Kruszewski is professor of political science at the University of Texas, El Paso; he is the author of *The Oder–Neisse Boundary and Poland's Modernization: The Socioeconomic and Political Impact* (Praeger, 1972).

Marcin Kula is professor of history at the Institute of History, the University of Warsaw; he is the author of a number of books dealing with contemporary Polish history.

John J. Kulczynski is a professor in the Department of History at the University of Illinois, Chicago; he is the author of *The Foreign Worker* *and the German Labor Movement: Xenophobia and Solidarity in the Coal Fields of the Ruhr, 1871–1914* (Berg, 1994).

Dr Elena Marushiakova is a specialist on the Romani of Bulgaria.

Susyn Yvonne Mihalasky is a doctoral student at the University of Toronto and teaches political science at Montclair State University in New Jersey; she has published articles on the Lemkos in such journals as *East European Quarterly* and *Nationalities Papers*.

Dr Vesselin Popov is a specialist on the Romani of Bulgaria.

Yuri Petrovich Shabaev is Vice-Director of the Komi Science Centre in the Urals Division of the Russian Academy of Sciences, Syktyvkar.

Alla Skvortsova is in the Institute for the Study of National Relations, Moldovan Academy of Sciences, Chişinău, and is IREX representative in the Republic of Moldova.

Ray Taras did his postgraduate work in England and Poland and was professor of political science at Tulane University; his many publications include *Postcommunist Presidents* (edited; Cambridge University Press, 1997).

Marcin Zaremba is at the Institute of Political Studies, the Polish Academy of Sciences, Warsaw, and teaches at the University of Warsaw.

I.L. Zherebtcov is at the Komi Science Centre in the Urals Division of the Russian Academy of Sciences, Syktyvkar.

1 Introduction

Ray Taras

The most serious challenge to the forging of a post-Cold War international order has come from the rise of nationalism in many states. Ethnic
conflict is hardly new to many societies, but the spread of ethno-
nationalist mobilisation in recent years reflects, on the one hand, an
aspiration on the part of ethnic minorities to reassert their 'right' of
self-determination and, on the other, a growing desire on the part of
ethnic majorities to define the state in more exclusory categories. Since
most countries in the world are ethnically heterogeneous, the potential
for conflict along ethnic lines is enormous.

The paradox is, of course, that nationalism has become 'international-
ised' in the 1990s: it has become a global phenomenon. One nation, one
ethnic minority or one region (all 'subgroups' within the state) sets for
itself the goal of self-determination, equates it with state sovereignty,
and pursues it by means of secession from an existing state. Whether it
is successful in realising its goal or not (only the constituent parts of
communist federations successfully attained independence but that was
the result of extraordinary conditions), 'subgroupism' has a demonstration effect.[1] Corresponding units in other states learn and mimic this
behaviour. Excepting regionalist movements for sovereignty, sub-
groupism generally overlaps with nationalism and its ethnically circumscribed offshoot, ethno-nationalism.

Thus Stephen Ryan noted how manifestations of ethno-nationalism
and ethnic conflict were visible in the first, second and third worlds.[2] In
the first world – the democratic West – an ethnic revival triggered
increased assertiveness among ethnic minorities such as the Basques and
Catalans in Spain, the Bretons in France, the Flemish in Belgium, the
Scots in the United Kingdom, the northern Italians (or 'Padanians' –
more a region than a distinct people) in Italy, African Americans in the
United States and French-speaking Québecers in Canada.

The rapid political and economic transformation of Eastern Europe
and the Soviet Union spurred the growth of ethno-nationalism in the
second world. Even though the original fault lines gave way to many
new states, ethnic trouble-spots continued to flare up. In the former

1

Yugoslavia, ethnic violence among Serbs, Croats and Muslims reached an intensity unknown in Europe since the Second World War. In the former Soviet Union, the break-up of central authority went hand-in-hand with nationalist mobilisation on the part of titular and non-titular nationalities. The culmination of the first phase of this process was the dissolution of the Soviet empire. It left new minority groups in newly-independent states, many having ethnic kin in other states.

As demonstrated by the brutal war that was launched in 1994 by Russia against one of its republics, Chechnya, the outcome of the second round of nationalist assertion remains unclear. The potential for new types of ethnic conflict, within and between the Soviet successor states, is increased by the proliferation of diaspora populations and the irredentist claims that follow. Ethno-nationalist conflict exploded not only in the Russian Federation but also in the other new states: Georgia (between majority Georgians and breakaway Abkhazians), Armenia and Azerbaijan (over the territory of Nagorny Karabakh), Moldova (between Trans-Dniester Russians and the majority Romanian-speaking population), Ukraine (over Crimea, involving a three-cornered struggle among Ukrainians, Russians and Crimean Tatars) and Tajikistan (between populations living in different valleys).

In most countries of the third world, the rise of ethno-nationalist movements is part of the legacy of colonialism which had created artificial boundaries – and even states – by ignoring cultural divisions and popular aspirations. In their post-colonial political history, many of these states had to confront ethno-nationalist mobilisation whenever minorities – and occasionally even majorities – felt unjustly treated. New dominant cultural groups were regarded as neo-colonialists. Very few ethnic conflicts, whether in Nigeria, Sudan, Ethiopia, Lebanon, Afghanistan, India, Pakistan or Sri Lanka, have been resolved satisfactorily. A growing polarisation has resulted between majorities and minorities along ethnic, religious, economic and cultural lines.

Nationalism may be the most powerful and recurring political idea of the past two centuries. It has been the central organising principle of the modern state system and has had a great impact on peoples in all modern societies. Nationalism's negative effects have invariably overshadowed its positive contributions. The practical difficulties associated with defining a 'collective self' and a national identity have been a major problem and a constant source of friction. The way the collapse of the USSR, Yugoslavia and Czechoslovakia was resolved fuelled rather than dampened expectations of self-determination of many nationality groups.

Not only did the nationalist idea create the problem of minorities, it was also instrumental in worsening the plight of minorities once the modern state-system was in place. Because they were sovereign, states insisted on absolute loyalty from their citizens. In consequence, this consideration not only precluded states from granting rights to minorities within their borders, it induced states to increase the assimilationist pressure on minorities. In some cases the reaction – immediate or delayed – of minorities has been to organise secessionist movements, and this has led to the outbreak of civil wars in various parts of the globe.

From this account it is clear that the study of nationalism and ethnic conflict has special importance for achieving international stability and peace at the turn of the twenty-first century. Studying nationalism, identity politics and ethnic conflict in Eastern Europe is particularly instructive in that this region can be considered a bellwether of more general political trends. Seeking to shed its authoritarian past, striving to overcome its long-standing backwardness and poverty and attempting to navigate within a complex ethnic mosaic, Eastern Europe shares characteristics with many other countries in the world. The purpose of this volume is to describe the diversity of peoples living in Eastern Europe who have recently asserted released or reconstructed identities in the aftermath of communism and to explain the consequences of new-found identities and mobilising minorities for the political life of the region.[3]

The book begins, accordingly, with two theoretical chapters addressing our major themes: national identity and ethnic minorities. Pamela Conover and Barbara Hicks are concerned with the problem of identity formation, citizenship and state building in Eastern Europe. They describe a paradigm in which four levels of identity may or may not overlap: ethnic, citizen, nation and Europe. Employing psychological theories of the self and social identities, the authors trace how individuals transform their membership of groups into political identities. Ethnic groups seem to provide the focus for the strongest identities, they suggest, while local communities, nations and Europe are neither as attractive psychologically to individuals nor as natural. Cultural context is crucial and a potentially unifying identity such as Europe might succeed among Czechs while producing a backlash among Serbs. Political discourse and leadership are also pivotal in determining which political identity will prove the most salient to people. Conover and Hicks outline how the peoples of Eastern Europe can reconcile and nest different identities, thereby achieving the psychological transition from communism, but they also draw attention to the complex make-up of identity formation.

There has been a wealth of scholarly research in the 1990s on nationalism and ethnicity, but it is easy to overlook the rich tradition of this subject and to underestimate the abundance and quality of the body of literature built up over the past century. Rajat Ganguly provides a comprehensive overview of this literature and identifies the principal schools and approaches that have emerged in the social sciences. From his analysis we are made aware that such commonly-used terms as ethnicity and nationalism are not in themselves unproblematic. Determining what constitutes an ethnic group is a prerequisite for understanding why ethnic mobilisation and ethnic conflict occur. Given the diversity of the case studies considered in this volume, Ganguly's chapter helps put into perspective the different stages of politicisation that these groups have reached.

Our cases begin with an examination of one of the pivotal new independent states of Eastern Europe, Belarus. Bogged down in bitter struggles between president and parliament, russophiles and nationalists and authoritarians and democrats, the country has seemingly faced greater difficulties in arriving at a clear sense of its ethnic, cultural and political identity. In order to examine more closely the political controversies that have beset Belarus, our volume contains three chapters dealing with identity politics in that country. In the first of these, Ed Jocelyn describes how the very formation of an independent state of Belarus has had an enduring effect on its politics. Since national consciousness here is a very problematic concept compared to, let us say, Lithuania or even Moldova, and the existence and use of a national language no less agreed upon, the author points to what he terms *res bureaucratica* as the source of a potential collective identity. The federal system of the Soviet Union bequeathed an administrative structure to the Belarus republic that was national in form. When the USSR collapsed, the administrative identity that Belarus was left with was also a national one. More so than a national awakening or nationalism as such, Jocelyn persuasively argues, Belarus statehood is the product of a bureaucratic legacy from Soviet times. It may well indeed become more than this in time, but it is this anomaly that makes Belarus a state different from other newly independent ones.

The next chapter compares the emergence of post-communist national identity in two nations whose history has intersected for centuries, Ukraine and Poland. The editor of this volume suggests that recapturing national identity for Ukrainians will be a much more challenging

and complex task than it is for Poles, given different patterns of domination, the presence or absence of an ethnic schism in their respective
contemporary societies and, perhaps most intriguingly, different subjective perceptions and stereotypes among respondents from the two
countries. Identity politics exist in both countries at the 'sub-national'
level – that is, among minorities and regions – but have greater political
salience in Ukraine. The chapter considers whether dominant interpretations of national identity in the two countries reflect liberal (civic)
or exclusory (ethnic) views. But the author concludes that, more   than
this issue, the longing to be like the West, discernable in key sections of
both societies, may prove the most difficult component   of identity
to reconcile with post-communist reality.

The following chapter applies Ernest Gellner's thesis that nationalism
helps forge large national markets, and therefore economic development,
to the cases of Poland and Russia. Małgorzata Budyta-Budzyńska
notes the paradox of Russian minorities, led by the former communist
nomenklatura, coming out in support of nationalist projects elaborated
by the titular nations of newly-independent states (such as Ukraine) and
even by those of newly-designated republics of the Russian Federation
(such as Tatarstan). Promoting economic development explains why the
leaders of Russian diasporas made common cause with titular peoples
and supported statist or regional variants of nationalism. Budyta-
Budzyńska reports on similar motives underlying the emergence of
regional movements in western Poland, in particular Silesia. Even
though inhabitants stop short of supporting political movements committed to independence or integration with Germany, they recognise
how regional mobilisation can prove a shortcut to full integration into
European structures and serve, therefore, as an agent of economic modernisation.

The economic pull of Germany for many Poles is also apparent
in John Kulczycki's study of Polish migrants to the Ruhr before the
First World War. He describes how Polish workers organised to defend
and promote their particular 'ethno-class' interests even when these
interests were frequently not shared by the broader Polish national
movement based in Poznań, in Prussian Poland. Indeed, during the
massive miners' strike of 1905, in recognition of its militancy and
commitment the Polish union received equal representation to that
of the principal German unions in the commission that led the
strike. The national interest of Polish migrants was thus identified
with class interest: Polish workers felt themselves to be more a part
of the German labour movement than of a national movement made

up of large landowners, the clergy, the intelligentsia and the nascent bourgeoisie. Kulczycki shows, then, how 'ethno-class consciousness' was neither a myth invented by socialists nor an unrealistic expectation. Still, it does not seem to have any counterparts in today's Europe.

It is illuminating to compare earlier forms of organisational life, as found among Polish migrants to the Ruhr, to emerging patterns discernible among Poles living in the newly-independent neighbouring states in the east. The Polish population now forms an important minority in Belarus, Ukraine and Lithuania, and Anthony Kruszewski examines the revival of Polish institutions and community life in these three states. Up until the Second World War western regions of these countries had formed part of and had been governed by Poland. But, as the author describes, Polish communities here had been decimated by Stalinist atrocities, the closing of Catholic churches – a central characteristic in the self-definition of Poles living on these territories – and assimilationist pressures. The political authorities in independent Belarus, as in Lithuania and Ukraine, now confront demands by more politically-active Polish communities for greater linguistic, educational and cultural autonomy. Where the Lithuanian government has, after initial difficulties, pursued a more liberal policy on minority rights, the two Slavic states have been more reticent about granting their Polish communities full educational and religious freedoms.

In her research note, Iwona Kabzińska focuses on forms of self-identity among Poles living in several villages in western Belarus. She suggests how complex are their perceptions of themselves – once we go beyond the Pole as Catholic stereotype – as well as of other peoples. For the Polish minority, the creation of an independent Belarus has necessitated the formation of new social networks. Internal to the community, new forms of organisation have had to be established as Poles have been cut off from one another by new state borders.

Studies of the political behaviour of Polish minorities might lead us to the conclusion that, if they subscribe to nationalist agendas and organisational life abroad, they would do so even more in their own country. Marcin Kula and Marcin Zaremba question this supposition. Indeed, they find that nationalism, contrary to popular perceptions dominant in the West, does not constitute the main language of social protest in Poland in the 1990s. To be sure, the authors report on some conflicts in certain localities that did take on ethno-nationalist overtones, such as mutual recriminations between Poles and Ukrainians in an eastern village over the fate of a church building claimed by each, and the *Samoobrona*   or ('Self-Defence') movement that engaged in militant action in 1994 and that had an ultra-nationalist character. But generally protests are connected with particular economic actors who rarely invoke a broader identity, whether these be unemployed urban youth, farm workers with declining living standards, or Polish entrepreneurs facing stiff foreign competition. In explaining the recourse to an economistic rather than nationalistic language of protest, Kula and Zaremba suggestively argue that nationalism had exhausted itself after serving as the dominant   form of discourse during opposition to and transition from communist rule.

The status of the Russian diaspora in the near abroad is a paramount political issue that has important implications for international security and regional stability. It has necessitated considerable diplomatic and even military intervention by the Russian Federation, as the Moldovan case attests. Considerable scholarship on the future of Russian minorities and, indirectly, on the future of the new states in the near abroad themselves has appeared in the 1990s. Alla Skvortsova's research on the Russian-speaking minority in Moldova begins with the important premise that movements on behalf of the Russian-speaking population were different from one republic to another, though all set as their objective equal rights for all peoples in the new states regardless of their nationality. In the case of Moldova, she argues that reactive nationalism came to characterise Russian speakers – other than ethnic Russians there were 200,000 Moldovans who considered Russian their native language – in the aftermath of what essentially was a greater Romania nationalism of Moldova's first political leaders in the Democratic Movement. By and large, from the outset Russian speakers supported Moldovan sovereignty even if many wished it to remain part of the USSR. Many Russian speakers were concerned about legislation, especially that dealing with the official language, that would have effectively turned them into second-class citizens. This anxiety gave General Alexander Lebed, commander of the Russian army in the country, his first opportunity to establish a political constituency. But with the ebb in Romanian nationalism after 1993, Russian-speakers voted in favour of an independent Moldova in the referendum held in March 1994. For Skvortsova Russians have participated, therefore, in the democratic processes initiated in Romania even if their level of political activeness has waned. She cautions, however, that a return to the issue of Moldova's possible unification with Romania would probably lead to activity beyond the realm of politics. At present, the Russian minority has reconciled itself to the many changes necessitated by the construction of an independent Moldovan state.

As with the study of Russians as new minorities in the former Soviet republics, so minority groups found in the Russian Federation have received considerable scholarly attention in the 1990s. This has occurred partly as a result of their new-found visibility as titular peoples (those who gave the name to a politico-territorial unit) – as opposed to non-titulars in the more labyrinthine structure of the Soviet Union – partly as a result of the need to craft new institutions at central and regional levels and to distribute powers among them equitably and commensurately. If the Chechens, Tatars and Yakuts have all, for different reasons, received the bulk of attention, there are several republics in the Russian Federation that are made up of Finno-Ugric peoples. In their chapter, Yury Shabaev and I.L. Zherebtcov provide empirical data on the political attitudes of these ethnic people that make up a combined 2 per cent of Russia's population: Komi, Komi-Permiaks, Mari, Udmurt, Mordva and Karelians. The authors argue that since Russia's independence considerable efforts have been undertaken to raise the status of these peoples even as language use, urbanisation and intermarriage indicate the impact of assimilationist pressure. Even ethnic self-awareness had declined and various Finno-Ugric national movements were set up in the 1990s to struggle for greater self-determination and sovereignty. The authors show how these movements embraced political ideas, such as those related to representative government and to citizenship, that did not always reflect the interests or the views of a majority of these peoples. In sum, Shabaev and Zherebtcov seek to debunk the approach favoured by many Western scholars that all nationalities, regardless of size, aspirations, or degree of assimilation, should achieve the same political outcome – national self- determination.

The volume includes two chapters on a much-misunderstood minority group found throughout Eastern Europe, the Gypsies. Both studies focus primarily on one case, however: the nomadic Gypsy community known as the *Kardarashi* in Bulgaria. Vesselin Popov describes how nomad traditions survived the forced settlement imposed by the communist authorities in the 1950s. To be sure, there were modifications to the wandering tradition that ensued, but the wandering way of life was revived in the 1990s, not least prompted by the economic hardships, including large-scale unemployment, that accompanied free-market economic reforms in the country. By contrast, Elena Marushiakova examines the internal organisational structure of Gypsy communities, in particular the institution of self-government known as the *Meshare* in Bulgaria. Made up of the elders in the group, it regulates social relations and seeks to uphold the traditional value system. Here, too, economic changes have affected the role of Gypsy self-government. The desire for 'ethnic emancipation' has led much of the country's Gypsy population to adopt new forms of social and political life and to integrate more closely into Bulgarian society.

Finally, the fall of authoritarianism and the rise of identity politics have allowed us to learn of the fate of many transitional communities seemingly on the road to full assimilation into a dominant culture. Can decades of assimilation, whether pursued deliberately as state policy or a result of overt contempt or benign neglect, be undone when a change of regime occurs? We may obtain a better idea about the answer by considering Susyn Mihalasky's study of the Lemkos in Poland. Caught between a Polish and Ukrainian identity, and therefore for a long time not recognised in their own right, the resurrection of a Carpatho-Rusyn ethnic identity in other former communist states – Ukraine, Slovakia, Hungary – has given inspiration to Poland's Lemkos as well. Mihalasky uses survey data to document differences in self-identity among Lemkos living in their historical mountainous home region, territories in Silesia they were resettled to in 1947 and other parts of Poland to which Lemkos moved. Even though a large majority of respondents agreed that Lemkos had a distinct language and literature, exactly the same proportion said it was not necessary to live in the Lemko homeland to preserve Lemko heritage. Other concrete material manifestations of Lemko identity, such as language and religion, were also not viewed by respondents as absolutely necessary to maintaining identity. Rather, identity was defined mainly in terms of parental heritage and emotional attachments to the homeland.

Here we arrive at the apogee of identity politics that have marked the 1990s throughout the world and especially in Eastern Europe. Identity is principally a subjective quality that can, as effectively as objective ones, mark off one group from another. In no way do such markers need to be negative or ill-intentioned ones, as the Lemko experience clearly demonstrates. Neither are they imagined or contrived inter-group boundaries, for subjective, psychological criteria can be as materially influential as objective ones. What we learn from ethnic groups at different stages of integration into a dominant culture is that sense of identity is enough to form the basis of politics.

Notes

1. The term 'subgroupism' is borrowed from James N. Rosenau, *Turbulence in World*

Politics (Princeton, NJ: Princeton University Press, 1990), p.403.

2. Stephen Ryan, *Ethnic Conflict and International Relations* (Aldershot: Dartmouth, 1990), pp.x–xi.

3. While most of the case studies included in this volume deal with traditional Eastern European peoples and regions, the Finno-Ugric peoples may seem to be an exception. However, most of them live in the European part of Russia and, as the chapter indicates, have taken their political cues from the Baltic states.

2 The Psychology of Overlapping Identities: Ethnic, Citizen, Nation and Beyond

Pamela Johnston Conover and Barbara E. Hicks

The recent changes sweeping across the European landscape have focused attention on the nature of political identities – ethnic, citizen, national and European – the relationships among them, and their effects on European politics. In the east, the development of stronger national identities seems inevitable given the focus on state-building. But across Europe, national identities are being challenged from below by the growing potency of regional and ethnic identities, and from above by the emerging reality of European identity. It is unclear, then, whether European integration will create a meaningful European identity or simply encourage cross-national regional groups and ethnic groups within European states to develop their own identities and seek greater autonomy. This is particularly problematic for Eastern Europe where the revitalisation of national identities may inhibit the emergence of the European identity. Thus our key analytic question is: how can these different kinds of political identities fit together? Can they be substituted for one another? Are they inevitably in conflict with one another or can they coexist comfortably together? And what are the implications of this for East European politics?

In the European context, the topic of political identities has been approached from a number of perspectives (see Haesly, 1995). Three of these are particularly relevant to understanding the contemporary situation: socio-historical analyses of political identities, particularly national and ethnic ones; social theory treatments of multi-culturalism and the 'politics of identity and recognition'; and psychological studies of the self and 'social identity' theory.

The oldest approach taken to the study of citizen, national and ethnic identities is sociological and historical (recent examples include Connor, 1994; Greenfield, 1992; Smith, 1991). Researchers employing this viewpoint focus on particular case studies or on comparative analyses. Often their analyses have been guided by the central question: 'what makes a nation?' Typically, such studies argue that the basis of national identities is a psychological bond among citizens that is sustained by a shared history and a common culture. But, that said, they seldom investigate the nature of that psychological bond or the manner in which ethnic, national and supra-national identities might fit together.

In recent years political theorists have devoted considerable attention to exploring the role of political identities in democratic states (for example, Calhoun, 1994; Kymlicka, 1995; Spinner, 1994; Tamir, 1993; Taylor, 1994). They have considered both the general question of 'what kinds of identities are essential to sustain a democratic political community', and the problematic question of 'how should we reconcile the demands of particular identities – rooted in ethnicity, race and gender and sustained by a need for recognition – with the need for a common identity?' Their analyses have led some to criticise sharply historical continuity and ethnic homogeneity as fundamental building-blocks of political communities (for example, Habermas, 1995). While their approach has been that of normative theory, embedded within their theories are ontological claims that should be subjected to empirical testing.

Finally, psychologists who study conceptions of the self and 'social identity' draw attention to the psychological mechanisms underlying political identities (for example, Brewer, 1991; Tajfel, 1981; Turner *et al.*, 1987). Their work tends to be experimental and more general in its focus with considerably less attention devoted to the specific nature of ethnic, citizen and national identities. Guiding their analyses is the fundamental question: 'What is the nature and development of social identities?' In addressing this question, political psychologists often treat individuals as if they were unconstrained by the social forces of culture and history. Consequently, they seldom explore the implications of their research for understanding present-day political developments, despite the fact that the changing political terrain of Eastern Europe represents an ideal real world laboratory for exploring the relationships among different kinds of identities.

Our primary goal here is to begin the work of bringing together, in a mutually beneficial fashion, these different strands of research. The sociological–historical approach would benefit by greater attention to the psychological mechanisms that shape the functioning of political identities; social theory would be improved by empirically grounding its claims and bringing current research to bear on them; the psychological approach would be enriched by greater attention to the social and political context within which identities develop; and all the empirical approaches would be richer for their attention to normative questions. Finally, we should all benefit by developing a more comprehensive understanding of the ways political identities are developing and shaping the changing face of Europe.

We start by outlining contemporary psychological theory as it applies to conceptions of the self and social identities. Then we sketch out the implications of this psychological theory for understanding how political identities – ethnic, citizen, national and European – develop and are used. Finally, we apply our theoretical arguments to understanding present-day Eastern Europe.

Conceptions of the Self and Social Identities

The nature of the self

Social psychological theories of the self are our foundation for understanding political identities. Psychologists now see the self as a 'multi-faced phenomenon' – a collection of traits and attributes – shaped by a dynamic, ever-changing process of categorisation (see Markus and Wurf, 1986; Greenwald and Pratkanis, 1984). At any point in time, we define who we are by placing ourselves in specific categories, thereby establishing a basis of social comparison – a means of determining whom we are like and from whom we are different. Those categories that are emotionally significant form the basis for our core identities; they provide us with answers to the question 'Who am I?'. As elements of the self, political identities can be distinguished from one another along three key dimensions: centrality, relational quality and social nature (see Markus and Nurius, 1986; Markus and Wurf, 1986).

Elements of the self differ in their continuing importance to the individual. This is readily understood by adopting a dynamic, information- processing interpretation of the functioning self that distinguishes elements currently in the 'working self' from those that are not.[1] The 'working self' is a temporary structure of elements that are currently 'accessible' or ready for information processing (see Markus and Kunda,

1986). Therefore, the content of the 'working self' is variable, adjusting to both contextual cues and internal motivations. To a certain extent, then, we can be different people at different times and in different places. but within that context of malleability, there is a stable self, a 'core' of self-conceptions that is 'chronically accessible' in the working self (see Markus and Kunda, 1986, p.859).

Elements of the self are also either non-relational or relational in that they pertain either to the self alone or to the self in relationship with others.[2] For example, attributes such as *trustworthy, kind, pretty* would be non-relational elements whereas *son, friend, sister* would be relational elements. The non-relational elements constitute the 'private' inner self while the relational elements make up the 'collective' outer self (see Greenwald and Pratkanis, 1984; Markus and Kitayama, 1991; and Triandis, 1989).

Finally, elements of the self constitute either personal or social identities. Personal identities distinguish a person from other *individuals* within a particular social context: they have an individuating effect. In contrast, social identities are relational elements, part of the collective self, which 'define the individual in terms of his or her shared similarities with members of certain social categories in contrast to other social categories' (Turner *et al.*, 1994, p.454). Social identities compel us to think as 'we', not 'I', and lead to an experience in which the self is defined in terms of *'others who exist outside the individual person doing the experiencing'* (Turner *et al.*, 1994, p.454). Thus social identities 'depersonalise' the self by extending the bounds of the self beyond the individual.

To this point, we have focused on individual elements of the self. But self-structures are potentially quite complex. The political landscape is populated by a variety of possible social identities – different 'we's' – that alone, or in combination with one another, could play a major role in defining the self. What are the consequences of these many possible social identities for public life and politics? We shall address the political aspects of this question below, but for now we focus on its purely psychological side which requires that we take up a central ontological question: are we fundamentally independent or interdependent? Translated into psychological terms, the question becomes: how does the self, *taken as a whole*, shape our understanding of our relations with others?

To answer this question, Hazel Markus and Shinobu Kitayama (1991) have developed a psychological theory that focuses on the structure of the core self: what proportions of the core are made up of elements from the private self versus the collective self? With that information, conceptions of the self can be arrayed along a *dimension* of independence–interdependence that captures the overall orientation of the self to others. At one extreme, the independent one, all people whose core selves are made up mostly of non-relational elements from the private self; at the other extreme, the interdependent one, are those whose cores are composed mostly of relational elements from the collective self; the remaining people fall in between.[3] Thus when they have many social identities that are core elements, people are more likely to develop an interdependent sense of the self.

To be clear: interdependency is a matter of degree, not a dichotomous classification. Still, the extreme ends of the continuum can be characterised as polar types. The most 'independent' selves have a very atomistic conception: they view themselves as separate from others because few of their relationships are part of the core. Consequently, they determine their behaviour on the basis of attributes, thoughts and feelings that refer to the individual rather than to others. By contrast, the most 'interdependent' selves have a very holistic view: they see themselves as connected with others because relational elements, rather than private attributes, dominate their cores. Their behaviour is heavily motivated by their sensitivity to the desires and interests of others.

Markus and Kitayama have compiled an impressive body of empirical evidence to support their theory. There are substantial psychological differences between more independent and more interdependent selves that fundamentally determine the general understanding and character of our social relations. The origins of these differences lie in the basic shift in focus from self to self-in-other, from 'I' to 'we', that occurs as one moves across the dimension from independent to interdependent conceptions of the self.[4] From a cognitive perspective, more interdependent selves are more sensitive to others. The expression and even experience of many emotions also varies markedly between independent and interdependent selves. Ego-focused emotions (for example, anger, frustration and pride) are expressed more frequently by those with more independent selves; conversely, other-focused emotions (such as sympathy and shame) are more likely to be expressed by more interdependent selves. Finally, more interdependent selves are more likely to express social motives – deference, affiliation, nurturance – than are independent selves. Thus interdependent and independent selves will make very different kinds of citizens. Arguably, 'interdependent' citizens should be better suited *naturally* for a public life of civic activity that flourishes when individuals are attentive to one another's needs and the norms that govern social interaction (for further discussion see Conover, 1995).

Because of this, it is important to determine how independent and interdependent selves are formed. We are probably *not* biologically 'hard-wired' towards interdependency or independence. More likely, beginning very early in life we are socialised towards a particular way of understanding our relationships with others.[5] Thus the creation of independent or interdependent selves begins on the macro level with cultural views of personhood that define a 'collective reality' sustained by and expressed in a variety of social customs, practices, norms and institutions. Such core cultural values are transformed by social institutions and practices into the immediate micro-level environments or local worlds where people live their lives. To become a valued member of those local worlds – communities, workplaces, schools, families – individuals must respond in culturally appropriate ways to the demands and expectations of the relevant social institutions, and thus unknowingly they often automatically live out the core cultural values of interdependence or independence. And in so doing, they develop a set of 'habitual psychological tendencies' that define their subjective experience and predispose them to view the world independently, in terms of their personal identities, or interdependently, in terms of their social identities (Markus and Kitayama, 1994).

The nature of social identities

To what extent are political identities – be they ethnic, citizen, national or supra-national – likely to constitute social identities in the psychological sense of the term? Specific types of political identities will be dealt with below, but for now we focus on clarifying the meaning of social identities and how they fit with political groups.

The concept of 'social identity' is often misunderstood, particularly in the United States where it is sometimes presumed that *any* self-categorisation involving a group constitutes a 'social identity' according to the theory of Henri Tajfel and his colleagues (see Brewer, 1991; Taijfel and Turner, 1986). But this is not the case. For example, a national identity as 'Polish' does not automatically function as a 'social identity' as defined by social identity theory. Self-categorisation as a member of a group may result in *either* a personal *or* a social identity. What is critical in determining whether a political group identity is 'personal' or 'social' is not, therefore, the abstract level of inclusiveness of the category but is instead the *immediate experience of the level of self-categorisation.* Is the perceiver defining herself or himself as an individual person or as an inextricable part of the political group *at that particular moment*? Is the current psychological perspective one of 'I' or one of 'we'? For example, a person may think of herself as a Czech compared with other individuals – a personal identity – or as a Czech compared with other nationalities – a social identity. How the self is being defined in the specific instance is what is crucial to determining whether a political group identity is personal or social. Thus political group identities can be either 'I' personal identities or 'we' social identities. As we shall see, contextual factors as well as conceptions of the self influence which level of categorisation is adopted in a particular instance.

But the *nature of the political group* also shapes whether group identities are experienced as 'I' or 'we' identities. Two related aspects of the group are particularly important. First, is the group a 'common-bond group' in which individual members have reciprocal ties linking them together as members or is it a 'common-identity group' in which members are not necessarily bound to one another *qua* members? In common-bond groups, social identity is heavily dependent on the individual's attachment to other group members, whereas social identity is independent of attachment to group members in 'common-identity' groups (Prentice, Miller and Lightdale, 1994). Ethnic groups, for example, are frequently common-bond groups in which members are bound to one another through social networks and traditions that generate strong ethnic social identities; nations, by contrast, are 'imagined communities' in which people identify directly with the nation in such a manner that the strength of their identities is independent of their attachment to other members of the nation.

Second, what kind of collective good does the group share, and why is it valued? As the philosopher Charles Taylor points out, there is a critical distinction between two kinds of collective goods: 'convergent goods' that 'have value to me and value to you', and 'common goods' that 'essentially have value to us' (Taylor, 1989, p.168). Many collective goods are convergent goods because their value is not enhanced by their collective provision. For example, neither clean air nor trash collection is valued *because* it is collectively provided. By contrast, 'common goods' derive some of their essential value from the fact that they are shared. Concerts or holiday traditions are common goods in this sense. Some common goods derive only part of their value from their shared nature. But for others, which Taylor calls 'immediately common goods', their shared nature is what matters most: 'the good is that we share' (Taylor,

1989, p.168). The central value of close friendships, for example, lies in the actions and meanings shared with friends.

There is, then, some 'sharing' of interest in all collective goods. But the nature of the 'sharing' is fundamentally different for convergent and common goods, so much so that it demands a different ontology and promotes a different level of categorisation in each case. The 'weak sharing' of convergent goods is atomistic: it requires only that the good be valued in a 'for me – for you' fashion. All that we 'share' is that we each have an individual interest in the collective good. Both common-good and common-identity groups can sustain the 'weak sharing' of convergent goods for it requires at most a contingently shared relationship between two people, and at a minimum no relationship at all. By contrast, the 'strong sharing' of common goods cannot be adequately conceptualised in terms of this same atomistic viewpoint. A holistic ontology is necessary to capture the 'for us' perspective that is involved in the sharing of common goods. For when we share them, we actually experience them together and value them for that experience (see Taylor, 1989). Thus common-bond groups are more likely than common-identity groups to generate common goods immediately because their members are connected and thus more capable of sharing *together* the experience of the collective good. Arguably, group identities will inevitably take the form of 'we' social identities when they are based on the sharing of immediately common goods; the shared *experience* pushes the individual to adopt a group level of categorisation that promotes social or 'we' identities. In contrast, where group identities are based on the 'weak sharing' of convergent goods, it is easier to treat group identities as personal or 'I' identities.

The self-categorisation process and the use of social identities

Conceptions of the self are both dynamic and stable: the working self changes and adjusts to meet the demands of specific situations, but stability is provided by a set of relatively permanent core elements. Determining when and how social identities influence behaviour is thus a matter of understanding how the working self functions: whether it includes social identities, and if so which ones and to what effect? How can we predict, then, when and how people will define themselves in terms of social identities?

John Turner and his colleagues (Turner *et al.*, 1994) argue that this question is best addressed by analysing the general principles that guide how people use self-categories to make sense of particular situations.

For descriptive purposes, the perceptual task can be thought of as having two parts: the individual's decision to focus on the personal or social level of categorisation and the selection of particular categories from those that are salient.[6] Both the level of categorisation and the categories themselves are selected in an interactive process that is a function of the individual's 'readiness' to use a particular category and the 'fit' of the category to the objective reality that must be represented (Turner *et al.* 1994; Oakes, 1987). Let us consider briefly each of these factors.

'Perceiver readiness' is determined by the relative accessibility of different categories within the self. It influences both the level of categorisation and the selection of specific categories, and reflects the active role of the perceiver in constructing responses to particular situations. As described above, overall conceptions of the self can habitually shape 'perceiver readiness' by predisposing an individual towards a particular level of categorisation: interdependent selves are more likely to adopt a group level of categorisation, and independent selves are more likely to choose a personal level. Similarly, the selection of particular categories at either level is influenced by a host of internal factors, including values, goals, needs, current motives, past experiences and present expectations (Turner *et al.*, 1994). To the extent that social identities constitute a part of the core self, they will be chronically accessible or salient and thus more likely to influence perception and behaviour.

Cognitive 'fit' has two components: normative and comparative (Turner *et al.*, 1994). Normative fit concerns the content of a category and the extent to which it matches the stimuli that need to be represented. For example, activating a European identity would require the perceiver to categorise a group of people (including the self) as 'Europeans' as opposed to 'non-Europeans'. But to do so, the differences between the two groups and similarities between them *in a particular instance* would have to 'fit' the perceiver's *existing* beliefs about the substantive social meaning of the category 'European'. Thus people employ only categorisations and activate social identities that are consistent with their background knowledge and implicit theories of the meaning of categories. Normative fit, therefore, directly engages the resources of the self with the demands of the external environment.

But the task of achieving normative fit is more complicated than simply comparing and matching the content of existing categories with that of the stimuli, because the *meaning* of relevant social categories is not fixed but also varies across situations. There is not, for example, a precise correspondence between the long-term knowledge stored about Europeans, and the meaning of the category 'European' that is constructed to represent them in a particular instance. Instead, the context of the application actually shapes the immediate meaning of the category itself (Turner *et al.*, 1994; also see Haslam, Turner, Oakes, McGarty and Hayes, 1992). Thus social identities will come into play *only* if the categories on which they are based can be construed as 'fitting' or 'making sense' in the particular terms characterising a specific context.

Comparative fit is defined by the 'meta-contrast principle' which proposes:

> a collection of stimuli is more likely to be categorized as an entry to the degree that the average differences perceived between those stimuli are less than the average differences between them and the remaining stimuli that make up the frame of reference. (Turner *et al.*, 1994, p.455)

Comparative fit involves the perceiver's ability to develop for the focal group an adequate contrast against some background. Fundamentally, it posits that where *inter-group differences are perceived as greater than intra*group differences people are more likely to categorise the self as 'we' rather than 'I'. Embodied within the 'metacontrast principle' is the critical idea that the process of categorisation is inherently *comparative*, and consequently the meaning of self-categories is variable and partially dependent on the frame of reference. Thus the processes of achieving comparable and normative fit are inextricably linked. Moreover, the demands of achieving comparative fit ensure that context plays a substantial role in shaping perception and behaviour. *If social identities are to be important, then, they must be made* salient *by the features of the situation.*

The metacontrast principle suggests a number of ways in which the context can be varied so as to heighten the general salience of social identities by influencing the level of categorisation. First, the process of self-categorisation is likely to move to a social or group level of categorisation when the 'comparative context is extended to include others who are different from the self and prior others' (Turner *et al.*, 1994, p.456; see also Gaertner, Mann, Murrell and Dovidio, 1989; Haslam and Turner, 1992; and Wilder and Thompson, 1988). For example, in a multicultural setting if public discussion shifts from a focus on specific ethnic groups to talk about an inclusive nation, more individuals should shift to a group level of categorisation. Where social identities are nested one within another, shifting the focus to a more inclusive identity forces more people to a group level of categorisation. Second, social identities become more important in *inter-group contexts, whereas personal identities are usually more salient in intra-*group situations (Hogg and Turner, 1987; Turner *et al.*, 1994). Therefore, collective conflicts that accentuate inter-group differences and promote within-group homogeneity are forceful determinants of social categorisation (Oakes, 1987). Third, the relative extremity of one's own and others' positions affects the level of categorisation: extremists – self and others – are more likely to adopt a group level of categorisation than are moderates because they differ more from the majority of others within the context (Haslam and Turner, 1992). Thus extremists, because they think more frequently in 'we' terms, could be more likely to aspire to leadership positions, to promote the group good, and even to instigate inter-group conflict.

Not only is the level of categorisation influenced by principles of contrast, but so is the selection of particular categories for contrast. Marilyn Brewer (1991) has argued that perceivers seek an 'optimal level of distinctiveness' in the categorisation process: the place on a continuum of 'inclusiveness' that constitutes the point of balance between the need to assimilate the self with others through inclusive self-categorisations, and the competing need to differentiate the self from others through exclusive self-categorisations. The 'optimal level of distinctiveness' varies both between and within cultures, with the 'optimal level' for relatively interdependent cultures and selves being higher on the continuum of inclusiveness than that of independent cultures and selves. Brewer (1991) further argues that in many circumstances personal identities will *not* provide the optimal level of self-categorisation, and therefore people will seek a self-categorisation at some higher level of inclusiveness. By the same token, however, social identities that are all-inclusive provide little basis for self-differentiation, and therefore they, too, are less likely to be used. From this perspective, social categories with *intermediate* levels of inclusiveness are most likely to be psychologically useful (also see Abrams, 1994).[7] Thus level of inclusiveness is an important contextual determinant of precisely *which* social identities will become important in a given situation.

In summary, the process of self-categorisation is one in which comparative and normative fit interact with perceiver readiness to determine which categories are salient. There is, then, constant flux between self-categorisation at the personal and group level. In any particular instance, multiple categories of the self at both levels are likely to be salient, and they can conflict or reinforce one another, suggesting alternative conceptions of the self. Ultimately, context will play a major role in determining which competing self-conception is used; the dominant social identity in one instance may not be so in the next situation. This is not to suggest that self-conceptions vary wildly across situations. Stability arises from a number of sources: social institutions and processes of social influence encourage stability by making some self-categories chronically accessible; higher-order knowledge structures lend consistency to our patterns of normative interpretation and thus to the 'fit' of categories; and the stability of social reality itself is reflected in the similarity of the contexts that perceivers encounter (Turner *et al.*, 1994). Still, the inevitable conclusion must be: *the role of social identities in public life cannot be predicted or explained in the absence of a full understanding of the context.*

None the less, we can specify the general perceptual and behavioural effects of categorisation at the group level as opposed to the personal level (see Conover, 1984). Social identities affect the relationships among group members, cognitive perspectives and motivations to act. By definition, social identities reflect ties to the group, but they can also stimulate (or derive from) an emotional bond between group members. They can foster an attachment and social connection among citizens, as members of a *particular* political group. And this, in turn, can encourage solidarity and engender a sense of mutual responsibility which together provide the foundation for citizens to act sympathetically and empathetically towards other group members. Thus we-identities serve as a solid foundation upon which to build group-based activities. Social identities also condition the understanding of public life by inspiring group members to think from the viewpoint of the political group, and to pursue the collective interest. In effect, by engendering a self-*in*-other psychological perspective, social identities encourage an 'attending together' by the *members of the social group* to *their* problems, thereby promoting a 'for us' – 'for them' perspective (see Mouffe, 1992; Taylor, 1989). Finally, through their influence on social ties and the understanding of the meaning of the group, social identities can shape people's motivation or will to act as group members.

Understanding Political Identities

What are the implications of the psychological underpinnings of political identities – ethnic, citizen, national and supra-national? Several are important to consider: the importance of cultural and historical settings, the critical role of framing, and the manner in which these identities can be related to one another.

Cultural and historical setting

The potential interplay between ethnic, citizen, national and European identities cannot be understood in a cultural vacuum. Cultural views of personhood condition the collective practices that structure the social norms and institutions that shape the micro-level processes that determine the nature of individual lives (Markus and Kitayama, 1994). It is important, therefore, to ascertain whether cultural values emphasise more independent or more interdependent conceptions of the self. In recent years, a number of psychologists have begun to elaborate on the attributes that distinguish these types of culture, typically by focusing on the emphasis given to individualism rather than collectivism (see Hui, 1988; Markus and Kitayama, 1991, 1994; Triandis, 1990; Triandis, McCusker and Hui, 1990). Interdependent selves are more likely in *collectivist* cultures that can be identified by: treatment of social groups as the basic unit of analysis; a strong emphasis on in-groups like the family; behaviour regulated by in-group norms; emphasis on hierarchy and harmony within the group; and attention to the fate and achievement of the in-group. In contrast, independent selves are more likely in *individualist* cultures that can be identified by: treatment of individuals as the unit of analysis; behaviour regulated by individual likes and dislikes and cost-benefit analyses; conflict and confrontation as acceptable in-group behaviour; and attention to personal fate and achievement (Triandis *et al.*, 1990). Thus the place at which to begin an examination of political identities is the cultural conception of the self.

Within any given culture, there is potential for the development of a range of politically relevant identities – ethnic, citizen, national and sometimes supra-national – and it is important to know what those possibilities are in each cultural setting. But the groups underlying these identities also differ generically in important ways that affect the likelihood that such identities will develop. Both common-bond and common-identity groups can give rise to powerful social identities characterised by 'we' thinking. In both cases, such identities are grounded by a substantive understanding of the group and what members have in common – the collective good associated with the group. For common-bond groups, relationships among members often facilitate the deep sharing of a valued common good that sustains the development of 'we' group identities. For common-identity groups there must also be a collective good, but it is much less likely to be deeply shared by members.

As applied to political groups, this distinction between common-bond and common-identity groups evokes a distinction made by Benedict Anderson (1983) in his description of 'real' as opposed to 'imagined' communities. Ethnic groups have the potential to become common-bond groups – 'real' communities – thus enabling the shared *experiences* of everyday living to ground strong ethnic identities. Similarly, on a civic republican account (see Taylor, 1989), citizen identities must be rooted in a common good, in the shared living that characterises 'real' political communities – a possibility that arises only when citizen identities are defined at the local level. But citizen identities defined at the level of the state, national identities, and supra-national identities such as 'European', are all identities with common-identity groups – *'imagined' communities* of one sort or another. A more abstract, less tangible collective good – one that is not immediately shared – must, therefore, undergird such identities. Thus, in liberal states, citizen identities with the political community might be supported by patriotic traditions or commitments to a common defence. And European identities might be founded on a sense of a common economic fate. But arguably the 'we' identities to such 'imagined' communities, because they are constructed on the basis of collective goods that are not immediately common, are more fragile than those to 'real' communities (see Taylor, 1989). That is not to say that such group identities will fail to develop, but only that they may well take the form of personal 'I' identities rather than social 'we' identities. For example, being Polish or European may constitute a personal attribute, rather than a social identity. Critically, where citizen or national or European identities are experienced as 'I' personal identities, they cannot represent viable alternatives to divisive 'we' identities.

Finally, it is important to determine how individuals in a particular culture understand the nature of such groups: what are the salient features of a group, and how do people determine who belongs to it? In effect, what are the dimensions of meaning that define the understanding of a particular group category? This may seem like a trivial exercise for some groups, such as gender, where objective membership appears obvious; but for the kinds of groups being discussed here, it is not a trivial exercise – quite the contrary. To the extent, for example, that people can define a 'nation' or 'Europe' among many different dimensions, many kinds of identities become possible.[8] It is important, therefore, *not* to assume that territory is the defining dimension along which ethnic, national and European identities are defined and thus compared. While such identities are overlapping or nested from a territorial perspective, along other dimensions of meaning – cultural or religious, for example – there may be little overlap.

Framing

The cultural and historical settings define the group environment and the terms in which individual groups are understood. But ultimately, *at any particular moment*, whether these groups affect behaviour – whether they enter our immediate consciousness as groups – depends on the framing given to the situation. Such framing goes on both at the macro- and at the micro-level, and the two kinds of framing together determine which social categories, which groups, are salient at that particular moment.

'Macro-framing' reflects the long-term political reality as defined by who is in control, their values, and the transmission of those values through social institutions. Usually the process of 'macro-framing' contributes stability to perceptions and individual behaviour by making some social categories chronically accessible to perceivers; it is, therefore, typically a source of continuity in the impact of social groups. But now in Eastern Europe the factors that normally ensure stability in macro-framing are in considerable flux. Social institutions and the processes of social influence are in a period of profound transformation; understandings of the social world are rapidly changing; and individuals are forced to confront group contexts that differ considerably from those of a decade ago. All of this erodes the long-run stability in framing that usually exists. New social categories are emerging and old ones are being challenged. Thus it is a moment of enormous change in the way in which ethnic, political, national and European communities are understood in many Eastern European countries. *By substantially altering the understanding and saliency of these groups, political elites can produce either a more destructive or a more constructive social and political environment.*

The micro-framing of the situation is both external and internal. The external framing reflects the particulars of the situation. Specifically, the context of the situation and the nature of public discourse together determine the external framing and thus the *salience* of group categories (see Conover, 1988, for an elaboration). In contrast, the internal framing stems from the perceptual readiness of the individual. Let us briefly consider both kinds of framing.

Focusing first on external framing and context, we experience our lives locally; therefore, the social groups that populate everyday life automatically enter as background into the framing of particular incidents. Groups made chronically 'visible' by the context are more likely to become salient in the self-categorisation process, as categories either for identification or for contrast. The number of group members and their concentration (that is, density) are a key determinant of the visibility of groups. Large, concentrated groups will generally be more visible than small, dispersed ones. Thus individuals will be more likely to identify with a group of similar others to the extent they are geographically concentrated (Lau, 1989).[9] Visibility is also determined by a group's 'distinctiveness': the degree to which group members contrast with non-members (Lau, 1989). If group members are readily identifiable, they can be more easily contrasted with non-members. Therefore, groups based on perceptible physical characteristics such as sex, skin colour or language are the most naturally visible, and enter automatically into social perception (see Stangor, Lynch, Duan and Glass, 1992). Similarly, distinctive elements of culture such as dress or customs can render group members readily identifiable to one another and to non-members as well. But the simple fact that its members are easily identifiable does not ensure that a group will be distinctive in a particular setting, for contrast is essential to distinctiveness. Thus homogeneous settings render even the most vivid cultural groups indistinct. In sum, '*group visibility*' may be conceptualised as a function of the number of group members, their concentration and their distinctiveness. To the extent that groups are more visible, they are more likely to become salient categories in the self-categorisation process.

External framing is also determined by the public discourse surrounding situations. A specific event can heighten the saliency of a group. Situations vary in the extent to which they raise the saliency of groups by providing group cues; saliency increases with the clarity and frequency of the group cues in political discourse (see Conover, 1988). In some instances, political discourse is framed very explicitly in group terms so that most members of the public will pick up the group cues; indeed, they may find it impossible to avoid using group categories if the framing is very explicit and repetitive. For example, news stories concerning Bosnia speak specifically of Serbs and Croats. Alternatively, group cues in political discourse may be latent rather than manifest: here, groups are not mentioned explicitly in public discussion; instead the perceivers themselves must establish what is an inherently plausible link between the situation and the group. In such cases, perceivers 'read into' information various groups that are salient to them, either in-groups with which they identify or out-group s that evoke strong emotional reactions. For example, a discussion of European integration might contain latent cues to various nations. Finally, some discussions are framed so that group cues are neither manifest nor latent for most members of the public. In those instances, the external framing actually inhibits the use of group categories: even if a particular group is salient to the individual, the principle of normative fit dictates against its introduction into the perception of a situation.

Various kinds of political groups provide different opportunities for external framing. Ethnic groups are often quite visible in the local worlds where people live their everyday lives, because they are typically associated with a culture characterised by distinctive language, dress, customs and in some cases racial make-up. Where ethnic differences are distinctive, it is hard for perceivers *not* to use ethnic group categories in their perceptions. If ethnic groups are the most naturally visible, 'citizens' are the most naturally *in*visible because the grounds for determining membership in a political community are typically so abstract. Citizens *qua* citizens are especiallly *in*visible where citizenship is universal or nearly so. However, the category of citizen can be made more visible when conceived of at the local level or when some residents are denied citizenship and this exclusion is linked to visible categories such as is often the case with guest workers or resident aliens. 'National' and 'European' categories vary in their visibility depending on the presence of contrasting 'others' and the dimension of meaning defining the groups[10]; but in the day-to-day living that goes on in local worlds, both should be relatively *in*visible.

The relative *invisibility* of citizen, national and European groups in everyday contexts suggests the extreme importance of the framing of political discourse. Through public discussion, political leaders can raise the salience of these groups, and thereby make it more likely that the groups will enter into the self-categorisation process. Where public discussion does *not* include such references, these categories are likely to remain unused unless individuals introduce them through their internal processes of framing. But even if these groups are salient to the individual, they are unlikely to enter into the self-categorisation process if there is no latent or manifest group content in political discourse.

Internal micro-framing is shaped by forces inside the individual. Conceptions of the self determine whether personal or social identities lie at a person's core, and thus which kinds of identities are chronically accessible. Similarly, an individual's values, motivations and expectations all shape perception of the situations making some categories more salient than others. In the end, the internal and external framing work together to determine which categories – which groups – are salient in a particular circumstance.

In sum, the macro- and micro-framing together make salient a number of categories out of which different constructions of the self might be made to meet the demands of the particular situation. One or many possible categories likely are to be selected to represent the self. The process of selection is inherently *comparative* in that salient categories are compared in terms of their substantive meaning and level of inclusiveness. People seek an 'optimal level of personal distinctiveness' that determines the 'level of inclusiveness' at which they strive to categorise themselves (Brewer, 1991). This preferred 'level of inclusiveness' most likely varies across cultures, between individuals, and within individuals across situations depending in part on the dimensions of meaning that are relevant. Generally, interdependent selves should have a higher preferred level of inclusiveness than independent selves. For a particular situation, there may be several salient categories at the preferred level of distinctiveness. In those instances, individuals can apply all the categories if they are similar or non-conflictual in their meaning (Taylor and Dube, 1986; Wong-Reiger and Taylor, 1981). Accordingly, where groups have similar values, multiple group identities can be used in the same situation. For example, national and European identities might be conceptualised in a compatible fashion on a cultural dimension and both be easily evoked in the same situation.[11] Thus the macro- and external micro-framing make salient a range of categories, from which perceivers will select the ones that are internally salient and whose meaning and level of inclusiveness fit the cognitive demands of the situation and their own needs.

It is important, therefore, to understand how ethnic, citizen, national and European identities typically differ in their 'levels of inclusiveness'. Of these four kinds of identities, ethnic and citizen identities are potentially lowest in their levels of inclusiveness. Citizenship at the local level or ethnic conclaves in multicultural nations provide the opportunity for these identities to be used at relatively low levels of inclusiveness. In different settings, however, both might have substantially higher levels of inclusiveness. In particular, where the nation-state is nearly synonymous with a particular ethnic group or where citizenship in the nation-state is at stake, both identities become more inclusive. Thus ethnic and citizen identities are flexible in their inclusiveness. By contrast, national and European identities enjoy less flexibility, though their perceived level of inclusiveness can vary according to the dimension of meaning used to define membership. Generally, national and European identities should have higher levels of inclusiveness than ethnic identities, making them more attractive identities for people and cultures that are relatively interdependent.

Moving between political identities

Ethnic identities are demonstrating their potency all across Europe, though especially in Eastern Europe. Can their divisiveness be ameliorated by appealing to citizen, national or European identities? In posing the question, it is well to keep in mind why ethnic identities are so powerful in comparison with these other identities. Ethnic groups are often common-bond groups that can easily constitute 'real' communities. When this occurs, the common life they sustain is a valued common good that is shared in the deepest sense of the word. For this reason, they are capable of generating powerful 'we' identities that become salient features in the core selves of many people. From a perceptual or framing perspective, ethnic groups are often naturally visible in the local worlds in which people live their lives; consequently they form an inevitable part of the background context for much of politics. Moreover, in many instances, ethnic groups fall in the middle range of levels of inclusiveness, thereby providing an optimal level of distinctiveness to many perceivers.

Could citizen identities redirect the focus of Eastern Europeans away from ethnic identities? Given the variety of citizen identities, it is a real possibility. Citizen identities can be associated with the 'real' political communities of cities and villages, and therefore provide the same level of distinctiveness that ethnic identities have to offer. If they are linked to real political communities that produce common goods shared in the deepest sense, citizen identities may be powerful 'we' identities supplanting ethnic identities. For this to occur, however, the category of citizen would have to be made more meaningful and more visible through local political discourse. Leaders would have to stress the ways in which everyday public life involved the exercise of local citizenship in the form of practices such as civility and tolerance.

Citizen identities can also be associated with the 'imagined' political communities of the nation-state. But in those instances it is less likely that the identities will be linked with immediately common goods. Consequently, their viability is questionable. This is, of course, the question that communitarian critics pose to liberal theorists: can citizen identities with the liberal state be sustained in the absence of any deeply shared common good (Taylor, 1989)? On psychological grounds, it is unclear. Certainly, people readily develop 'we' group identities that are not grounded in attachments and connections with individual group mem-bers (see Prentice *et al.*, 1994). And nation-states provide collective political benefits – stability, peace, prosperity – that many people might value and associate with citizenship. But from a framing perspective, the category of 'citizen' is not *naturally* visible or salient; when tied to the national political community, it is pitched at a level of inclusiveness that may be too high for many people, and the meaning of 'citizen' is vague and unclear for many people. All these factors dictate against the category's use, and therefore against the prominence of citizen identities. If citizen identities with national political communities are to be a viable alternative to ethnic identities, external framing through political discourse must play a major role in making the category of 'citizen of the nation-state' visible, and in defining its meaning.

Do national identities represent a more practical psychological alternative to divisive ethnic identities than do citizen identities? National and citizen identities should have similar levels of inclusiveness to the extent that they are both linked to the nation-state. But the development and use of nation and citizen identities can vary considerably because people are likely to have very different understandings of those two categories, despite the fact that their members may be identical. Also, because it is easier to define concretely, the category of 'nation' should be more meaningful than that of 'citizen' for most people. Moreover, the meaning of a 'nation' can be defined on multiple dimensions – territorial, political, economic, social, religious and cultural – thereby creating a wide range of circumstances under which national identities might become salient. However, in practice in Eastern Europe, these circumstances are often narrowed significantly by the collective tendency to define the nation-state in historical terms or in ways serving the self-interest of particular leaders.

Regardless of the collective understanding of the meaning of the 'nation', factors internal and external to a nation influence the potential saliency of national identities. From an internal perspective, majority social groups should find it easier to shift their focus from ethnic to national identities than do minority groups. Because the difference in levels of inclusiveness between ethnic and national identities will be less for majority groups than for minority groups, the cognitive task associated with the shift is easier for majority group members.

Moreover, to the extent that the meaning of the 'nation' is non-territorial in cultural and social terms, it is more likely to reflect the cultural and social practices of the majority group rather than those of minority groups. Therefore, majority groups should find it easier than minority groups to value the nation, and thus to develop national identities. All this suggests that to entice minority groups to focus on their national rather than ethnic identities it is essential to frame the shared meaning of the nation in terms of broad appeal.

From an external perspective, the saliency of national identities can be raised in several ways. First, the category of 'nation' can be made more visible by comparing a nation to surrounding nations. Second, identifying groups at a higher level of inclusiveness will not only make the nation category more salient, but will also render its level of inclusiveness more optimal. For example, when political discourse draws attention to various regions or to Europe itself, it may also have the effect of making the nation a more salient and optimal category of identification. Ironically, then, political efforts aimed at raising the level of European identification are likely to have the side-effect of actually making national identities stronger, thereby to some extent undermining the effort. Finally, conflict between a nation and other nations or regions will especially heighten the saliency of national identities (Brewer, 1986).

Lastly, we turn to European identities. Are they a viable psychological alternative to ethnic and national identities? When thought of primarily in terms of territory, the category 'European' is a problematic basis of identity that is unlikely to represent for very many East Europeans a reasonable alternative to ethnic and national identities. To begin with, some East Europeans may have a territorial understanding of Europe that actually excludes them. By treating the categories of Western Europe and Europe as one and the same, they may conceive of the eastern boundaries of Europe in a way that, by definition, eliminates them from Europe. Even if they count themselves as members of Europe, the category still may not be identified with because its level of inclusiveness might be too high to be optimal, even for those individuals or cultures that are more interdependent. Moreover, the category of 'Europe' typically lacks a contrast adequate to make it salient, though this could be ameliorated somewhat if political discourse provided explicit comparisons of Europe with, for example, Russia or the United States. But perhaps most important, purely territorial understandings of Europe provide little sense of a collective good that is associated with the group, making it less likely that people will develop strong European identities.

But the category of 'Europe', like that of 'nation', can be understood in non-territorial terms. To the extent that people employ multidimensional understandings of Europe, it should psychologically facilitate the development of European identities. For one thing, classifying oneself as European should become easier for Eastern Europeans as concrete and rigid territorial criteria that are potentially exclusive are abandoned in favour of more flexible markers of group membership. Thinking about Europe in non-territorial terms also makes it easier to conceive of the collective goods associated with the group: being European becomes valuable because of the appealing practices of a common culture, or the economic benefits of a common market, or the strategic advantages of a common defence. Thus political leaders can encourage the use of European identities by focusing dialogue on the cultural, economic and security aspects of Europe and by consciously drawing contrasts with non-European entities. Finally, thinking about Europe in non-territorial terms makes it more likely that European identities will not be in conflict with national identities (see Smith, 1992).

Within Eastern Europe, the saliency of Europe as a category of identification should also vary across countries and within countries. European identities should be stronger in those countries and for those individuals that have more interdependent conceptions of the self, because they will be more likely to favour an optimal level of distinctiveness that is compatible with the inclusiveness of 'Europe' as a category. The visibility and thus saliency of 'European' as a category should also increase to the extent that there is interaction with other Europeans. Thus European identities should be stronger in those countries that have the highest levels of visitation by Europeans from other nations, and for those individuals who travel frequently within Europe or whose everyday lives bring them into contact with Europeans from other nations. We might expect, therefore, that European identities would be used more frequently in those East European countries bordering Western Europe, and that within countries, there would in all probability be regional and class differences in the use of European identities.

Still, despite the ability to raise the saliency of European identities through interaction and framing by political elites, the basic fact remains: European identities are difficult to create and sustain. In many ways the task of creating strong European identities is similar to that of developing powerful national identities. The nation-state and Europe are both 'imagined communities', and therefore, identities to both must be sustained by collective understandings that make evident the common meaning of the group and the basis for valuing it. But the creation of strong European identities must face an additional hurdle: Europe is a category whose level of inclusiveness is fairly high. For many, thinking of oneself as 'European' simply might not provide an optimal level of distinctiveness; thinking in such inclusive terms could be uncomfortable. In the long run, the increasing globalisation of everyday life in the twenty-first century could shift the frame of reference for thinking about inclusiveness: compared to a global 'citizen of the world' identity, European identities would provide a more optimal level of distinctiveness. And increasing interaction among the citizens of Europe is an important key to stimulating European identities. But in the immediate future, hopes for creating strong European identities must rest on political leaders – on what must be their deliberate and sustained effort to raise the saliency   of European identities both through political discourse that focuses on Europe and through the forging of true common European goods.

Some Applications to Eastern Europe

The theoretical propositions offered by political psychologists suggest several approaches to the study of East European political identities. To understand how the levels and dimensions of identity in these countries are actually formed and integrated would require research on individual perceptions and macro-level frames. Consequently, we only speculate about the ways in which the factors discussed in the chapter might fit together in some East European contexts. Our propositions, therefore, take the form of hypotheses rather than empirical statements.

Cultural and historical setting

The cultural and historical context of identity formation is crucial not only for establishing the universe of potential groups and identities and for influencing their formation, but also for shaping the very predilection to think of oneself in terms of social relations and groups. The cultural make-up and historical experience of this part of the world suggest in most countries a propensity towards interdependent identities, a plethora of possible in-groups, and easily accessible (frequently mobilised) group identities on a number of dimensions.

A collectivist strand in Slavic culture has been emphasised by a number of observers working in different disciplines.[12] Similarly, Eastern Orthodox religion is credited with fostering stronger collective and community-based identities, and also a tendency to place the good of the community above individual interest. If these observations are true, both the culture and the core selves of individuals should be more interdependent in countries that are predominantly Slavic *and* predominantly Orthodox – Russia, Ukraine, Belarus, Bulgaria, Macedonia, Serbia and Montenegro.[13] Other countries – Romania, Moldova, Bosnia, Slovakia, Poland, Croatia and the Czech Republic – that are less Slavic or less Orthodox might fall along the centre of the continuum of interdependence. Those that are neither – Latvia, Lithuania, Estonia, Hungary and Albania – should foster stronger independent bases of personal identity.

This coarse characterisation is problematic. The non-Slavic cultures of the region may have strong collectivist values as well. Likewise, other religions encourage community and individual identities to lesser or greater degrees: thus Islam and Catholicism are relatively more corporative, or predisposed to emphasising the community over the individual, than is Protestantism. As a starting-point, however, these two simple dichotomies can be taken as indicators of the propensity towards the development of more or less interdependent core selves. Later, we shall see that along the immediate periphery of Western Europe – the Czech Republic, Hungary, Poland, Slovenia and probably the Baltic states – geographical proximity to Western liberalism, with its emphasis on individual rights and responsibilities, and higher levels of economic development, complicates matters by fostering cultural norms favouring independent identities.

Culture and religion are only two facets of the context in which identities are formed. Also important are the populations that exist as potential bases for group identities and the presence or absence of group differences that serve as contrasts during the process of categorisation. Many of the countries of post-communist Europe – Russia, Ukraine, Latvia, Estonia, Moldova, Romania, Bulgaria, Slovakia and all the former Yugoslav republics except for Slovenia and Montenegro – contain strong mixes of populations that differ by ethnicity, language, religion, class or life-style, dress and custom. These differences are often visible or audible, and many of the groups are geographically concentrated enough to provide an arena for common bonds among group members and to be visible to others. These population patterns not only provide many substantive dimensions along which individuals can form identities by contrasting themselves with neighbours, but more importantly they are often configured in ways that make it easy for those identities to form. Some of the substantive dimensions for identity formation – ethnicity, religion and language, for example – often overlap almost completely, providing a number of possible cues for distinguishing oneself from others along ethnic lines.

Historical experience plays a strong role in defining which populations become actual groups and in keeping them 'readily accessible' for the shaping of social identities. Inter-group conflict sharpens group boundaries and provides a number of symbols or cues for political elites who wish to mobilise group identities. For example, the historical record of brutality between Croats and Serbs supplied recent leaders in Croatia and Serbia with powerful symbols for instilling fear and mobilising combatants in the current conflict (Banac, 1992). Moreover, many ethnic populations in this region also span national borders, allowing group identities to cut across state-based citizen identities and provoke inter-state conflict, thereby creating a context favouring strong ethnic group identification. Thus, the conflict between Romanians and Hungarians in Romania is strongly linked with conflict between the two states, making Romanians a more significant 'other' than they might otherwise be for Hungarians in today's Hungary.

Like conflict among groups, the existence of collectively-based repression enhances the salience of the group identity (or identities) used to achieve that repression. Minorities are prone to this dynamic within a state. But even the dominant groups in East European countries shared this experience on and off for centuries under imperial rule and again in the Soviet bloc.[14] The processes of being labelled and treated as a collective and strengthening collective identity as a means of defence were usually reciprocal. Thus, even though Poland is one of the most homogeneous states of post-war Europe, symbols of national identity, many of them developed during the earlier partition of the country, provided powerful cues for mobilising against Soviet domination and were reinforced in the process.[15]

Framing

Population patterns and history, of course, do not alone determine the use of specific identities at a given time and place.[16] The multitude of possible identities places a premium on the framing in a given context. For instance, the discourse within the League of Communists of Yugoslavia, carefully purged of nationalist rhetoric (even as the party was organised along republic – hence also ethnic – lines), turned in the course of a year (1986-87) or perhaps a single night, on Kosovo Pole. Conversely, where there are many visibly different populations, as in

Bosnia–Herzegovina and its capital Sarajevo, citizens may use different bases of identity – in this case multicultural citizenship – for extended periods of time. That the cultural and historical context makes some frames easier to propagate does not ensure their dominance over contradictory frames, but it does make the competition between frames asymmetrical.

When the agents of continuity in framing (institutions, norms and knowledge, daily life patterns) are undergoing change, volatility in identities increases, and with it the possibility for manipulation. Extremists and leaders are in advantageous positions to provide strong cues that can frame identities even if individuals reject their politics. Extremist parties, especially those that gain enough support to remain visible at the margins of politics, tend to have members with more interdependent identities and can often exert a strong influence on categorisation and therefore identity formation. Although together they won only 11–12 per cent of the 1992 vote for parliament, the Party of Romanian National Unity and the Greater Romania Party none the less shaped political discourse in the country. The issues of Romania's relationship with Moldova and of the place for Romania's ethnically Hungarian citizens provided these parties with ready vehicles for defining Romanian ethnic identity as the national identity and reinforcing the tendency to think in terms of ethnicity. These two issues were also more salient in Romania for the efforts of nationalists, and others in political life felt compelled to refer to nationalist positions. In Serbia the Serbian Radical Party maintained even stronger nationalist positions than Milosević's Socialist Party of Serbia, again forcing anyone trying to reframe social identities to combat the national frame, thereby effectively acknowledging its relevance.

Leaders, in general, tend to think more in interdependent terms and are often more extreme than their supporters. We have already alluded to the importance of Slobodan Milosević's speech in Kosovo in April 1987 for overtly casting politics into an ethnic frame. Vladimir Mečiar not only raised Slovak national consciousness but was able to push through the split of Czechoslovakia, even though public opinion polls in Slovakia showed a majority against becoming a separate state. Franjo Tudjman has also strengthened the national-as-ethnic framing of identities in Croatia even as he has attempted to assure the Serb minority of its citizenship rights. In Russia, Vladimir Zhirinovsky reinforces a more extreme ethnic frame for the Russian nation than do most of his voters. These leaders have been among the more radical factions of their parties and have succeeded in pulling their party towards more radically ethnic frames of 'nation'. Another prominent party leader, István Csurka of the Hungarian Democratic Forum, went beyond the Christian national values of his party to argue that liberals, Jews and Communists were obstructing democratisation (reported in Oltays, 1993). Rather than pulling the party with him, however, Csurka was eventually expelled (a common pattern of party fracturing in post-communist Europe). In this case, the leader failed to move the party in a more extreme direction, but he still sharpened the issue of Jewish identity in politics and in the continuing process of defining Hungarian identity. *The divisive or 'radicalising' role of leaders, however, is also a matter of choice and political dynamics.* Mircea Snegur in Moldova, Václav Havel in the Czech Republic, and to some extent Leonid Kuchma in Ukraine, have all tried to mitigate ethnically-based frames by emphasising other values, such as citizenship, and the tasks of state-building and governance. In some instances they have met with relative success; in others their approaches have been overpowered by other frames.

Some identities are easier to cue, because they are based on visible distinctions, tap common bonds, or produce common goods. Some identities are also complementary, while others are contradictory. We turn now to the possibilitities for integrating different identities.

Three examples of the possible layering of identities

Although we can develop general principles of identity and talk generally about the context(s) of Eastern Europe, ultimately we cannot say much about how particular identities are constructed without examining specific contexts. In this section we discuss three cases and suggest ways in which the salience of various levels of inclusiveness and substantive dimensions might combine. Ethnic identities are the primary focus of our analysis because they are often easier to establish, and because they have proved both current and tenacious in post-communist Europe. However, the viability of identity formation along other substantive dimensions will also be examined.

For the first case, take a woman of Hungarian ethnicity living in Romania. The Hungarians are a frequently cued minority in Romania, with a neighbouring state in which their ethnic group is dominant. Their Uralic language is completely different from Romanian, a Latin language. Ethnic Hungarians are sufficiently concentrated to be visible to other Romanians and to constitute a community capable of nurturing common-bond ties. As both a woman and a member of a minority, our subject is likely to have a more interdependent core self than her culture might otherwise suggest. Her most immediate social relationships will be with her family. If her family is not ethnically mixed, it is likely to practise Hungarian traditions and be tied to the ethnic community through these traditions, religious practices, the neighbourhood and daily interactions such as shopping. All these ties fall along complementary dimensions with successively higher levels of inclusiveness. They produce common goods, such as solidarity, companionship, perhaps even mutual self-help in a shortage economy (see Verdery, 1993, for an example of the importance of these ties for obtaining such ordinary things as hair colouring).

As a resident in a specific locality, our subject will also have links to residents of other ethnic groups. If her family is ethnically mixed, she could belong to both ethnic communities, and therefore emphasise her identity as a citizen of the local community in order to reduce competition between the two ethnic identities which are at the same level of inclusiveness. However, the particular content of ethnic categories in each of her communities, shaped by framing processes, might also exclude those of mixed heritage. Exclusion would then impel her towards an even stronger citizenship-based identity at the local level. Assuming, however, that our subject is not of mixed heritage and is well-integrated into her local Hungarian community, the strength of her local citizen identity will be shaped by several factors. If Hungarians are in conflict with local government and other local populations, it will be very difficult for her to embrace both ethnic and citizen identities, especially if local government is identified with Romanian ethnicity. If conflict levels are low and the local administration does not favour one ethnic group over another, the chances are reduced that our subject's identity as a local citizen will clash with her ethnic identity. Citizenship could involve both another dimension of identity and a higher level of inclusiveness than her local ethnic community. To the extent that citizenship can provide harmony between Hungarians and Romanians, better public infrastructure and perhaps a distinguishing local identity (similar to what some have referred to as the 'Spirit of Timişoara' at the beginning of the Romanian revolution), it also might become a salient part of our subject's self-understanding.

Moving to higher levels of inclusiveness, our subject might think of herself as a member of various 'imagined' communities. The strength of her ties with these larger 'communities' would increase to the degree that they are linked to her experienced identity at the local level, that they are framed as inclusive, and that they do not contradict other parts of her identity. The density of ethnic networks extending from her community to other Hungarian communities in Romania, and across the border to Hungary, might make a broader Hungarian identity quite salient. Repression or discrimination could also strengthen her self-perception as Hungarian and the salience of this identity. What about the potential of citizenship identities at the state level to supersede ethnic divisions? Local experience of the state will be an important factor shaping the relationship between her ethnic identity and her identity as a citizen of Romania. If her local community supersedes her ethnic identity and she perceives this to be typical for other communities, local ties may link her more strongly to her Romanian citizenship. If, however, attachment to the state is framed in terms of Romanian ethnicity or if it benefits primarily Romanians, it would be very difficult for our subject *not* to see herself as a Hungarian in the midst of ethnic conflict. Hungarian identity and Romanian citizenship would be mutually exclusive choices on the same dimension of identity (ethnicity). Crucial here would be the extent to which 'nation' is associated with state citizenship or linked to a corporate ethnic body. If citizenship in the nation-state does not have strong ethnic content, citizen identity will not contradict ethnic identity, as the two will now be on different dimensions and at different levels of inclusiveness.

Finally, what are the chances for our subject to develop an identity with Europe? Europe is at a much higher level of inclusiveness; consequently, although European identity does not clash with her other identities, it may not be very salient. As a vague territorial identity, Europe would most likely remain of low salience unless Romania's inclusion in that area were challenged from outside, say from Russia or Turkey. However, for our particular subject, both the territorial and other aspects of Europe – culture, norms, economic advantage, institutional power – might help integrate her ethnic and state identities by overarching Romanian and Hungarian citizenship. Being part of Europe could be another angle from which to deal with an ethnically-rooted Romanian state. Europe might provide resources for addressing the problems faced as an ethnic minority in Romania, and thus European identities could become more salient.[17]

As our second case, let us take perhaps the best-case scenario for developing a salient European identity, the Czech case. Czechs are the majority in their country, and there is neither a very salient minority group within the country nor a significant concentration of Czechs outside the country who might influence identity. Although they possess a Slavic culture, Czechs are not generally Orthodox. Secularism and Protestantism have made significant inroads into this former part of the largely Catholic Habsburg empire. The Czech lands are more developed than other areas of post-communist Europe (and have been for a longer period of time), and the country not only borders but juts into liberal Western Europe. One would expect, therefore, to see more independent core selves than in most of the neighbouring countries.

Our Czech man's closest common-bond groups are his family and his local community (perhaps reinforced by the internal migration following 1968). Given the small size of the Czech state, and the predominance of Prague and a plethora of small towns, local identities may be relatively strong. If he lives in one of the few big cities of the country, his attachment may be to his neighbourhood and probably his occupational circle. Since the split of Czechoslovakia into two states, ethnicity has become a less salient element in national identity. And unless he lives in one of the communities with a strong German or Romany minority,[18] where land restitution or citizenship issues might provoke conflict, his ethnicity will probably not be a major factor at the local level either. If he does live in one of these situations, ethnicity will play a stronger role. In either case, his Czech identity should be compatible with his citizenship in the Czech nation-state, so he might not feel much of a challenge to his ethnic identity or a resulting need to defend it. Thus, in most cases, local citizenship frames have a good chance of superseding frames based on local ethnic communities.

How well does local citizenship travel up a level of inclusiveness to identity with state citizenship? Probably quite well. The lack of a significant intervening level of administration between the centre and the locality facilitates ties to the centre: the nation-state. Perhaps more influential for our subject's citizen identity, however, is the heightening of its salience in the discourse surrounding the splitting of Czechoslovakia and in the provision of goods by the national government. While not dismantling its welfare net, the Czech Republic has distributed partial ownership rights in the economy to all citizens via voucher privatisation. Of all the countries in the area, it has the lowest unemployment and inflation rates, and its population has experienced relatively little disruption given the degree of economic transformation undergone – common goods identified with the central state.

The substantive framing of Czech citizenship also makes it compatible with parts of European identity. In terms of territory and culture, the Czechs have labelled themselves 'Central European' and stressed their place at the heart of Europe and in the development of (West) European culture. The government, and President Havel, have couched the discussion of citizenship in liberal terms and most parties are on the liberal side of the political spectrum (even if they vary in their approach to the economy). This framing is compatible both with the European paradigm and with the core values of Czechs. Moreover, these values are clearly visible in the government's policies leading the Central European move towards integration with the European Union. In sum, Czechs in the Czech Republic can probably nest their ethnic, citizen, national and European identities more easily than their neighbours. These identities are on compatible substantive dimensions and ranged in successive levels of inclusiveness.

A less favourable case for European identity might be the case of another majority, but one that faces salient minority issues: Serbia. The recent war heightened conflict, ethnic framing and contrast to Europe, but even without war the prospects for a European identity in Serbia were slim. Slavic culture, Orthodoxy, historical experience of rule by the Ottoman empire, and contrast with other distinctive groups, all heighten the degree to which Serbs might be socialised to develop interdependent core identities. Our Serb is part of a highly-cued ethnic majority in his country. His closest common-bond groups are his family and his local ethnic community, perhaps centred on an Orthodox church.

We shall assume that he is *not* one of the few Serbs living in Kosovo or another area where he would find himself in a local minority, which would increase even further the salience of his ethnic identity and ties to his local and broader ethnic community.[19] His local citizen identity would be shaped by the same factors as our Hungarian in Romania: the degree to which other ethnic groups are present and in conflict with Serbs, and the degree to which local government supersedes ethnic difference and supplies common and convergent goods. The difference in the two cases is that the Serb subject is in the ethnic majority in his town, region and state. Thus, even if local government does reflect Serb ethnic preference, there should be no normative incompatibility between his ethnic and local citizen identities. Perhaps he lives in a community with a visible and numerically significant minority and local government does not favour a particular ethnic group. If conflict is high and framing suggests that the government is Serbian, the lack of Serb favouritism may be a point for majority disaffection (for example, the government is 'not Serbian enough – bowing to others'). If, however, the local government manages community affairs in such a way as to mitigate tensions (particularly high with war-time population shifts) and provide for the common good, our Serb may find his ethnic identity and his local citizen identity compatible. That is, they would be located on different and non-conflicting substantive dimensions and they may or may not be at different levels of inclusiveness depending on the focus of ethnic identity at a particular time.

On the level of 'imagined communities' an ethnically-based framing of Serbian (or rump Yugoslav) citizenship would be compatible with our subject's family and ethnic identities. A citizenship-based identity at the state level should not contradict the other elements of his identity, unless its lack of 'Serbian' roots is cued in political discourse. This case of Serbia presents a challenge to our normal hierarchy of norms – one that is not unique, however. The imagined ethnic nation of 'Serbia' extends beyond the borders of the state. We recognise this as a root of the wars of Yugoslav succession, but the choice of matching borders to ethnic nations is a matter of framing and agency, albeit one that is implicit in the nineteenth-century concept of the nation-state. The jump in level of inclusiveness beyond state borders – from citizen to nation in this case – would be a significant challenge for identity formation. (The cognitive dissonance of war mobilisation and repulsion against war make this identity shift even more unstable.) It would require a strong framing, tapping ethnic identity and linking it to other salient issues. Citizenship identities based on co-operation at the local level might come into conflict with such framing or its policy implications, however much the relative ease of ethnic frame and a sense of threat might overcome them. Where threat is lessened and citizenship experience is broader, the frame could shift away from placing such salience on the all-inclusive nation.

For most Serbs, the move to European identity will be difficult. For the moment, the conflict between European powers and Serbia over the war and basic values probably makes European identity possible only for a small group of liberal dissidents in Serbia. Putting aside the war, European identity might find itself in contrast with Serbian identity as a Balkan power and with (historical) elements of pan-Slavic identity and ties to Russia. To the extent, then, that the Balkans are contrasted with Europe both from Serbia's vantage-point and from a Western vantage point (see Todorova, 1993, on the Balkans as Europe's 'dark other') or that Russia is counterposed to Europe or a combination of the two factors, any attempt to develop a European identity should produce cognitive dissonance. Such an attempt might even provoke a stronger Serb identity in contrast to Europe.

Conclusions

Psychological theories of the self and social identities provide a framework for understanding the processes through which individuals transform their membership of political groups into potent political identities. The ability of political groups to generate powerful 'we' identities depends, in part, on the nature of the groups themselves. Because they are frequently rooted in real communities and are capable of generating immediately common goods, ethnic groups are often visible and sufficiently salient to produce strong identities. As the basis of social identities, the other political groups that we have considered – political communities, nations, and Europe – are not *naturally* so attractive psychologically. They are 'imagined communities' that must trigger identities on the basis of collective goods that do not always stimulate 'for us' thinking. Still, at any particular moment, it is possible to construct situations that will make citizen, national and European identities salient.

The framing of situations occurs on both a macro- and a micro-level. The macro-level framing reflects cultural patterns and the nature of social institutions, and its presence makes essential comparative research for understanding the functioning of political identities. The micro-level framing is heavily influenced by context, and importantly by political discourse. Thus political leaders play a substantial role in structuring situations so that they evoke particular political identities. This suggests, then, the key strategy for dampening the effects of divisive ethnic identities: raising the salience of more unifying identities through the use of political discourse. But such discourse cannot be 'empty words'. The willingness of individuals to use political identities that are framed prominently in political discourse ultimately depends on finding something of value in the group. European identities cannot be forged out of merely symbolic common goods like sports teams: they must rest on real collective goods of substantial value to Europeans.

Notes

An earlier version of this chapter was published in 'Identity Formation, Citizenship and Statebuilding in the Former Communist Countries of Eastern Europe', Papers presented at the ARENA Seminar, Oslo, 7–8 December 1995: Oslo: ARENA Working Paper 20/96, October 1996.

1. While comtemporary social psychological theory consistently supports the idea that the self is dynamic and varies with the context, there is disagreement over whether

there is a permanent structure of the self. John Turner and his colleagues argue that there is no permanent self-structure; at any point in time, the self reflects the immediate application of cognitive categories to the individual: see Turner, Oakes, Haslam and McGarty, 1994. But others, following the arguments of Hazel Markus, would suggest that there is some continuing structure of the self: see Markus and Wurf, 1987. For our purposes, it is unnecessary to settle this theoretical dispute. What is important here is to recognise the dynamic nature of the self and its responsiveness to context.

2. The relational quality of an attribute or category should not be confused with the social origins of its meaning. The meaning of all categories is socially defined, but not all categories imply a *relationship* between the self and others.

3. Others (Shweder and Bourne, 1984; Triandis, 1989; Triandis *et al.*, 1988) have identified a similar dimension in self-conceptions although they have not necessarily used the same terminology.

4. For a summary of these effects see Markus and Kitayama, 1991.

5. The description of the socialisation process which follows summarises the argument made by Markus and Kitayama, 1994.

6. Although these two acts may be distinguished for descriptive purposes, they are likely to be inextricably linked in the actual process of perception.

7. But what constitutes an 'intermediate' level of inclusiveness is likely to vary cross-culturally.

8. Certainly given the wide range of conceptualisations of 'nation' that scholars have come up with, we should not be at all surprised that citizens, too, have many different ways in which they think about nations. For a discussion of the multiplicity of meanings that 'nation' or 'Europe' might assume, see Smith, 1992.

9. Large groups of concentrated 'others' should be more visible than those that are dispersed, although their proximity and concentration will not necessarily trigger in-group–out-group hostilities. The proximity of concentrated 'others' might facilitate inter-group contact and thus reduce the likelihood of conflict or it might fuel inter-group conflict. The degree to which there is interaction between the two groups will play a significant role in determining the outcome (see Brewer, 1986). Overall, the relationship between social density and group identification is an inverted U function. At some point, social density becomes so great that the category becomes so inclusive that it ceases to be optimally distinctive (Lau, 1989).

10. Where the meaning of membership of both categories is defined in terms of territory, it is difficult to make the categories visible in everyday life. However, if their meaning is defined culturally or religiously, for example, it becomes more likely that there will be within-nation contrasts between nationals and non-nationals, and Europeans and non-Europeans.

11. Defined strictly in territorial terms, this would be unlikely because the two identities would be at quite different levels of inclusiveness. However, defined in non-territorial terms, the levels of inclusiveness could be closer together and the substantive meanings similar enough that the two identities could be evoked simultaneously.

12. Studies of Russian and Soviet political culture point especially to the experience of the *mir* – a pre-revolutionary agricultural community – as formative: see Tucker, 1987. In the Balkans, a smaller co-operative unit, the *zadruga*, fulfilled a similar function (Wolff, 1978). Our argument here is that Slavic culture, shaped by experiences among those peoples, heightens the propensity for individuals to form interdependent identi-

ties. We do not mean to imply that this propensity has anything to do with 'authoritarian' or 'democratic' mind-sets (see Petro, 1995, for an argument against an emphasis on 'collectivism' in Russian culture as anti-democratic). The communal orientations of Orthodoxy are discussed in *inter alia* Miliukov, 1960 (1942); Berdyaev, 1960 (1937); Tucker, 1987; and White, 1979.

13. Belarus and Montenegro are unusual cases of strong identity interdependence with Russia and Serbia, respectively.

14. It can be argued that Russia as an imperial power and the core nation of the Soviet empire was not subjected to this sort of repression. Although external repression of Russians is probably a lesser factor in identity formation, many Russian and Western scholars argue that Russian culture and identity were suppressed or distorted by the Soviet regime.

15. The effect of these cases on personal identities was vislble in the profound confusion and resentment resulting from the split of Solidarity in 1990 and the breakdown of national unity.

16. Thus, we fully support Verdery's argument (1993) against the analogy of Soviet decline having 'taken the lid off the pot' of perpetually brewing ethnic strife.

17. This condominium of European and domestic norms might also be perceived as working against minority interests, though. For some Slovaks, Czech emphasis on Europe's liberal political and economic values may have been yet another avenue of cultural imperialism and a mechanism for maintaining the Czechs' privileged status in a united Czechoslovakia. The asymmetrical patterns of political parties and political party support in the two countries after the split suggest such a dramatic difference regarding liberal norms.

18. The Czech Republic also has a Slovak minority, but the challenge of this minority to Czech ethnic identity is lessened by the recent creation of a Slovak state and thus the separation of Slovak political aspirations from the Czech polity.

19. A mixed ethnic heritage would reduce this salience, leading to identity politics similar to those mentioned in the first case. In order not to complicate this illustration further, we shall assume that he is not of mixed heritage and is included by the current predominant framing of Serb ethnicity.

References

Abrams, Dominic (1994). 'Political Distinctiveness: An Identity Optimizing Approach', *European Journal of Social Psychology* **24**, pp.357–65.

Anderson, Benedict (1983). *Imagined Communities* (London: Verso).

Banac, Ivo (1992). 'Post-Communism as Post-Yugoslavism: The Yugoslav Non-Revolutions of 1989–90', in Ivo Banac (ed.), *Eastern Europe in Revolution* (Ithaca, NY: Cornell University Press), pp.168–87.

Berdyaev, Nicolas (1960). *The Origins of Russian Communism* (Ann Arbor, MI: University of Michigan Press); first published in 1937.

Brewer, Marilyn (1986). 'The Role of Ethnocentrism in inter-group Conflict', in Stephen Worchel and William G. Austin (eds), *The Psychology of Inter-Group Relations* (Chicago, IL: Nelson Hall).

—— (1991). 'The Social Self: On Being the Same and Different at the Same Time', *Personality and Social Psychology Bulletin* **17**, pp.475–82.

Calhoun, Craig (1994). *Social Theory and the Politics of Identity* (Cambridge, MA: Blackwell).

Connor, Walker (1994). *Ethnonationalism: The Quest for Understanding* (Princeton, NJ: Princeton University Press).

Conover, Pamela Johnston (1984). 'The Influence of Group Identifications Political Perception and Evaluation', *Journal of Politics* **46**, pp.760–85.

—— (1988). 'The Role of Groups in Political Thinking', *British Journal of Political Science* **18**, pp.51–76.

—— (1995). 'Citizen Identities and Conceptions of the Self', *Journal of Political Philosophy* **3**, pp.133–65.

Gaertner, S.L., J. Mann, A. Murrell and J.F. Dovidio (1989), 'Reducing In-Group Bias: The Benefits of Recategorization', *Journal of Personality and Social Psychology* **57**, pp. 239–49.

Greenfield, Leah (1992). *Nationalism* (Cambridge, MA: Harvard University Press).

Greenwald, A.G. and A.R. Pratkanis (1984). 'The Self', in R.W. Wyer and T.K. Srull (eds), *Handbook of Social Cognition* (Hillsdale, NJ: Lawrence Erlbaum), vol.3.

Habermas, Jürgen (1995). 'Citizenship and National Identity: Some Reflections on the Future of Europe, in Ronald Beiner (ed.), *Theorizing Citizenship* (Beverley Hills, CA: Sage), pp.255–81.

Haesly, Richard (1995). 'The Components of National Identity: Towards a Political Psychological Understanding of National Identity' (paper presented at the annual meetings of the International Society of Political Psychology, Washington, DC, 5–7 July).

Haslam, S. Alexander and John C. Turner (1992). 'Context-Dependent Variation in Social Stereotyping 2: The Relationship Between Frame of Reference, Self-Categorization and Accentuation', *European Journal of Social Psychology* **22**, pp.251–77.

——, Penelope J. Oakes, Craig McGarty and B.K. Hayes (1992). 'Context-Dependen Variation in Social Stereotyping 1: The Effects of Inter-Group Relations as Mediated by Social Change and Frame of Reference', *European Journal of Social Psychology* **22**, pp.3–20.

Hogg, M.A. and J.C. Turner (1987). 'Inter-Group Behaviour, Self-Stereotyping, and the Salience of Social Categories', *British Journal of Social Psychology* **26**, pp.325–40.

Hui, C. Harry (1988). 'Measurement of Individualism-Collectivism', *Journal of Research in Personality* **22**, pp.17–36.

Kymlicka, Will (1995). *Multicultural Citizenship* (Oxford: Oxford University Press).

Lau, Richard R. (1989). 'Individual and Contextual Influences on Group Identification', *Social Psychology Quarterly* **52**, pp.220–31.

Markus, Hazel and Shinobu Kitayama (1991). 'Culture and the Self: Implications for Cognition, Emotion, and Motivation', *Psychological Bulletin* **98**, pp.224–53.

—— (1994). 'A Collective Fear of the Collective: Implications for Selves and Theories of Selves', *Personality and Social Psychology Bulletin* **20**, pp.568–79.

Markus, Hazel and Ziva Kunda (1986). 'Stability and Malleability of the Self-Concept', *Journal of Personality and Social Psychology* **51**, pp.858–66.

Markus, Hazel and Paula Nurius (1986). 'Possible Selves', *American Psychologist* **41**, pp.954–69.

Markus, Hazel and Elissa Wurf (1987). 'The Dynamic Self-Concept: A Social Psychological Perspective', *Annual Review of Psychology* **38**, pp.299–337.

Miliukov, Paul (1960). *Outlines of Russian Culture, Part I: Religion and the Church*, edited by Michael Karpovich (New York: A.J. Barnes); first published in 1942.

Mouffe, Chantal (1992). 'Democratic Citizenship and the Political Community', in Chantal Mouffe (ed.), *Dimensions of Radical Democracy: Pluralism, Citizenship, Community* (London: Verso), pp.225-39.

Oakes, Penelope J. (1987), 'The Salience of Social Categories', in J.C. Turner, M.A. Hogg, P.J. Oakes, S.D. Reicher and M.S. Wetherall (eds), *Rediscovering the Social Group: A Self-Categorization Theory*, pp.117-41.

Ottay, Edith (1993). 'Hungarian Democratic Forum Expects Radical Leader', *Radio Free Europe/Radio Liberty Research Report* **2**, no.31 (30 July), pp.24-9.

Petro, Nicolas N. (1995). *The Rebirth of Russian Democracy: An Interpetation of Russian Political Culture* (Cambridge, MA: Harvard University Press).

Prentice, Deborah A., Dale T. Miller and Jenifer R. Lightdale (1994). 'Asymmetries in Attachments to Groups and to Their Members: Distinguishing Between Common-Identity and Common-Bond Groups, *Personality and Social Psychology Bulletin* **20**, pp.484-93.

Seroka, Jim (1993). 'Yugoslavia and Its Successor States', in Stephen White, Judy Batt and Paul G. Lewis (eds), *Developments in East European Politics* (Basingstoke: Macmillan, and Durham, NC: Duke University Press), pp.98-121.

Shweder, R.A. and E.J. Bourne (1984). 'Does the Concept of the Person Vary Cross-Culturally?', in R.A. Shweder and R.A. Levine (eds), *Culture Theory: Essays on Mind, Self, and Emotion* (Cambridge: Cambridge University Press), pp.113-55.

Smith, Anthony D. (1991). *National Identity* (Harmondsworth: Penguin).

—— (1992). 'National Identity and the Idea of European Unity', *International Affairs* **68**, pp.55-76.

Spinner, Jeff (1994). *The Boundaries of Citizenship: Race, Ethnicity, and Nationality in the Liberal State* (Baltimore, MD: Johns Hopkins University Press).

Stangor, Charles, Laure Lynch, Changming Duan and Beth Glass (1992). 'Categorization of Individuals on the Basis of Multiple Social Features', *Journal of Personality and Social Psychology* **62**, pp.207-18.

Tamir, Yael (1993). *Liberal Nationalism* (Princeton, NJ: Princeton University Press).

Tajfel, Henri (1981). *Human Groups and Social Categories* (Cambridge: Cambridge University Press).

—— and John C. Turner (1986). 'The Social Identity Theory of Inter-Group Behavior' in S. Worchel and A. Austin (eds), *Psychology of inter-group Relations* (Chicago: Nelson-Hall), pp.7-24.

Taylor, Charles (1985). 'Alternative Futures: Legitimacy, Identity and Alienation in Late Twentieth Century Canada', in Alan Cairns and Cynthia Williams (eds), *Constitutionalism, Citizenship and Society in Canada* (Toronto: University of Toronto Press), pp.183-229.

—— (1989). 'Cross-Purposes: The Liberal-Communitarian Debate', in Nancy L. Rosenblum (ed.), *Liberalism and the Moral Life* (Cambridge, MA: Harvard University Press), pp.159-82.

—— (1994). *Multiculturalism* (Princeton, NJ: Princeton University Press).

Taylor, Donald M. and Lise Dube (1986). 'Two Faces of Identity: The "I" and the "We"', *Journal of Social Issues* **42**, pp.81-98.

Todorova, Maria (1994). 'The Balkans: From Discovery to Invention', *Slavic Review* **53**, pp.453-82.

Triandis, Harry C. (1989). 'The Self and Social Behavior in Differing Cultural Contexts', *Journal of Personality and Social Psychology* **96**, pp.506-20.

—— (1990). 'Cross-Cultural Studies of Individualism and Collectivism', in John J. Berman (ed.), *Cross-Cultural Perspectives* (1989 Nebraska Symposium on Motivation) **37**, pp.41–143.

——, Robert Bontempo and Marcelo J. Villareal (1988). 'Individualism and Collectivism: Cross-Cultural Perspectives on Self–In-Group   Relations', *Journal of Personality and Social Psychology* **54**, pp.32–338.

Triandis, Harry C., Christopher McCusker and C. Harry Hui (1990). 'Multimethod Probes of Individualism and Collectivism', *Journal of Personality and Social Psychology* **59**, pp.1006–20.

Tucker, Robert C. (1987). *Political Culture and Leadership in Soviet Russia* (Brighton: Wheatsheaf).

Turner, John C., M. Hogg, P. Oakes, S. Reicher and M. Wetherell (1987). *Rediscovering the Group: A Self-CategorizationTheory* (Oxford and New York: Basil Blackwell).

Turner, John C., Penelope Oakes, S. Alexander Haslam and Craig McGarty (1994). 'Self and Collective: Cognition and Social Context', *Personality and Social Psychology Bulletin* **20**, pp.454–63.

Verdery, Katherine (1993). 'Nationalism and National Sentiment in Post-Socialist Romania', *Slavic Review* **52**, pp.179–203.

Wilder, D.A. and J.E. Thompson (1988). 'Assimilation and Contrast Effects in the Judgments of Groups', *Journal of Personality and Social Psychology* **54**, pp.62–73.

White, Stephen (197 9). *Political Culture and Soviet Politics* (London and Basingstoke: Macmillan).

Wolff, Robert Lee (1978). *The Balkans in Our Time*, rev. edn (New York: Norton).

Wong-Reiger, Durhane and Donald M. Taylor (1981). 'Multiple Group Membership and Self-Identity', *Journal of Cross-Cultural Psychology* **12**, pp.61–79.

3 Why Do Ethnic Groups Mobilise?

Rajat Ganguly

As is clear from events taking place in Eastern Europe and elsewhere in the world in the 1990s, ethnic disputes have become a central feature of politics. An obvious factor behind such conflict is the greater political assertiveness of 'ethnic groups'. Hence, a proper understanding of what the term 'ethnic group' means is an important research priority. A related question is why, in the last quarter of the twentieth century, we have witnessed political mobilisation of ethnic groups in all parts of the globe, including those groups considered in this volume. A proper understanding of the causes of ethnic political mobilisation and conflict is crucial, and we must move beyond simplistic discussions of 'ancient hatreds' to search for more systematic explanations.

The Debate Over Ethnicity

The word 'ethnic' derives from the Greek word *ethnikos*. There is, however, a wide divergence of opinion among scholars regarding the meaning and interpretation of the term 'ethnic group'. For some, it refers to a small community with archaic characteristics.[1] For others, the term refers to both small and large communities not only in backward societies but also in advanced industrialised ones.[2] The present-day political usage of the term is restricted primarily to 'a quasi-national kind of "minority group" within the state, which has somehow not achieved the status of a "nation"'.[3] If understood in this sense, an ethnic group is distinct from a nation. While a nation is a broader and more inclusive concept and can be defined culturally ('cultural nation') as well as politically ('political nation'), an ethnic group is smaller and more exclusive, and is confined in membership to those who share certain common attributes.[4] Similarly, 'ethnocentrism' – sentiment and bias towards one's ethnic group and against other such groups – can be distinguished from 'nationalism' – sentiment for one's nation.[5]

Scholars are also divided in their opinion regarding the basis of ethnicity. In general, one may speak of four viewpoints: the *objective*, the *subjective*, the *syncretist* and the *constructivist*. For the objectivists, such as Geertz and Isaacs, ethnic identity is a 'given' or 'natural' phenomenon.[6] Understood in this sense, ethnic groups 'constitute the network into which human individuals are born' and where 'every human infant or young child finds itself a member of a kinship group and of a neighborhood' and therefore comes to share with the other members of the group certain common cultural attributes.[7] Some of these common cultural attributes are language, religion, customs, tradition, food, dress and music.[8]

For their part, the subjectivists, such as Glazer and Moynihan,[9] without dismissing the importance of cultural markers in the manifestation of ethnic identity, stress the psychological aspect of self- and group-related 'feeling of identity distinctiveness and its recognition by others' as a crucial determinant of ethnic identity selection and its persistence.[10] The exact nature of these psychological feelings is not very clear. Rex, for instance, argues that in psychological terms three things are important for group creation. First comes the emotional satisfaction, or warmth, that one gets from belonging to the group. Second, a shared belief in a myth of origin or the history of the group is important because it sets the boundaries of the group. Finally, the members of the group must 'regard the social relations, within which they live, as "sacred" and as including not merely the living but the dead'.[11] Subjectivists, therefore, without ruling out the importance of cultural attributes, put more emphasis on the psychological aspect in the formation of ethnic boundaries and the development of 'we' versus 'them' feelings among a group of people.

Identifying the shortcomings of both these perspectives – the failure of objectivists to account for social adaptation and the difficulty faced by subjectivists in explaining when and how groups arrive at self-ascriptive feelings – the syncretists stress the complementarity of the two approaches. They defined ethnicity as a 'subjectively held sense of shared identity based on objective cultural or regional criteria'.[12] In other words, the syncretists view ethnicity as a complex phenomenon comprising many components and, therefore, not reducible to a single-factor explanation.[13] Anthony Smith exemplifies this approach when he examines six 'bases' or 'foundations' of ethnic identity. First, an ethnic group must have a name in order to be recognised as a distinct community, both by its members and by outsiders. The other five bases include a belief in or myth of common ancestry, the presence of historical memories (as interpreted and diffused over generations by group members, often verbally) among members of the group, shared culture (including dress, food, music, crafts and architecture, laws, customs and institutions, religion and language), attachment to a specific territory and a sense of common solidarity.[14]

Discussing the conditions that promote the formation and survival of ethnic groups, Smith pointed out that in pre-modern times four factors favoured ethnic crystallisation and survival. The first condition was 'the acquisition (or, later, the loss) of a particular piece of territory, which was felt to "belong" to a people as they belonged to it'.[15] Second, a history of struggle with various enemies not only led to a sense of community but also served (through historical myths and beliefs) as a source of inspiration for future generations. Third, some form of organised religion was necessary 'for producing specialists in communications and record-keeping, as well as for generating the rituals and traditions that formed the channels of continuity for ethnic communities'.[16] Finally, 'the proximate cause of ethnic durability and survival was the rise and power of a myth of "ethnic chosenness"'.[17] Smith concluded that the factors which promote one's sense of ethnic identity have become more influential in modern times. Of crucial importance have been the increasing cultural and civic activities of the modern state, activities of intellectuals and intelligentsia within the ethnic group, and the development of the ideology of nationalism – particularly ethnic nationalism in contradistinction to a territorial or civic one.[18]

The constructivists, in turn, categorically reject the notion that ethnic identity is a 'natural' or 'given' phenomenon. Pointing out that the presumption of 'naturalness' of the nation and national identity distinctions obscures the human 'hand' and 'motivations' behind these processes and that the terms ethnic identity and ethnic group mean quite different things in different places and among peoples, constructivists contend that these concepts are *social constructions* – 'the product of specific historical and geographical forces rather than biologically given ideas whose meaning is dictated by nature'.[19] From the constructivist perspective, ethnic identity and ethno-nationalism should be viewed as the 'product of processes which are embedded in human actions and choices' rather than as 'natural' or 'given'.[20]

One of the earlier influential writers who stressed the social construction of ethnic identity was Max Weber. He viewed ethnic groups as 'human groups' whose belief in a common ancestry, in spite of its origins being mostly fictitious, is so strong that it leads to the creation of a community.[21] Ethnic groups are, therefore, based more on beliefs and less on any objective cultural or biological traits. Weber concluded that ethnic membership by itself 'does not necessarily result in ethnic group formation but only provides the resources that may, under the right circumstances, be mobilized into a group by appropriate political action'[22]

Charles Keyes has argued that ethnic identity derives from a 'cultural construal of descent',[23] and distinguishes between 'social descent' and 'genetic descent'. Social descent is a form of kin selection by which human beings seek to create solidarity with those whom they recognise as being 'of the same people' or as 'sharing descent'. Its formation depends upon the cultural construal of those characteristics that indicates who does or does not 'belong to the same people as oneself'.[24] Genetic descent, on the other hand, consists of 'biological characteristics transmitted through genetic inheritance'.[25]

Keyes further argues that while the cultural construal of descent – social descent – leads to the formation of ethnic identity, '[there] is no invariable pattern as to which cultural differences will be seized upon by groups as emblematic of their ethnic differences'.[26] But generally speaking, the type of cultural markers that are put forward as 'emblematic of ethnic identity depends upon the interpretations of the experiences and actions of mythical ancestors and/or historical forebears. These interpretations are often presented in the form of myths or legends in which historical events have been accorded symbolic significance'.[27] The forms that these myths and legends can take vary. They can be found, for example, in 'stories, both oral and written, songs, artistic depictions, dramatisations, rituals'.[28] But no matter how these myths and legends are created and presented, 'the symbols of ethnic identity must be appropriated and internalized by individuals before they can serve as the basis for orienting people to social action'.[29]

Keyes cautions that the cultural construal of ethnicity and its internalisation by individuals do not necessarily make it an explanatory variable of social action. Rather, ethnicity becomes a variable 'only if access to the means of production, means of expropriation of the products of labour, or means of exchange between groups are determined by membership in groups defined in terms of nongenealogical descent'.[30] At such moments, ethnicity can be 'a device as much as a focus for group mobilisation by its leadership through the select use of ethnic symbols for socio-cultural and politico-economic purposes'.[31] Ethnic identity, therefore, is the social and political creation of 'élites, who draw upon, distort, and sometimes fabricate materials from the cultures of the groups they wish to represent in order to protect their well-being or existence or to gain political and economic advantage for their groups as well as for themselves'.[32]

From this discussion, it becomes clear that the most contentious issue between the primordialists and the social constructivists concerns the role of culture in the formation of ethnic identity. Primordialists consider culture to be more integrally connected with ethnic identity formation, 'although even they recognize that some behaviors and emblems may change independently of basic identity'.[33] This view, by and large, is reflected in the writings of Geertz, Isaacs, Naroll, Gordon, Mitchell, Epstein and Furnivall.[34]

This primordialist viewpoint assigning primacy to culture in the formation of ethnic identity came under attack after the late 1960s. Kuper was one of the first scholars who questioned this 'a priori dependency relationship between cultural and other forms of social and political grouping, including the racial and the ethnic'.[35] Subsequently, Barth, together with Glazer and Moynihan, also argued that 'there is no necessary continuity or congruence, in time or space, between social (including ethnic) groups and cultural practice'.[36] This analytical distinction and separation between ethnicity *per se* and culture is now generally accepted by most social scientists. From this viewpoint, culture is 'a mere epiphenomenon of ethnicity, dependent on more basic organisational and strategic factors'.[37] Social constructivists, however, have taken this particular viewpoint to an extreme level 'where culture is relegated to a very secondary position in the ethnic scheme of things, as a series of symbols that justify the existence of particular (ethnic) interest groups'.[38] Some constructivists have even suggested that cultural markers can be 'manipulated to rationalise the identity and organisation of the ethnic group'.[39]

The Concept of Ethno-nationalism

In spite of the attention recently accorded it, the concept of 'ethno-nationalism' remains contentious. Most scholars agree that a fundamental distinction exists between ethnic politics and nationalist politics, but they disagree over the conditions when, and if at all, this distinction can be overcome and ethnic and nationalist politics can coincide. Anthony Smith, for instance, in spite of accepting the distinction between ethnic politics and nationalist politics, nevertheless suggests that ethnic nationalism ... unlike the territorial and civic versions of nationalism ... conceives of the nation as a genealogical and vernacular cultural community. Whereas civic and territorial conceptions of the nation regard it as a community of shared culture, common laws and territorial citizenship, ethnic concepts of the nation focus on the genealogy of its members, however, fictive; on popular mobilisation of 'the folk'; on native history and customs; and on the vernacular culture. As a vernacular community of genealogical descent, the ethnic nation seeks to create itself in the image of an ancestral *ethnie*. In doing so, it often helps to recreate that *ethnie*.[40]

Not all scholars agree with this interpretation. Walker Connor, for one, believes that nationalism refers to loyalty to one's nation or ethnic group.[41] From his perspective, any political activity undertaken by individuals on the basis of their loyalty to their ethnic group is a manifestation of ethno-nationalism. By and large, however, the consensus among scholars is that, although ethnic and nationalist politics are differentiated, this differentiation can be overcome if the political goal of an ethnic group coincides with the political objective of the nationalist doctrine, namely self-determination. Kellas, for example, points out that 'Nationalism focuses on "national self-determination," or home rule in a national territory. Ethnic politics in contrast is largely concerned with the protection of rights for members of the group within the existing state, with no claim for a territorial "homeland"'.[42] In similar fashion, Frye notes: 'Ethnic groups may or may not feel a sense of nationalism, that is, they may or may not seek the creation of a nation-state that corresponds to a given territory. The sense of nation has a territorial aspect absent from ethnicity, since a member of an ethnic group living abroad can share a sense of identity with a co-ethnic in the home country quite apart from feeling an attachment to a nation-state'.[43]

For these scholars, ethnic groups exhibit ethno-nationalist sentiment only when their political agenda hinges on 'ethnic self-determination' and the creation of a nation-state corresponding to their specific territorial homelands. Frye stresses that while the core objective of a nationalist movement is to achieve political sovereignty within a given territory, 'not all nationalist movements are driven by a single ethnic group, nor do all ethnic revivals lead to a campaign for national sovereignty'.[44] But ethnic groups may often form the core of nationalist movements, and when they do, they shift from being ethnic to ethno-nationalist groups. This interpretation also is favoured by Ted Gurr when he defines ethno-nationalist groups as large politicised groups of people sharing a common language and ethnicity who are territorially concentrated and exhibit a history of making demands for political autonomy or separate statehood.[45]

If we understand ethno-nationalism as one specific type of ethnic politics – the movement by an ethnic group for self-determination in the form of political autonomy or the creation of a separate state corresponding to its ethnic homeland – then it becomes obvious that there can be different types of ethnic political movements. In *Minorities at Risk*, Gurr has provided a detailed description of the various types of ethnic political movements currently active in the world.

Gurr used the term non-state communal groups to refer to peoples sharing language, ethnicity, region of residence and history but not necessarily constituting nations or states. Thus, 'communal groups are cultural and psychological entities rather than bounded political communities'.[46] Politically salient communal groups are those which either suffer or benefit from systematic discrimination, engage in political mobilisation to promote self-defined interests, or combine these characteristics. Gurr further subdivided politicised communal groups into national and minority peoples. National peoples can be ethno-nationalist groups – large, regionally concentrated peoples with a history of organised political autonomy and separatist movements – as well as indigenous peoples – the conquered descendants of the original inhabitants of a region. In turn, minority peoples are made up of three groups: (a) ethno-classes, that is, usually low-status, ethnically distinct peoples; (b) militant sects, or groups focused on defence of their religious beliefs (reconceptualised in Gurr's book with Barbara Harff as the less pejorative-sounding politically active religious minorities); and (c) communal contenders, or culturally distinct groups aspiring to exercise a share of state power. Communal contenders may be given advantages over other groups and therefore represent dominant minorities, or they may be disadvantaged, suffer various forms of discrimination and be drawn into ethnic struggles of a particularly bloody kind.

Of 233 communal groups identified by Gurr as functioning between 1945 and 1989, over two-thirds were national groups: 81 (such as Croatians and Québecois) were ethno-nationalist and 83 (native Americans, Australian aboriginals) indigenous peoples. There were 45 ethno-classes, ranging from African-Americans in the US and in nine Latin American societies to Muslims in France and Koreans in Japan. Most of the 49 militant sects consisted of Muslim minorities (Turks in Germany, Malays in Thailand). There were 25 advantaged minorities (such as the Tutsis of Burundi and the Sunnis of Iraq) and 41 disadvantaged communal contenders (many of the tribal groups in sub-Saharan Africa).

The world of ethnic groups and ethnic politics is thus vast and varied. This makes the task of formulating a general explanation of ethnic politics more difficult. One way out of this difficulty is to adopt Charles Ragin's approach and ask the question: what factors account for the political mobilisation of ethnic groups?[47] While such an approach does not tell us much about the type of group and the nature of its demands, by focusing on causes it allows for a general explanation of what drives ethnic politics. We turn to this subject next.

Indirect Theories of Ethnic Political Mobilisation and Conflict

Negative theories of integration

One of the best known and most influential theories in this category is that of Karl Deutsch. In *Nationalism and Social Communication*, he constructed a paradigm of national integration employing two key concepts: mobilisation and assimilation. His argument was that, first, modernisation leads to a greater mobilisation of the population, and second, increasing urbanisation and the spread of communication (a consequence of modernisation) results in the assimilation of those mobilised into the national mainstream. The outcome is national integration, the basis for nationalism.[48]

Deutsch, however, signalled the dangers of disruption of the integrative process. Using the same concepts of mobilisation and assimilation, he argued that parochialism or regionalism (including their ethnic forms), with their concomitant instability and national fragmentation, could result from situations in which mobilisation outpaced assimilation. The mobilisation–assimilation gap created when mobilisation preceded assimilation was the root cause of national fragmentation and the rise of parochialism.[49]

Related points have been made by such other scholars as Samuel Huntington and Daniel Lerner. Both have referred to the significance of the tension between 'rising expectations' and 'rising frustrations', caused primarily by modernisation in developing countries, in accounting for disintegrative tendencies in these states. In most of these societies, the process of modernisation, by causing rapid social mobilisation, the breakdown of the traditional order, and the expansion of communications and transportation networks, led to an increase in the number of political participants who were sensitive to the poverty in which they lived. Hence demands on the political system greatly increased as new groups entered the political arena. However, since economic growth was slow in most cases, and because élites were concerned that an equitable distributive response to demands could further slow down economic growth, the capacity of the political system to respond to demands was restricted. As a result the initial euphoria that was generated by the 'revolution of rising expectations' was soon replaced by the despair of the 'revolution of rising frustrations'. As political participation increased and economic conditions degenerated, many Third World societies and, more recently, parts of the former Soviet Union, witnessed political fragmentation and decay and the rise of parochial and ethno-nationalist sentiments.[50]

Another explanation for the rise of ethnic political mobilisation has been provided by *strain theorists* such as Clifford Geertz, who argued that

> during the disorienting process of modernisation ... unintegrated citizens, looking for an anchor in a sea of changes, will grab hold of an increasingly anachronistic ethnic identity, which bursts onto the scene and then recedes as the process of structural differentiation moves toward a reintegrated society. Thus, ethnicity might resurge temporarily, but like suicide, it is a manifestation of anomie that would inexorably disappear.[51]

Hence ethnic political mobilisation, as seen by strain theorists, was possible only in the event of 'some failure to draw subnations into national economic life ... and ... because of the growing economic, cultural and political divergence of the sub-nation from the rest of the nation'.[52] Although regional economic inequality as a cause of ethnic political mobilisation was compatible with the developmental perspective, the failure to integrate the subnation was considered the underlying cause.[53] At the same time, since this school considered strain in society caused by modernisation to be a temporary phenomenon, ethnic political mobilisation was expected to be short-lived, too.

In a similar fashion, in accounting for the rise of ethnic political mobilisation, parochialism and recognition, Stein Rokkan highlighted the salience of three related factors: territorial concentration, social isolation and economic isolation. All indicated the failure of the state to draw ethnic groups into national life.[54] But the underlying assumption that ethnicity is a primordial sentiment and ethnic political mobilisation an aberration which would disappear when the structural reintegration of society is completed remained in his analysis.

Negative theories of cohesion

Negative theories of cohesion include three models of control. The first is *incompatibility theory* or the *plural society approach*. Second, scepticism about the plural society approach has led to the theory of *consociationalism*. Finally, shortcomings in the consociational model has produced development of the theory of *hegemonic-exchange*.

(a) The plural society approach. The failure of the modernisation paradigm and various assimilationist theories to account for growing fragmentation in multi-ethnic societies led to disillusionment with the optimistic predictions of nation-building theories and renewed interest in the 'theory of the plural society, which posited that multi-ethnic societies could not remain both stable and democratic'.[55] Although the most systematic version of the plural society approach was developed by the British economist J.S. Furnivall and later modified by the West Indian anthropologist M.G. Smith, indications of the approach could be found in the writings of the Duke of Sully in the seventeenth century and of John Stuart Mill.[56]

The main argument of the plural society approach, as elaborated by Furnivall, is that in plural societies – where different ethnic groups live in close proximity to but separately from each other – intercommunal relations are characterised by unchecked economic competition. Since relations between the various groups remain confined to the market place, these societies fail to develop a sense of common loyalty that would overcome the cultural and ethnic differences between the various groups. Unrestrained competition and competing nationalisms that follow between different cultural groups cause society to fragment. Furnivall argued that the only way such societies could be held together was through the application of external force. For him, this external force was provided by colonialism.[57]

M.G. Smith modified the plural society approach. He argued that a plural society could be created by incorporating members of different cultural groups into a multi-ethnic state in one of three ways. The first type of incorporation is termed *uniform*, where individuals are incorporated as equal citizens with equal civic and political status irrespective of ethnic or cultural affiliation. The second is called *equivalent* where different collectivities are incorporated into a single society with equal or complementary public rights and status. This is the consociational democracy model. The final type of incorporation is labelled *differential*, where a dominant group exercises power and maintains its superior position by excluding other groups from power.

Although Smith identified the ways in which different cultural groups could be incorporated into multi-ethnic states, he harboured serious doubts about the stability and durability of such states. First, uniform incorporation would result in assimilative policies resented by the targeted groups. Second, differential incorporation would lead to domination and subordination of relations among groups and the exclusion of some groups from real power. Hence, this arrangement would also not be conducive to stable, democratic multi-ethnic societies. Finally, although the equivalent or consociational method seemed to hold the most hope, in practice it was unlikely to produce stable, democratic, multi-ethnic societies because most often 'the components of a consociation are unequal in numbers, territory and economic potential'.[58] As a result, real or perceived grievances may lead to ethnic unrest and undermine the stability of the union.

(b) The theory of consociationalism. Because the plural society approach painted a bleak picture of multi-ethnic societies, some scholars expressed grave doubts about 'the incompatibility view of ethnic relations within a single sovereign state'.[59] They therefore developed 'at least two alternative approaches to the issue of stability and democracy in multi-ethnic states'.[60] One was the consociational democracy approach pioneered by Arend Lijphart; the other was Donald Rothchild's theory of hegemonic exchange.

In *Democracy in Plural Societies: A Comparative Exploration,* and *Democracies: Patterns of Majoritarian and Consensus Government in Twenty-One Countries,* Lijphart offered a framework and stipulated the conditions that could lead to stable, democratic, multi-ethnic societies. He rejected the traditional Westminster majoritarian model with its 'one-party cabinets, a two party system, a first past the post electoral system, a unitary and centralised government and an unwritten constitution'.[61] Instead, he opted for a consociational framework involving executive power-sharing and grand coalitions, formal and informal separation of powers, balanced bicameralism and special minority representation in the upper chamber, a multi-party system, a multi-dimensional party system reflecting the various lines of cleavage in society, proportional representation, territorial as well as non-territorial federalism and political decentralisation, and a written constitution protecting certain rights of minority groups by laying down extremely difficult procedures for amendment.[62]

Out of this list of characteristics, Lijphart considered four to be the 'pillars' upon which a stable, consociational democratic society could rest. Of primary importance was the formation of a grand coalition of leaders representing all the communities. The other three important characteristics included the provision of a veto power to all communities on legislation affecting their vital interests, a system of proportional representation in parliament, and a high degree of autonomy for each community to run its own affairs. The success of the consociational model was to be seen in states such as Switzerland, Canada, Malaysia, Belgium and Holland.

After setting up the model of consociationalism, Lijphart provided a list of conditions which he felt promoted élite co-operation. These included a power balance between the various groups so that none could form a majority by itself, a multi-party system, small state size, cross-cutting societal cleavages, feelings of patriotism or a common religion, clear group boundaries and a tradition of co-operation among group élites.

Some of these conditions are clearly contradictory – such as the existence of cross-cutting societal cleavages and clear group boundaries – while the sum of them is convoluted. Moreover, considering the fact that some of the worst cases of ethnic violence have occurred in small states like Cyprus, Lebanon and Sri Lanka, it is doubtful if small state size really promotes co-operation among élites. To be sure, Lijphart did emphasise that the presence or absence of these conditions was not decisive and therefore they were neither necessary nor sufficient by themselves to determine the success of consociational democracy.[63]

The absence of some or all of Lijphart's conditions may unleash ethno-nationalistic feelings and conflict among various groups in a multi-ethnic state. The empirical evidence suggests that the record of consociational democracy has been mixed. Whereas it has produced relatively stable multi-ethnic democracies in some states (such as Switzerland and Holland and to a lesser degree Belgium and Canada), it has failed to prevent the outbreak of ethnic conflict elsewhere (Sri Lanka, Cyprus, Lebanon).

An attempt to refine the consociational democracy model of Lijphart has been made by Eric Nordlinger in his *Conflict Regulation in Divided Societies*. Nordlinger also stressed élite co-operation and structured élite predominance as ways to prevent conflict in multi-ethnic societies.[64] He maintained that élite co-operation and conflict regulation is possible through any of the following strategies: stable coalition, the proportionality principle, de-politicisation, mutual veto, mutual compromise and concessions. He further observed that certain conditions may motivate élites to regulate conflict through co-operation. These include their desire to thwart external threats to the state, the presence of a sufficiently large commercial class dedicated towards the promotion of economic values, the inability of any group to acquire political power and office without the support of others, and the threat of civil violence in the event of élite non-co-operation.[65]

Unlike Lijphart, however, Nordlinger was sceptical about the positive impact of cross-cutting pressures and segmental isolation of groups on élite co-operation. He argued that there is simply not enough evidence to suggest that cross-cutting cleavages positively reduce violence in divided societies. Moreover, since an individual's cultural identity is often more salient than cross-cultural ties, cross-cultural cleavages are more likely to be catalysts of ethnic violence than its moderators. Indeed, geographical isolation may actually 'increase conflict by increasing unequal development and by encouraging calls for greater autonomy, which can raise the stakes of the conflict'.[66]

(c) The theory of hegemonic exchange. The inability of consociational arrangements to prevent ethnic conflict led to the development of the hegemonic exchange theory, which supplemented consociational democratic ideas with control and dominance theory. This approach is associated primarily with Donald Rothchild, who has applied it to African states.

Rothchild found that although a number of African states were able to impose a limited amount of hegemony over the ethnic groups within their borders and thus prevent open ethnic conflict, these states were 'soft' states because they lacked the capacity to impose solutions on all groups. Accordingly, these states had to engage in a process of exchange with them. The result was a hegemonic exchange system of state–group relations in which 'a somewhat autonomous central-state actor and a number of considerably less autonomous ethno-regional interests engage, on the basis of commonly accepted procedural norms, rules, or understandings, in a process of mutual accommodation'.[67]

Like the consociational approach, the hegemonic exchange system does not regard ethnic relations within a state as 'a primordial clash of exclusive identities. Rather it posits that ethnic groups have overt, tangible interests that can be pursued in a rational, utility maximizing manner. Therefore, tradeoffs and bargaining are possible, and ethnic violence can be ended by changes in policies of allocation of power and wealth'.[68] The role of the state in this scheme is not as 'an oppressor, but as a mediator and facilitator; and in order to play this role it must reject an exclusivist approach to access to power in favor of an inclusive strategy based on ethnic balancing'.[69] Rothchild's examples of hegemonic exchange include post-civil-war Nigeria, Mauritius, Togo, Ivory Coast, Zambia, Kenya and Zimbabwe after 1987.

The problem with theories of cohesion and control are threefold. First, as the theories of consociationalism and hegemonic exchange indicate, the maintenance of cohesion in multi-ethnic states is a difficult task, and cohesion, even when achieved, remains precarious. At any moment it can be shattered by the emergence of new counter-élites which cannot be incorporated into the system, or by the emergence of new demands by groups which cannot be accommodated. Second, the existing balance of power between the various groups may change over time, thereby undermining co-operative arrangements arrived at by groups. Finally, inter-ethnic cohesion achieved through institutionalised control and domination is difficult to maintain when   the legitimacy of state authority cannot be taken for granted. We are drawn to the conclusion, then, that not only are the various models of cohesion and control unlikely to preserve political stability in multi-ethnic states, they may actually facilitate the rise of ethno-nationalist feelings.

Indirect theories of disintegration

The indirect theories of disintegration subsume 'the various interpretations of revolution, inter-group conflict and aggression, all of which contain clues which can lead to a general theory of disintegration'.[70] The most important explanations come from those theories of revolution that stress socio-economic factors such as relative deprivation, resource scarcity and the sudden rise in aspirations that are frustrated, and also political approaches dealing with interest group competition, mobilisation, breakdown of institutions and revolutionary organisation and leadership.[71]

By far the most important theory in this category is that of relative deprivation developed by Gurr in *Why Men Rebel*. Relative deprivation refers to 'the perceived discrepancy between value expectations and value expectancies in a society'.[72] What this means is that 'the inclination to revolt is most likely to be present when people perceive an inequity in the wretchedness of their condition – when they receive less (their expectations) than they feel they deserve (their expectancies)'.[73] Gurr points to four stages in the process by which relative deprivation leads to revolt. First, people must recognise that deprivation exists. Second, they must also become aware that the wretched conditions they experience are not universal and that others enjoy what they lack. Third, people must develop the feeling that a situation of deprivation is unfair. The final step is the recognition that political action may be able to change the situation. This is the stage for mass political activity and revolution.[74]

The theory of relative deprivation is useful for explaining the rise of ethnic political mobilisation not only among economically backward groups but also among relatively prosperous ethnic groups. For example, Czechs wanted to escape from Czechoslovakia precisely because they were the better-off nation. When a group perceives a threat to its privileged position or becomes a victim of state discrimination, it may undertake militant action. After all, as the theory suggests, it is the realisation by a group that it is receiving less than it deserves and that others are receiving more that motivates the group to take political action. Applying this concept to ethnic conflict, as Gurr does in his later work, *Minorities at Risk*, it is easy to understand why perceived disadvantage or discrimination (real or imaginary) by a group regarding its status (socio-cultural, economic, political) is an underlying cause for political action.[75]

Direct Theories of Ethnic Political Mobilisation and Conflict

Direct theories of ethnic political mobilisation were developed chiefly in the 1970s and 1980s as a result of dissatisfaction among scholars with inadequate conceptual tools with which to explain the persistence and proliferation of ethnic political mobilisation. Thus the failure of strain theory to account for the persistence of ethnic conflict led to its eventual abandonment. Moreover, scholars realised that, although the various indirect theories offered some insights regarding the causes of ethnic political mobilisation, they did so more through inference and induction. Their primary focus remained modernisation and its associated problems – stability and democracy in plural societies and the issues of violence and revolution.

Particularly in the 1980s, scholars who were not yet prepared to discard the salience of the modernisation process in the rise of ethnic nationalism tried to reformulate these theories. Two paradigms dealing directly with the causes of ethnic political mobilisation and state disintegration emerged: *internal colonialism* or the *reactive ethnicity* approach, and the *primordialist* or *developmental* approach. A third, older approach, the *communalist* or *ethnic competition* approach, sought to explain state disintegration in underdeveloped societies brought about by ethnic and communal conflict.

The primordialist or developmental approach

The primary focus of the primordialist approach is on ethnic identity and consciousness, which it treats as 'the essential independent variable that leads to political assertiveness and militant separatism, regardless of the existence of inequality or dominance'.[76] Primordialists argue that distinct communities prefer to be governed poorly by their ethnic brethren rather than wisely by aliens since rule by foreigners is degrading.

Although the primordialists put more stress on cultural markers as sources of ethnic identity and consciousness, they nevertheless do not discount the role of socio-economic variables. They continue to recognise the salience of the modernisation process in the rise of ethnonationalism. At the same time, they are unwilling to accept the general conclusion of the modernisation approach that ethnicity is a vanishing tradition. In reformulating modernisation theories, they acknowledge that socio-economic factors may form the basis of discontent but 'only discontent founded on ethnic symbols, such as language, religion, culture, origin or race can lead to separatism'.[77]

This was a significant breakthrough for research on ethnicity. For some time, ethnicity and ethnic identity were regarded as a *dependent* variable. Now the primordialists turned the argument around by claiming that ethnic identity was an *independent* or explanatory variable triggering political action. The primordialist approach is illustrated in the scholarship of Walker Connor, Nathan Glazer and Daniel Moynihan, Cynthia Enloe, Donald Horowitz, Anthony Smith and John Armstrong.[78]

Connor, an early exponent of the primordialist perspective, has traced the etiology and manifestation of ethnic political mobilisation. He contended that modernisation, by increasing interaction and competition among ethnic groups for the same economic and political rewards, actually sharpened ethnic divisions in society in four ways. First, rapid social communication and mobilisation increased cultural awareness and exacerbated inter-ethnic conflict.[79] Second, improvements 'in communications and transportation' increased 'the cultural awareness of the minorities by making their members more aware of the distinctions between themselves and others'.[80] Third, the rise of militant ethnic consciousness in many parts of both developed and developing worlds could be explained not in terms of the 'nature or density of the communications media, but the *message*'.[81] The reference here was to the doctrine of self-determination of nations which, in its pristine form, made ethnicity 'the ultimate measure of political legitimacy, by holding that any self-differentiating people, simply because it *is* a people, has the right, should it so desire, to rule itself'.[82] This doctrine not only provided justification but also acted as catalyst for ethnic political movements.[83] Finally, changes in the global political environment also contributed to the upsurge in ethnic consciousness by making it 'much more unlikely that a militarily weak polity will be annexed by a larger power'.[84] In this context, Connor pointed out that the achievement of nuclear parity between the superpowers caused '*independence* to appear as a more enduring prospect for even the weakest of units'.[85]

In *The Ethnic Revival*, Anthony Smith posited that ethnic conflict is the outcome of incongruence between economic modernisation and processes of political development associated with the birth of the modern state. Starting from the same perspective as Weber and Durkheim but arriving at a diametrically opposite conclusion, Smith concluded that the modern bureaucratic state seeks legitimacy in scientific rationality. When coupled with the economic and educational modernisation of society, the rationality imperative produces an expanding stratum of secular intelligentsia. However, the inability of the state bureaucracy to absorb the entire body of secular intellectuals causes them to identify with their ethnic groups, which help legitimate their perceptions of injustice.[86]

Saul Newman has pointed out that a major shortcoming of Smith's argument was his failure to explain why secularising intellectuals or élites, when faced with a lack of opportunities, should revert to their ethnic identities 'instead of radical secular ideologies such as Marxism'.[87] While it is true that cultural markers and primordial sentiments play a crucial role in the development of human personality, we can question whether ethnic identity alone constitutes a powerful factor triggering ethno-political movements. Moreover, as we noted above, culture has a multiplicity of components which are given differentiated stress over time. Another criticism of Smith's approach is that by concentrating on élites his framework failed to address the question of how such élites mobilise mass support. More importantly, he did not explain how the popular classes ended up with a political agenda that suited the personal needs of a narrow élite.[88] Finally, Smith paid little attention to the political obstacles faced by new ethnic movements and to such other factors as demographic, socio-economic and political power at the disposal of ethnic groups that often accounted for different levels and types of ethnic political activity.[89]

Internal colonialism or the reactive ethnicity approach

Lack of agreement on the effect that modernisation had on ethnic political mobilisation led to the development of the internal colonialism or reactive ethnicity approach. The main proponent of the internal colonialism approach is Michael Hechter, although the idea was derived from Marxist social theories expounded by Lenin and Gramsci.

At the crux of Hechter's argument is the concept of *exploitation*. It characterises the relationship between members of a dominant cultural group and those of peripheral ethnic groups in advanced industrial states. Using the Celtic minority in the United Kingdom as a case study, Hechter contended that such exploitation results in 'a particularistic allocation of valued roles and resources to the dominant ethnic group', thereby causing political mobilisation of the peripheral ethnic group.[90] Faced with infiltration of their region by the core group, its stunted development caused by its being treated as an appendage of the national economy, and the destruction of the social fabric of the peripheral region as a result of modernisation, the peripheral ethnic group engages in protests and forms separatist movements based on cultural and ethnic differences. To be sure, Hechter pointed out that the selective co-optation of potentially destructive or divisive leaders from such peripheral ethnic groups by the core ethnic group can often weaken ethno-political movements, thereby ensuring the continuity of the cultural division of labour.[91]

Although Hechter studied Celts in the United Kingdom, his theory can explain the rise of ethnic political mobilisation among peripheral minorities in many parts of the world. Good examples would include the nationalist movements in the Central Asian republics of the former Soviet Union.

Hechter added an important dimension to the analysis of politicised ethnicity by combining economic explanations with cultural ones. But the independent variable – the cultural division of labour – was in his view only a necessary and not a sufficient condition for the formation of ethno-political movements.[92] His model also falls short in explaining ethno-political assertions on the part of economically privileged ethnic groups.

The ethnic competition or communalist approach

The communalist approach is much older than others we have been considering here. It explains ethnic political mobilisation by focusing on modernisation, scarcity of resources and élite competition. The process of modernisation, from this perspective, affects both peripheral and core ethnic groups in two ways. First, it reduces ethnic diversity within both dominant and subordinate ethnic groups by eroding local identities. Second, as a result of this erosion of local identities large-scale ethnic identity-formation is promoted because of the altered conditions of political competition between groups and élites.[93]

Although the communalists posit that large-scale ethnic identity-formation occurs when groups are forced to compete with each other for the same rewards and resources, the roots of ethnic political mobilisation leading to ethnic violence and even ethnic separatism lie in 'élite disputes over the direction of change and grievances linked with the scarcity of resources' and also 'when previously acquired privileges are threatened or alternatively when underprivileged groups realise that the moment has come to redress inequality'.[94] The communalists argue that this phenomen is more pronounced in modern states, particularly those in the middle ranks of economic development. Such states, which include Ukraine and Kazakhstan, often lack the capacity and resources to manage social mobilisation and to satisfy the increased aspirations which mobilisation creates. Hence, these states are particularly vulnerable to intense competition and conflict between élites and groups.

An important example of this approach to ethnic identity-creation and to the rise of ethnic political mobilisation as a result of élite competition in pre-modern and modern societies is the work of Paul Brass.[95] Using case studies of ethnic and communal conflict from India, the former Soviet Union and parts of Eastern Europe, Brass has shown how altered conditions of élite competition, the emergence of new élites, resource scarcity and centralising tendencies of states (all a result of modernisation) have combined to generate intense élite competition and ethnic polarisation in many of these societies.

The communalist approach to ethnic political mobilisation enhances our understanding of the causes of large-scale ethnic identity-formation in modernising societies, of the competition for resources that this process entails, and of the dynamics of élite interaction behind the politicisation of ethnicity. But its major shortcoming is that it tends 'to overemphasise the element of greedy élites and manipulative, power-seeking regional leaders who take advantage of the communal spirit for their own ends'.[96] As a result, communalists often ignore 'the element of inequality and communal identity as well as the degree of ingroup legitimisation' that is required for ethno-political and secessionist sentiments to develop.[97]

Although the direct theories offer a wider variety of explanations for the rise of ethno-nationalism than the indirect ones, they nevertheless suffer from major defects. Whereas the internal colonialism or reactive ethnicity approach fails to account for the rise of separatist sentiments on the part of economically rich sub-nations, the primordialist or developmental approach is flawed by its minimalising of the significance of economic inequality as a source for the rise of separatist movements. In turn, the communalist or ethnic competition perspective over-emphasises the role of manipulative élites driven by their own needs and aspirations, and it underestimates the importance of ethnic consciousness in the rise of separatist sentiments. It also fails to explain adequately why such movements at times acquire a high level of in-group legitimisation for secession.[98]

On their own, none of these theoretical approaches can explain all cases of ethnic political mobilisation. Our discussion has revealed the importance of diverse factors – cultural, economic, political – for the politicisation of ethnicity. Attempting to combine these factors in one explanatory framework may allow for a better understanding of the reasons for the awakening and politicisation of various ethnic groups in the world today, including many in Eastern Europe.

Notes

A more detailed version of this chapter appears in Rajat Ganguly and Ray Taras, *Understanding Ethnic Conflict* (New York: Longman, 1998).

1. Raoul Naroll, 'On Ethnic Unit Classification', *Current Anthropology* 5 (October 1964), p.1.
2. See Frederick Barth, *Ethnic Groups and Boundaries: The Social Organisation of Cultural Difference* (London: George Allen & Unwin, 1970); Nathan Glazer and Daniel P. Moynihan (eds), *Ethnicity: Theory and Experience* (Cambridge, MA: Harvard University Press, 1975); R.A. Schermerhorn, *Comparative Ethnic Relations* (New York: Random House, 1970).
3. James G. Kellas, *The Politics of Nationalism and Ethnicity* (New York: St. Martin's Press, 1991), p.4.
4. Ibid.
5. Ibid.
6. Clifford Geertz, *Old Societies and New States: The Quest for Modernity in Asia and

Africa (Glencoe, IL: The Free Press, 1963); Harold Isaacs, 'Basic Group Identity: The Idols of the Tribe', *Ethnicity* **1** (1974), pp.15–42.

7. John Rex, 'Ethnic Identity and the Nation-State: The Political Sociology of Multi-Cultural Societies', *Social Identities* **1**, no.1 (1995), pp.24–5; see also Judith Nagata, 'In Defense of Ethnic Boundaries: The Changing Myths and Charters of Malay Identity', in Charles F. Keyes (ed.), *Ethnic Change* (Seattle: University of Washington Press, 1981), p.89.

8. See Anthony H. Richmond, 'Migration and Race Relations', *Ethnic and Racial Studies* **1** (January 1978), p.60; and Anthony Smith, *Theories of Nationalism*, 2nd edn (New York: Holmes & Meier, 1983), p.180, cited in Urmila Phadnis, *Ethnicity and Nation-building in South Asia* (Newbury Park, CA: Sage, 1990), p.14, n.11. For a stimulating discussion of the role of food in the formation and – more importantly – the stereotyping of ethnic identity, see Uma Narayan, 'Eating Cultures: Incorporation, Identity and Indian Food', *Social Identities* **1**, no.1 (1995), pp.63–86.

9. Nathan Glazer and Daniel P. Moynihan, *Beyond the Melting Pot: The Negroes, Puerto Ricans, Jews, Italians and Irish of New York* (Cambridge, MA: MIT and Harvard University Presses, 1963), pp.13–14, cited in Phadnis, *Ethnicity and Nation-buildin in South Asia*, p.14, n.14.

10. Ibid.

11. Rex, 'Ethnic Identity and the Nation-State', p.25.

12. Timothy M. Frye, 'Ethnicity, Sovereignty and Transitions from Non-Democratic Rule', *Journal of International Affairs* **45**, no.2 (Winter 1992), p.602.

13. Ibid.

14. See Anthony D. Smith, 'The Ethnic Sources of Nationalism', *Survival* **35**, no.1 (Spring 1993), pp.50–51.

15. Ibid., p.52.

16. Ibid., p.53.

17. Ibid.

18. Ibid., pp.53–5.

19. Peter Jackson and Jan Penrose, 'Introduction: Placing "Race" and Nation', in Peter Jackson and Jan Penrose (eds), *Constructions of Race, Place and Nation* (London: UCL Press, 1993), p.1; see also Jan Penrose, 'Reification in the Name of Change: The Impact of Nationalism on Social Constructions of National, People and Place in Scotland and the United Kingdom', in Jackson and Penrose, *Constructions*, p.28.

20. Ibid., p.2.

21. John Stone, 'Race, Ethnicity, and the Weberian Legacy', *American Behavioral Scientist* **38**, no.3 (January 1995), p.396.

22. Ibid.

23. Charles F. Keyes, 'The Dialectics of Ethnic Change', in Keyes (ed.), *Ethnic Change*, p.5.

24. Ibid., p.6.

25. Ibid., p.5.

26. Ibid., p.7.

27. Ibid.

28. Ibid., p.9.

29. Ibid.

30. Ibid., p.11.

31. Phadnis, *Ethnicity and Nation-building in South Asia*, p.16.

32. Paul R. Brass, *Ethnicity and Nationalism: Theory and Comparison* (Newbury Park,

70 *Rajat Ganguly*

CA: Sage, 1991), p.8.

33. Nagata, 'In Defense of Ethnic Boundaries', p.90.
34. See Geertz, *Old Societies and New States*; Isaacs, 'Basic Group Identity', pp.15–42; Naroll, 'On Ethnic Unit Classification', pp.283–312; Milton Gordon, *Assimilation in American Life: The Role of Race, Religion and National Origins* (New York: Oxford University Press, 1964); J. Clyde Mitchell, *The Kalela Dance: Aspects of Social Relationships Among Urban Africans of Northern Rhodesia* (Manchester: Manchester University Press, 1956); A.L. Epstein, *Politics in an Urban African Community* (Manchester: Manchester University Press, 1958); J.S. Furnivall, *Netherlands India: A Study of Plural Economy* (New York: Macmillan, 1944).
35. Nagata, 'In Defense of Ethnic Boundaries', p.90. For details of Kuper's criticism of primordialism see Leo Kuper, 'Plural Societies: Perspectives and Problems', in Leo Kuper and M.G. Smith (eds), *Pluralism in Africa* (Berkeley: University of California Press, 1969), pp.7–26.
36. Ibid., for details see Barth, *Ethnic Groups and Boundaries*, and Glazer and Moynihan (eds), *Ethnicity: Theory and Experience*.
37. Ibid.
38. Ibid.
39. Ibid.
40. Smith, 'The Ethnic Sources', p.55.
41. Walker Connor, 'Nation-Building or Nation-Destroying?', *World Politics* 24, no.3 (April 1972).
42. Kellas, *The Politics of Nationalism and Ethnicity*, p.6.
43. Frye, 'Ethnicity, Sovereignty and Transitions', pp.602–3.
44. Ibid., p.603.
45. Ted Robert Gurr, *Minorities at Risk: A Global View of Ethnopolitical Conflicts* (Washington, DC: United States Institute of Peace Press, 1993).
46. Ibid., p.10.
47. See Charles Ragin, *The Comparative Method* (Berkeley: University of California Press, 1987).
48. Karl W. Deutsch, *Nationalism and Social Communication* (Cambridge, MA: MIT Press, 1953), pp.86–130.
49. Ibid.
50. See, for example, Samuel P. Huntington, *Political Order in Changing Societies* (New Haven, CT: Yale University Press, 1968), and Daniel Lerner, 'Communications and the Prospects of Innovative Development', in Daniel Lerner and Wilbur Schramm (eds), *Communication and Change in the Developing Countries* (Honolulu: East–West Center Press, 1967), pp.305–17.
51. Saul Newman, 'Does Modernization Breed Ethnic Political Conflict?', *World Politics* 43, no.3 (April 1991), pp.454–55. For a detailed exposition of this view of strain theory see Neil J. Smelser, 'Mechanisms of Change and Adjustment to Change', in Bert F. Hoselitz and Wilbert E. Moore (eds), *Industrialization and Society* (The Hague: UNESCO and Mouton, 1963), p.41, and Geertz (ed.), *Old Societies and New States*.
52. Ragin, *The Comparative Method*, p.134.
53. Ibid.
54. Stein Rokkan, *Citizens, Elections, Parties* (New York: McKay, 1970), p.121, cited in ibid., pp.134–5.

55. Stephen Ryan, *Ethnic Conflict and International Relations* (Aldershot: Dartmouth, 1990), p.1.
56. Ibid., pp.1–2.
57. Ibid., pp.3–4. For details of Furnivall's idea on plural societies, see Furnivall, *Netherlands India*, pp.446–69.
58. M.G. Smith, 'Some Developments in the Analytic Study of Pluralism', in Kuper and Smith (eds), *Pluralism in Africa*, p.442.
59. Ryan, *Ethnic Conflict and International Relations*, p.12.
60. Ibid., pp.15–16.
61. Ibid., p.16.
62. See, for example, Arend Lijphart, *Democracy in Plural Societies: A Comparative Exploration* (New Haven, CT: Yale University Press, 1977), and *Democracies: Patterns of Majoritarian and Consensus Government in Twenty-One Countries* (New Haven, CT: Yale University Press, 1984), pp.23–30.
63. Ryan, *Ethnic Conflict and International Relations*, p.17.
64. E.A. Nordlinger, *Conflict Regulation in Divided Societies* (Cambridge, MA: Harvard Center for International Affairs, 1972), p.87.
65. Ryan, *Ethnic Conflict and International Relations*, p.17.
66. Ibid., p.18.
67. Donald Rothchild, 'Hegemonic Exchanges: An Alternative Model for Managing Conflict in Middle Africa', in D.L. Thompson and D. Ronen (eds), *Ethnicity, Politics and Development* (Boulder, CO: Lynne Rienner, 1986), p.72.
68. Ryan, *Ethnic Conflict and International Relations*, pp.19–20.
69. Ibid., p.20.
70. Alexis Heraclides, *The Self-Determination of Minorities in International Politics* (London: Frank Cass, 1991), p.6.
71. Some of the most important works in this area include Ted Robert Gurr, *Why Men Rebel* (Princeton, NJ: Princeton University Press, 1970); James C. Davis, 'Toward a Theory of Revolution', *American Sociological Review* **27** (February 1962), pp.5–19; Mancur Olson, *The Logic of Collective Action* (Cambridge, MA: Harvard University Press, 1965); Chalmers Johnson, *Revolutionary Change* (Boston, MA: Little, Brown, 1966); Samuel P. Huntington, *Political Order in Changing Societies*; Charles Tilly, *From Mobilization to Revolution* (Reading, MA: Addison-Wesley, 1978); Theda Skocpol, *States and Social Revolutions* (Cambridge: Cambridge University Press, 1979).
72. Donald M. Snow, *Distant Thunder* (New York: St. Martin's Press, 1993), p.60.
73. Ibid.
74. For details see Gurr, *Why Men Rebel*.
75. Gurr, *Minorities at Risk*.
76. Heraclides, *The Self-determination of Minorities*, p.8.
77. Clifford Geertz, 'The Integrative Revolution: Primordial Sentiments and Civic Politics in the New States', in C.E. Welch, Jr (ed.), *Political Modernization* (Belmont, CA: 1967), p.170.
78. See, for example, Connor, 'Nation-Building or Nation-Destroying?', and Walker Connor, 'The Politics of Ethnonationalism', *Journal of International Affairs* **27** (January 1973); Glazer and Moynihan, *Ethnicity: Theory and Experience*; Cynthia H. Enloe, *Ethnic Conflict and Political Development* (Boston, MA: Little, Brown, 1973); Donald L. Horowitz, *Ethnic Groups in Conflict* (Berkeley and Los Angeles: University

of California Press, 1985); Anthony D. Smith, *The Ethnic Origins of Nations* (Oxford: Basil Blackwell, 1986); John A. Armstrong, *Nations Before Nationalism* (Chapel Hill: University of North Carolina Press, 1982).

79. Connor, 'Nation-Building or Nation-Destroying?', p.328; original emphasis. Similar views can be found in Connor, 'The Politics of Ethnonationalism', pp.1–21.
80. Ibid., p.329.
81. Ibid., p.331; emphasis added.
82. Ibid.; original emphasis. For a detailed exposition of Connor's views on the doctrine of 'self-determination of nations' see Walker Connor, 'Self-Determination: The New Phase', *World Politics* **20**, no.1 (October 1967), pp.30–53.
83. Ibid.
84. Ibid., pp.331–2.
85. Ibid., p.332; emphasis added.
86. For details, see Anthony D. Smith, *The Ethnic Revival* (Cambridge: Cambridge University Press, 1981).
87. Newman, 'Does Modernization Breed Ethnic Political Conflict?', p.458.
88. Ibid.
89. Ibid., p.459.
90. Ragin, *The Comparative Method*, p.135.
91. For details see Michael Hechter, *Internal Colonialism: The Celtic Fringe of British National Development, 1536–1966* (London: Routledge & Kegan Paul, 1975), p.41.
92. Michael Hechter and Margaret Levi, 'The Comparative Analysis of Ethnoregional Movements', *Ethnic and Racial Studies* **2** (July 1979), p.272.
93. Ragin, *The Comparative Method*, pp.135–6. For a detailed exposition of how the process of modernisation affects nations and sub-nations from this perspective see also Michael Hannan, 'The Dynamics of Ethnic Boundaries in Modern States', in Michael Hannan and John Meyer (eds), *National Development and the World System: Educational, Economic and Political Change, 1950–1970* (Chicago: University of Chicago Press, 1979), pp.253–77; François Nielsen, 'The Flemish Movement in Belgium after World War II: A Dynamic Analysis', *American Sociological Review* **45** (1980), pp.76–94, and 'Toward a Theory of Ethnic Solidarity in Modern Societies', *American Sociological Review* **50** (1985), pp.133–49; Charles C. Ragin, 'Class, Status, and "Reactive Ethnic Cleavages": The Social Bases of Political Regionalism', *American Sociological Review* **42** (1977), pp.438–50, and 'Ethnic Political Mobilization: The Welsh Case', *American Sociological Review* **44** (1979), pp.619–35.
94. Heraclides, *The Self-determination of Minorities*, p.9.
95. See Brass, *Ethnicity and Nationalism*.
96. Heraclides, *The Self-determination of Minorities*, p.9.
97. Ibid.
98. Ibid., pp.8–9.

4 Nationalism, Identity and the Belarusian State

Ed Jocelyn

Nationalism and the formation of nation-states in Europe are usually treated in the context of the evolution and political mobilisation of 'national consciousness'.[1] This collective, national identity may be considered to derive from recognition of a primordial, 'natural' phenomenon (that is, the 'nation'); it may be treated as both a result of and an actor in the interplay of socio-economic and political forces; or it may be reduced to what Anthony Smith describes as 'a communion of imagery', whose basis is a 'text' made up of images and cultural constructs.[2] However, while the existence of different 'levels' of national consciousness is accepted, with the exception of analyses proceeding from this final conception (which Smith labels as 'post-modernist') the phenomenon of national consciousness itself tends to be taken as undifferentiated and unproblematic, and this has certainly been the case with studies of the former Soviet Union.

In the case of Belarus, however, national consciousness is a highly problematic concept. Study of the formation of national consciousness, defined according to ethnic or ethno-linguistic criteria, and its subsequent political mobilisation provides neither the only nor necessarily the most useful context in which to analyse the processes leading to the realisation of a Belarusian nation-state. Indeed, talk of the 'development of a national consciousness' can be deeply misleading. The Republic of Belarus is the ultimate political expression of a Belarusian 'nation', but this term in itself does not really tell us anything useful with respect to the establishment of such a state. National identity, and hence national consciousness, is far from a monolithic phenomenon – many sources flow into it, and many consequences may spring from it. So although it is by definition a collective identity its internal differentiation may be very great. Analyses have typically focused on the collective identity seemingly embodied by Nationalist political movements, which is principally defined according to ethno-linguistic criteria, but although this identity certainly exists in Belarus, I do not think that by itself it can be considered sufficient as a basis for the establishment and maintenance of an independent Belarusian state. Strong evidence of its political weakness came in the results of the referendum held in May 1995 on the status of the Russian language in the Republic, in which only 12.7 per cent of the Belarusian 'Nation' opposed the granting of official status to a 'foreign' language – and this in the teeth of vehement opposition from Nationalists and others who defined a Belarusian national consciousness fundamentally in ethno-linguistic terms.[3]

Once we recognise the subtlety and complexity inherent in the simple label of 'national identity', we risk finding ourselves unable to conclude anything at all – for example, how is one to qualify the impact of the Chernobyl disaster on several million individuals, and realistically assess the consequences as it relates to their subsequent activity and psychology? It is, I think, important to accept that generalisation and simplification often provide our best resource for interpreting the world for the benefit of others. For this reason I propose to restrict my attention to two sources of Belarusian collective (that is, that may be defined as national) identity which I believe are *actively* defined by their relationship to state power, and have had a demonstrable bearing on developments at the state level. The first of these is the identity associated with Nationalist political activity, while the second is that which I believe evolved as a consequence of the administrative structure of the Soviet state, and which proved largely antagonistic to the first. I do not expect this to provide any definitive answers, but I do think that it will help point the way to more profitable areas in which to seek out the foundations upon which the Republic stands.

Characterising Belarus Nationalism

The spur to Nationalist activity is a perception that the Nation is disenfranchised, or that its interests are otherwise damaged by the existing political order. This perception is not necessarily shared by all, or even many, imagined members of the Nation; indeed, not all those whom Nationalists imagine to be included in the Nation may identify themselves in such a way. In such a situation Nationalist political activity is likely to be insignificant. This should not present a theoretical problem for nationalist activists, however, since it need not indicate that their perception of the Nation and its interests is a fallacy, but that among a number of its members either (i) there is an absence of national consciousness, or (ii) national consciousness is dormant, that is, not politcally active. For this reason the rise of strong Nationalist movements tends to be characterised (by themselves and by outsiders who do not really question the phenomena of nation and national consciousness) in two main ways:

(a) as marking the 'birth' of national consciousness/the Nation;
(b) as signalling the 'awakening' of national consciousness/the Nation.

The markers by which one member of a Nation recognises another are usually distinctive enough to avoid confusion, although difficulties may well arise on the margins where, for example, skin colour or religious affiliation could prevent some members of a Nation from recognising the validity of another's claim to membership. In the European context, the chief marker has been language. Membership of a Nation has mostly been associated with knowledge of the Nation's 'mother tongue', and the German Romantic philosophers of the late eighteenth and early nineteenth centuries in particular established a strong intellectual tradition arguing that this association is only natural.[4] The fact that this tradition has long been familiar in Belarusian intellectual circles is clear from early writings expressing a sense of Belarusian collective identity: to quote just one well-known example, in the foreword to his *Dudka bielaruskaya* ('The Belarusian Fife', published in Cracow in 1891), Francišak Bahuševic (the 'father of modern Belarusian literature'[5]) wrote that 'People recognise others by their face and dress. Language is the face and dress of the soul', and he admonished his fellow Belarusians: 'Do not abandon our Belarusian language, lest you die'.[6] This phrase appears today on the masthead of the newspaper of the Belarusian Language Society, *Nasha slova*, and its apocalyptic tone is echoed throughout Nationalist writing on the subject of the Belarusian language, the disappearance of which is linked with the death of the Belarusian Nation. The key marker according to which members of the Belarusian language Nation may recognise one another has therefore been the Belarusian language. The national consciousness, whose (a) existence and (b) politicisation would have been prerequisites for a strong Belarusian Nationalist movement, had to be shared through the medium of the Belarusian language, without which there could indeed be no Nation.

For this reason, in the late Soviet period there was generally assumed to be a low level of national consciousness in the Belorussian Soviet Socialist Republic (BSSR). Not only was little dissidence associated with Belarusian nationality, and little anti-Russian feeling was to be

found in anecdotal evidence, but all the available evidence suggested that
the Belarusians[7] were progressively abandoning their 'own' language for
that of another Nation: Russian. Any visitor to the capital of the
BSSR, Minsk, would have been unlikely to hear a single word uttered
in Belarusian. Among the diaspora, and in most Western scholarship
that considered the matter, the BSSR was 'the test-bed for a policy
of ethnic and linguistic fusion into a single Russophone "Soviet"
people'.[8] And the figures on the decline of the Belarusian language and
the rise of the use of Russian created widespread acceptance of the
success of this policy, nowhere more so than in the putative Nationalist
movement.

It is the acceptance of this problem that is one of the defining characteristics of Belarusian Nationalism. Whereas, for example, a Lithuanian
nationalist would have little difficulty recognising another member of the
Lithuanian Nation, the collective identity sought by a Belarusian Nationalist has been devastated by the abandonment of Belarusian as the
mother tongue by a huge proportion of the population. I would almost
go so far as to say that the Belarusian Nation does not exist: although the
people are still there, they are shorn of the characteristic that makes them
recognisable as members of the Belarusian Nation. The Belarusian collective identity recognised and appealed to by Belarusian Nationalists is a
lapsed collective identity. Belarusian national consciousness is explicitly
appealed to as a force *in absentia*, a latent collective identity which
unites the Nation in forgetting – for a Belarusian Nation which speaks
Russian is an irreconcilable paradox. Consider the following statement,
from the electoral platform of the Belorussian Popular Front (or BPF, the
principal locus of Nationalist political activity in the BSSR, and subsequently in the independent republic) for the elections to the Supreme
Soviet and local soviets of the BSSR in March 1990:

> Decades of Stalinist genocide and the bureaucratic de-nationalisation of Belorussia –
> resulting in the destruction of its cultural heritage, historical monuments, humanistic
> morality, religion, and national history and language – have brought our nation to the
> brink of disaster. Saving and reviving our language should be a noble task. The BPF
> calls for the granting of the status of state language to the Belorussian language, with
> the realisation that this endeavour will require considerable time, *conditioning*, good-
> will and effort on the part of the entire population of Belorussia.[9]

Belarusian Nationalists *accept* the lack of national consciousness (that
is, they do not speak of awakening it), and seek power to implement policies that would restore the lapsed marker of Belarusian collective identity and hence return the people to the nation which they,

the Nationalists, recognise. Thus it is appropriate that the principal Nationalist movement was named *Adradzhen'ne*, meaning re-birth or renewal.

This made the movement very different in character from Nationalist movements in, for example, the Baltic republics, where the idea of 'awakening' was dominant and the mutual recognition of Nation and Nationalists was un-problematic. There, problems arose when it became a matter of deciding the political status of those who were not recognised as members of the Nation, principally the Russian diaspora. The Belarusian movement's political stance in the dying days of the Soviet Union also differed considerably from that of the analogous movements in the Baltic region, which took on the leading role in the move towards independence and carried their leaders, however briefly, into positions of power. The Belarusian movement played no more than a marginal role in the eventual move to independence, and its leaders gained no political benefit from this development. As I have argued above, national consciousness as it is understood by the Nationalist movement does not exist among much of the population, hence the need for 'rebirth', and this was surely confirmed in stark fashion by the results of the referendum held in May 1995, where the pleas of BPF (*Adradzhen'ne*) to vote 'no' to the questions put before the electorate – notably on the status of the Russian language *vis-à-vis* Belarusian and the 'historic symbols' of Belarusian statehood were overwhelmingly rejected, or ignored.[10] To quote the leader of the BPF, Zyanon Paznyak, popular support has been given (or, at least, popular opposition has not been voiced) to policies aimed at 'aiding the seizure of Belarus by Russia, destroying our sovereignty, undermining the basis of the state'.[11]

Yet, from a certain viewpoint, the result of the collapse of Soviet power looks much the same from Minsk as it does from Vilnius, Tallinn or Kiev. There is an independent nation-state whose legitimacy is drawn from a Belarusian nation, and whatever one might think of the nature of that state's relationship with Russia, from an institutional point of view its independence is just as real as that of the Baltic countries, and probably more so than that of a member of the European Union. Whatever the government's crimes against the Nation, the republic has refused to fall; Belarusian 'nationhood' continues to be incarnated by the state declared independent on 25 August 1991 and given its current name on 19 September of that year. Since the collective identity represented by the Nationalist movement has proved less than politically dominant, this would suggest that in terms of state power there is another, politically significant, collective identity in Belarus which is also 'national', but is not necessarily congruent with any idea of exclusive ethnic identity.

Res bureaucratica

Study of Soviet census data reveals an interesting point, which is the lack of congruence between identification with Belarusian nationality for the benefit of the census – a clear manifestation of collective identity – and use of the Belarusian language, going right back to the early days of the BSSR: 39.3 per cent of the urban population in 1926 claimed Belarusian nationality, but only 20 per cent gave Belarusian as their native tongue[12]; in 1989 only 80.22 per cent of those claiming Belarusian nationality gave Belarusian as their mother tongue.[13] This in itself demonstrates the existence of a sense – or perhaps senses – of Belarusian identity which are not linked to the language. There is nothing particularly unusual in this – there are plenty of examples of national identities which are not fundamentally defined by language use. My question is, which, if any, of these identities may have had political significance with regard to the state?

The establishment of the BSSR in 1919 created the first effective political–administrative unit that used reference to Belarus (Belorussia) as its identifying principle, and therefore created a potential collective identity based on recognition of membership of the group which inhabited the boundaries of the BSSR.

I say 'potential' collective identity because I make no pretence of knowing whether or not the mass of inhabitants of the BSSR ever sensed this or placed any importance upon it if they did. If so, it has manifested no positive political significance up to now. However, there is one group which events suggest did develop a collective identity linked directly to the administrative-territorial unit, whose political significance is undeniable, and that is the administration itself.[14]

Imagine a bureaucrat (I include the 'elected' members of soviets in this category) in the administration of the BSSR. What kind of a career path could he or she imagine? The BSSR possessed all the institutions of a state bureaucracy, centred in Minsk, such that from one point of view the career of our bureaucrat is circumscribed by the boundaries of the BSSR, and its pinnacle of aspiration lay at the centre of power in the capital. However, there was an alternative focus of aspirations, the All-Union bureaucracy, which ultimately targeted the centre of the federal apparatus, namely Moscow. It would be wrong to imagine these two bureaucracies as discrete systems – personnel could and did move from one to the other and back again, and the central powers in Moscow theoretically had ultimate control over personnel decisions in the BSSR, but in actual fact the circulation of the bureaucracy in the BSSR was largely self-regulating. According to Michael Urban's research on elite circulation in the BSSR, 'the actual career patterns of officials in the BSSR primarily had been determined by factors indigenous to the Republic, principally, the patronage of former partisans and rival groups. Within the framework of the Soviet order, then, the BSSR had been since the mid-sixties, if not earlier, a self-governing republic'.[15] Where personnel moved out of the BSSR into the Soviet bureaucracy, this was often a temporary move, eventually leading to a return to the system centred in Minsk, but this capacity for mobility outside the BSSR (aided, no doubt, by the fact that a bureaucrat in the BSSR was almost certain to be Russian-speaking) was significant in allowing our bureaucrat to imagine him- or herself as a member of either of two groups – the one bounded by the BSSR, and the other touching all points of the Union.

So our bureaucrat could imagine him- or herself as a member of two different communities linked to two different political-administrative units. I suggest, however, that the group identity defined by the BSSR had more reality for more people than that which was defined by the boundaries of the Soviet state. For one thing, the sideways move into the Soviet bureaucracy was simply made by fewer people, and the integrity of the BSSR group remained unchallenged by such moves, as vacancies were filled from within the BSSR's infrastructure (see note 14). Secondly, the relationship of the BSSR to the Soviet apparatus had at least this much in common with the developed colonial system of, for example, the late British Empire: the administration of the region was carried out overwhelmingly by people born and educated there (even if educated on lines set by the 'metropole', that is, Moscow – for the Western culture instilled by the higher educational institutions of the British Empire, read Russian–Soviet culture), whose prospects of moving beyond the 'colonial' boundaries were relatively small. So there exists a huge bureaucracy whose jobs and career paths gave it a group identity defined by the boundaries of the BSSR,[16] and a clear interest in preserving those boundaries and the internal structure of the state. The dual identity of our bureaucrat meant, nevertheless, that while the overall system remained stable there was no tension at the margins between a BSSR bureaucrat identity and the All-Union apparatus. Here contests were fought out on a factional basis.[17]

The progressive weakening of the federal centre brought about by

Gorbachev's attempts at reform meant that by 1991 the system had long ceased to appear stable. The collective with which our bureaucrat could confidently identify was increasingly bounded solely by the BSSR; the proposed new Union Treaty, in aiming for a massive transfer of power from the central ministries to the Union Republics, looked set to continue this trend. Here, I suggest, is one explanation for the easy adoption of certain features of Nationalist rhetoric ('sovereignty', 'independence') by an anti-Nationalist Establishment, to which they were useful as symbols, not of ethnic identity but of political identity, and as political resources. Soviet federal organisation had bequeathed an administrative structure that was national in form, so that when the federal centre of power collapsed in August 1991, burying the dual identity as it fell, the administrative identity that was left in Belarus was also national in form.

I think that this goes a long way towards explaining the ease with which the BSSR was transformed into and maintained as an independent nation-state, in the absence of a strong Nationalist movement. It was the vested interests in the administration, a hangover from Soviet bureaucratic organisation, which actually provided the foundation of Belarusian *state*hood. Note that the republic's independence was and is supported by the Establishment and has never been tested in a referendum, as was the case, in Ukraine for example,. This simple fact, of the Establishment's support for an independent Republic, is enough to prove that there *is* a politically significant sense of Belarusian identity, and the continuing struggle for power of the parties of the 'national-democratic' or 'patriotic-democratic' opposition shows that Belarusian national consciousness is far from the simple unifying force its name suggests; and, furthermore, that what Michael Urban and Jan Zaprudnik called the 'accomplished fact' of Belarusian nationhood[18] remains a highly problematic concept.[19]

Conclusion

In looking for answers to the questions posed by the demise of the Soviet Union and the inheritance it bequeathed, much has been made of the role of national consciousness. In its relationship to the state are clues to explaining the shape of the map of contemporary Europe. Belarus, I believe, presents something of a special case, in that study of the national consciousness represented by the contemporary Nationalist movement proves so unenlightening when it is related to the development and activities of the state. Belarusian national identity is fragmented, and its roots lead in different directions. I do not think we can uncover the foundations of Belarusian statehood, or 'nationhood', by examining the contemporary *Adradzhen'ne* and attempting to place it in some kind of historical continuity. If the Republic of Belarus fits into a historical continuity, it is the one that leads directly in and out of the Soviet experience – the foundations of the Belarusian state ultimately lie in the origins of the BSSR, and it is at this historical juncture that the relationship of national consciousness and Nationalist activity to state power, and its influence on the federal arrangement of the USSR, requires attention if Nationalism's role in the foundation of a Belarusian nation-state is to be properly assessed.

Glossary of Terms

Much of the criticism that can be levelled at writing on nationalism springs from a lack of clarity on the part of the writer as to what he or she understands by the term and, moreover, by its associated phenomena (nation, national consciousness etc...). All these are things which can and do mean different things to different people; there is no objective definition to which we can usefully make reference. Making assumptions about the reader's perceptions is something of which we should always be wary. Because of the importance of subjectivity, and also the emotive power of the word, a debate on the 'real' meaning of nationalism would be somewhat futile, and therefore the best the writer on the topic can do is to set out clearly what he or she understands by the word and its related terminology. If the analysis is then bound by those definitions, the chances of engendering meaningful discussion instead of sterile quibbling ought to be much greater. In the hope of making my position clear, therefore, here is a brief summary of the principal definitions upon which my analysis is based.

I distinguish between two kinds of nationalism, which will be denoted by the use of upper and lower case 'n' according to the variant to which I am referring. Thus:

*N*ationalism = activity in promotion or defence of the perceived interests of a 'nation', imagined as a unified, homogeneous political interest group.
*N*ationalist (n.) = (i) a person who believes in the primacy of their nation's interests;

(ii) a person engaged in political activity in promotion or defence of the perceived interests of a nation, imagined as a unified, homogeneous political interest group.

Nation = a group which shares a collective identity which allows each member to imagine him- or herself as part of a wider community, and to recognise other members who are not personally known. This community is known as the nation. This identity, thus the definition of the nation, is subjectively determined (such that one person may disagree with another over the validity of their claim to membership of the nation).

national = a rather misleading term, which implies an 'awareness' of membership of a nation., as if the nation is a natural, *a priori* phenomenon. Where I mention it in connection with a nationalist point of view, this is what I take it to mean. Otherwise, I use it to mean the identification with a collective identity, and the *belief* that this constitutes membership of a nation.

national identity = (i) the name given to the 'nation' of which membership is claimed;
(ii) the identification of oneself with a 'nation';
(iii) the identification of oneself with a nation-state.

nationalism = a complex social, political and economic process by which nation-states are formed. In this case the 'nation' is not to be defined subjectively, but is described as the body of people in the defence of whose interests the state bases its legitimacy. Thus, for example, the French nation is made up of those whom the French state exists to protect and serve.

Notes

1. Please refer to glossary of terms (above) for definitions of nationalism and related terminology.
2. Anthony D. Smith, 'Gastronomy or Geology? The Role of Nationalism in the Reconstruction of Nations', *Nations and Nationalism* 1, no.1 (1995), pp.3–23 (p.9).
3. See note 9 below.
4. As just one example, Friedrich Schleiermacher (1768–1834) wrote: 'Only one language is firmly implanted in an individual. Only to one does he belong entirely, no matter how many he learns subsequently. ... For every language is a particular mode of thought, and what is cogitated in one language can never be repeated in the same way in another ... Language, thus, just like the church or the state, is an expression of a peculiar life which contains within it and develops through it a common body of language': quoted in Elie Kedourie, *Nationalism* (London: Hutchinson, 1960), p.63.
5. Anthony Adamovich, *Opposition to Sovietisation in Belorussian Literature (1917–*

1957) (Munich: Institute for the Study of the USSR, 1958), p.180.

6. Quoted in V. Lastouski, *Shto treba vedats' kazhnamu belarusu* (Minsk: Tararystva belaruskai movy, 1991), p.11.

7. For the sake of convenience and consistency I shall retain the use of this appelation throughout, although when writing of the Soviet era the term in use at the time – Belorussian – would be more appropriate.

8. Vera Rich, 'Belarusian Books Axed', *News International*, 14 June 1995, p.9.

9. Walter Stankievich, 'Belorussian Popular Front Announces its Electoral Platform', *RFE/RL Report on the USSR*, 12 January 1990, pp.20–23 (p.22).

10. The questions were the following:
    (a) Do you support giving the Russian language equal status with Belarusian?
    (b) Do you support the establishment of a new state flag and symbol of the Republic of Belarus [to replace the white–red–white flag and 'Pahonya' symbol held by nationalists to be the historic symbols of Belarusian statehood]?
    (c) Do you support the actions of the President towards economic integration with the Russian Federation?
    (d) Do you agree with the necessity of changing the Constitution of the Republic of Belarus to provide for the possibility of the President disbanding the Supreme Soviet before the end of its term in the case of systematic or serious breaches of the Constitution?

    The result was a massive vote in favour of every one of the proporals: 83.3 per cent voted in favour of giving Russian equal status as a state language (only 12.7 per cent voted against this – and it was this issue that was credited by the nationalists with posing the gravest danger to 'the nation'); 75.1 per cent voted for the new flag and symbol; and 83.3 per cent supported 'economic integration with the Russian Federation'; 77.7 per cent supported the final proposition; this was on a turnout of only 53.8 per cent: see *Narodnaya gazeta*, 19 April 1995, p.1; 16 May 1995, p.1.

11. *Narodnaya gazeta*, 14 June 1995, p.1.

12. S.L. Guthier, 'The Belorussians: National Identification and Assimilation, 1897–1970', *Soviet Studies* **XXIX**, no.1 (1977), p.55.

13. *Natsional'nyi sostav naseleniya SSSR* (Moscow: Finansy i statistika, 1991), p.88.

14. For much of what follows I should declare my indebtedness to Benedict Anderson's *Imagined Communities*, 2nd edn (London: Verso, 1991).

15. Michael Urban and J. Zaprudnik, 'Belarus: A Long Road to Nationhood', in Ian Bremmer and Raymond Taras (eds), *Nations and Politics in the Soviet Successor States* (Cambridge: Cambridge University Press, 1993), pp.99–120 (p.108).

16. Between 1966 and 1986, 1368 vacancies occurred in the jobs that Urban numbers among the top three strata of the elite, but he records only nine instances of those jobs being taken by individuals having no career history within the BSSR: see Michael J. Urban, *An Algebra of Soviet Power: Elite Circulation in the Belorussian Republic, 1966–86* (Cambridge: Cambridge University Press, 1989), p.21.

17. Ibid., chapters 5 and 6.

18. I should note that I am rather unsure of what is meant by this term: I take it to mean the achievement of a sense of collective identity, defined as national, which is politicised to support the demand for or exercise of state power.

19. Urban and Zaprudnik, 'Belarus: A Long Road to Nationhood', p.117.

5 Redefining National Identity After Communism: A Preliminary Comparison of Ukraine and Poland

Ray Taras

The disintegration of the Soviet empire and the withering away of Communist ideology had many consequences for members of the Soviet bloc. One of them was to trigger a search for a new, or renewed, sense of national identity. With the ability of Russia to interfere in the internal affairs of other states now limited, and with the discrediting of an ideology that had promulgated a contrived form of internationalism, it was natural for post-communist states to become introspective and to search for what was unique and distinctive in their histories.[1]

This chapter attempts a preliminary comparison of this process of national introspection in Ukraine and Poland. The history shared by these two Slavic peoples – in particular, their partial incorporations into tsarist Russia throughout the nineteenth century and their subjugation by the Soviet empire for various periods of the twentieth century – makes the two cases comparable.[2] To be sure, Poland's extended periods of statehood and, in addition, its dominion over parts of western Ukraine, also make the two nations' histories different. Poles' sense of national identity would not seem to have been as completely obliterated during periods of tsarist and Soviet colonialisation as that of Ukrainians, who never even enjoyed the equivalent of a Duchy of Warsaw or Congress Poland. This suggests that, under post-communist conditions, national identity would be more easily re-acquired by Poles, while it would require considerable reconstructing by Ukrainians. We should expect that

84

Ukrainian independence, achieved in December 1991, would precipitate a more intensive search for historical identity and lead to efforts to delineate boundaries between ethnic groups residing on its territory more sharply. This chapter therefore looks more closely at the more complex Ukrainian case.

Why should the way a nation mounts its quest for national identity be important? First of all, it can tell us whether an exclusive (ethnic) or inclusive (civic) understanding of identity is adopted. Second, it can suggest whether the rights of minority groups will be closely respected. Third, examining how a people search for national identity can reveal whether it is secure, self-confident and tolerant, or displays symptoms of insecurity, paranoia and xenophobia. All three questions bear on the subject of creating liberalism in societies that have recently cast aside communist authoritarianism. The progress recorded towards engendering liberal societies is considered at the conclusion of this chapter.

Beyond these issues, a study of national identity can indicate whether the process of party formation is shaped by nationalist agendas. Furthermore, it can shed light on the actual policy programmes that parties of the left, the centre and the right pursue. For the effort to depict national identity, national interest and national *raison d'état* may turn out to be a policy priority for parties across the political continuum and can overshadow other issues, such as economic reform and constitution-making. If identity politics are central to a party's platform, to what extent are they formalised into a quasi-ideology? For it seems that defining identity theoretically is an important part of the more general process of rethinking and *soznanie* taking place in lands of the former Soviet empire. Finally, we might be better placed to answer the question that students of political culture have invariably asked: what are the foci of identification of various social groups in a given state? Is class identity submerged by a national one? Can there be regional identities, or identities based on other types of sub-groupism?

The Concept of National Identity

National identity is not a new concept for political scientists and it has been the subject of considerable research. In the 1960s Dankwart Rustow identified four objective characteristics of a nation: geography, history, language and popular will. It was his account of the role of history, however, that was iconoclastic. Rustow wrote:

For all his preoccupation with history, the early nationalist, like other historical romanti-
cists, is straining for a break with his living past, with his immediate social and cultural
context. The historical themes he invokes are significant not as hypotheses of historic
causation but as part of a psychological search for symbols of confidence in the present.[4]

The mythology of history is pieced together by nationalists, Rustow
claimed, primarily because of lack of confidence in and a sense of
insecurity about the nation's present and future.

While the number and permutation of factors to be considered in the
study of national identity can be greatly increased from that proposed by
Rustow, one in particular rarely appears in social science research, even
though it has been employed for centuries: the symbiotic relationship
between national identity and alterity. Alterity is the image of a foreign
nation – positive or otherwise – that is juxtaposed with self-image. In
many cases of constructing a national identity, there is an assumed
oppostion between national traits and those ascribed to another nation.
Thus, the twelfth-century opposition between Christian and pagan nations is illustrated in a series of symmetrical binomes found in the
Chanson de Rolland. Similarly, in the fourteenth century, Petrarch's
Prosa juxtaposes Germans and Italians in a highly systematised way. A
century later, in her polemical *Ditie de Jeanne d'Arc*, Christine de Pizan
depicted religious and national alterity as found between English and
French nations.[5] While this chapter only briefly examines images of
alterity in our two case studies, it is a subject that merits greater attention.

Leading US social scientists, such as S.M. Lipset and Samuel Huntington, have written about the specific case of American national identity.
Huntington, for example, concluded that the tenets of individualism 'are
at the very core of national identity. Americans cannot abandon them
without ceasing to be Americans in the most meaningful sense of the
word – without, in short, becoming un-American.'[6] George Lodge
described two ideal-type ideologies in the contemporary world that
affected national competitiveness: individualism and communitarianism.
To equal degrees, both could serve as the core value system defining
national identity, for the cosy relationship between communitarian and
nationalist values was in practice no more likely to enhance identity than
the more tenuous relationship between individualism and nationalism.
The case studies in Lodge's volume in large measure succumb to the
alterity temptation: the claim is that US individualism and Japanese
communitarianism have long histories, each contributing to contrasting
senses of national identity.[7]

Even though the connection seems obvious, national identity studies have seldom been based on identification theory – a paradigm that would seem to complement such a research focus well. Identification theory has for many decades been central to research undertaken by psychologists, and only recently has it begun to make a mark in political science. William Bloom is one of the first social scientists to apply the paradigm – designed for the study of individual psychology – to research on international politics. Summarising the findings of Sigmund Freud, George Herbert Mead, Erik Erikson, Talcott Parsons and Jürgen Habermas (the latter two, of course, not psychologists), he arrives at an apparently banal conclusion:

> *National identity* describes that condition in which a mass of people have made the same identification with national symbols – have internalized the symbols of the nation – so that they may act as one psychological group when there is a threat to, or the possibility of enhancement of, these symbols of national identity.[8]

Bloom specifies the necessary condition for national identity to emerge: 'the people *en masse* must have gone through the actual psychological process of making that general identification with the nation'. Bloom sees no chicken-and-egg problem with his approach: 'As an idea, nationalism has no intrinsic power to create any national identity. It may, however, be appropriate to, and harness, a sense of national identity which already exists'.[9]

One of the few issues on which the psychoanalytic and behavioural schools of psychology would seem to agree is the bio-psychological drive to internalise the behaviour of significant others in order to create identity. The exposition of this multi-step psychological process and its linkage with political maturation is, arguably, the most stimulating part of Bloom's study. Let me list his key propositions:

1. Identification – the mechanism of internalising the attitude, mores and behaviour of significant others – is a psycho-biological imperative based in the earliest infantile need to surive.
2. Identification is a dynamic adaptive mechanism as much at work in adults as in infants.
3. A satisfactory synthesis of identifications, or identity stability, is crucial for a sense of psychological security and well-being. Identity enhancement leads to a greater sense of well-being; identity diffusion leads to anxiety and breakdown.
4. As life circumstances change, individuals may make new and

appropriate identifications. Individuals may also seek to protect and
enhance identifications already made.

5. As the individuals enter more fully into society, identifications are
    made with more diffuse symbolic entities... These are Mead's 'gen-
    eralized others', Erikson's 'ideologies' and Habermas's 'identity-
    securing interpretive systems'.
6. In as much as a group of individuals shares a common identification,
    there is the potential for that group to act together to enhance and
    protect that shared identity.[10]

Nation-building occurs when the mass of citizens experiences the actions
of the state and concludes that this experience has been beneficial to
them, especially, that it has provided them with psychological security so
that identification with the nation becomes a form of gratification. When
he links national identity to foreign policy (a subject not of concern
here), Bloom probably exaggerates the importance of national identity:
'identity is as tangible a factor as territory or property in situations of
conflict; in fact, it can well be argued that territory is only a blatant
symbol of national identity.'[11]

   There are both more general and more particularist forms of identity
than the national one, for example, a psychological association with the
international working-class as posited by Marxism, a parochial identity-
securing interpretative structure such as the Hindu caste system where
even the deprived enjoy a secure cosmological place. But Bloom imputes
special social-psychological powers to the national identity dynamic in
its unique ability to mobilise a mass public.

   Having considered one systematic approach to the study of national
identity adapted for political science, let me turn to the case studies. I
wish to enquire whether these propositions are substantiated by political
development in two nations which have reasserted their identities following the discrediting of previous, externally-imposed identities. A list of
the factors that contribute to identity enhancement, security in the collective psyche, and national mobilisation can include: historical memory,
language, religion, regional integration, self-perceptions and use of stereotypes (alterity), governmental policies and political party platforms.
While it is impossible to provide a comprehensive analysis of all of these
variables, let me identify the most salient aspects of each of these for
Ukraine and Poland in the 1990s.

Ukrainian National Identity

Collective memory

When faced with pressures for assimilation, national identity can survive when a people's collective memory of a common history is continuously reinforced. Many students of the former USSR accept an understanding of identity that goes beyond simple primordialism. Gregory Gleason, a specialist on Soviet nationalities, is one: 'National identity – the "rapport of the people", as Walt Whitman put it – has its roots in the "old ways", the habits of thought and practice that are handed down from one generation to the next.'[12] The eminent Ukrainian specialist and Harvard University historian Roman Szporluk made a similar point: 'During their national revival of the nineteenth century, the Ukrainians created their own conception of national history as a process that followed its own inner dynamic.' That is, this history was not driven simply by the dynamic of Russian history. The concept of a distinct Ukrainian historical process was developed in detail, of course, by Mykhailo Hrushevsky in the early part of the twentieth century, but it has come under challenge. Recently, for example, Mark von Hagen provocatively argued that because contemporary Ukraine has a future it *will* have a history, though it may not have one yet.[13]

Szporluk stressed Ukrainians' different approach to the role of the state, a reaction to tsarist and bolshevik use of the state apparatus to crush national culture. As an example, 'The "tsar liberator", Alexander II, in Ukrainian historical memory is associated with the decrees that banned the use of Ukrainian in print, in school, and on the stage.'[14] The author grounded modern Ukrainian national identity in the historical convictions that: (1) Kievan Rus' had been an ethnically pluralist entity; and, (2) the Muscovite state was neither the only nor the principal successor of Kiev. Szporluk endorsed Mykola Kostomarov's thesis of 'two Russian nationalities' (advanced in 1861) and lent support to the proposition that 'the basis of Ukrainian–Russian differentiation is historico-political rather than ethno-linguistic.'[15] Indeed, as we see below, the purported linguistic schism between Ukrainian and Russian speakers is all too often exaggerated.

The questions asked by Tomas Masaryk near the end of the First World War, therefore, remain pertinent: 'Are the Ukrainians a separate nation or a Russian tribe? Is the Ukrainian language a separate language or a Russian dialect?' Masaryk implied that even if the answer to the second question was negative, it did not preclude the recognition of

Ukraine as a separate nation. For what appear as 'merely' cultural differences can become politicised and form the basis for separate social and economic development when a centralising empire is oppressive.[16]

To summarise the role of collective memory as a unique historical dynamic, Szporluk invoked both the socialist thinker Mykhailo Drahomanov and the conservative monarchist Vyacheslav Lypynsky to support his position. Ukrainian national identity is rooted, the argument goes, in the nation's past participation in Europe's cultural progress as well as in its political structure that differs from that of Russia. In particular, this structure is based on very different relations between state and society and the elite and the lower social classes. Szporluk also cautioned against catching the 'Polish infection,' but he accepted that that dimension of the infection which would establish statehood *à la polonaise* was not to be condemned.[17]

The issue of national identity is compounded where a people's name has been appropriated by another group. Up to the eighteenth century Ukrainians were known as Rusyns, derived from the original Kievan Rus' state. Peter the Great had claimed that Muscovites had their ancestral homeland in Kievan Rus' and they constituted the original Rusyns, or Russians. The people living on Russia's periphery were to be called Ukrainians, that is, those who live on the periphery of the country. The very connotation of the name implies a negative definition, then: what Ukrainians are is that they are not Russians. For the most part, such a conceptualisation of Ukrainians is rejected by the collective memory.

Language

Given a contested history, national identity would seem unviable without the existence of a national language. Arnold Toynbee claimed this need not be so and warned against searching for 'the criterion of Nationality in the shibboleth of Language.'[18] Language was an unsatisfactory criterion of nationality largely because consequence and cause of, for example, literary nationalism could not be distinguished. Dante and Luther were *both* creating new literary idioms *and* were products of increasing Italian and German cultural unity.[19]

Some linguists and political leaders have contended that Ukrainian is a dialect of Russian. However controversial this claim may be, this status alone may be sufficient to define identity when the dialect is perceived by those using it as a national language. In this way, the sense of national identity is sustained through a distinct living language (or even dialect). In addition to being a means of communication and serving symbolic functions, language orders a group's conceptualisation of the world and its understanding of its role within the world. It is difficult to agree with Walker Connor, then, when he claims that language has had chiefly a symbolic value for Ukrainian nationalists.[20] Language and identity – including political identity – are interdependent. Not surprisingly, in the former Soviet Union communist leaders made efforts to decouple the two in order to defuse Ukraine political self-awareness.

Given its centrality (though not its essentiality) in determining national identity, it is to be expected that even within the Marxist tradition scholars would disagree about national identity and language change. Lev Yurkevych (whose *nom de plume* was L. Rybalka) was the first Ukrainian national communist to challenge Lenin.[21] A book published in 1987 under the auspices of Kiev State University was concerned with 'analysing the most important results of Leninist nationality policy.' Vladimir Zamlinskii and his co-authors argued pointedly that Lenin himself had believed that language change had to be natural and could not be imposed 'by means of a stick.'[22] It followed that any policy of russianisation was anti-Leninist – a form of argumentation very characteristic of the period of *glasnost'*.

An issue more complex than the relationship between national identity and language is the subjective perception of citizens concerning language use. Both the 1989 Soviet census and a 1992 Ukrainian Sociological Association survey discovered that about two-thirds of citizens in Ukraine identified Ukrainian as their native language. Seventy per cent of Ukrainian speakers said they also knew Russian, while 60 per cent of Russian speakers also knew Ukrainian. In sum, 85 per cent of respondents living throughout Ukraine spoke Ukrainian as a first or second language, and slightly less (78 per cent) spoke Russian.[23] This remarkably high rate of bilingualism indicates that a linguistic divide hardly exists in the new country.

When we examine the extent to which Ukrainians perceive themselves as different from Russians, however, it seems important to treat the phenomenon of bilingualism with some scepticism. Writing before the Soviet collapse, Zvi Gitelman made the point that 'members of ethnic minorities learn to adapt their language and mores to specific social situations, appearing "assimilated" in one kind of situation, but "going native" in a different situation.' Regarding the specific question of language use, Gitelman contended that 'A non-Russian who uses the Russian language may be hostile to Russians, and may insist on maintaining a non-Russian identity.'[24]

Since independence, native Ukrainian and Russian speakers have disagreed whether Ukrainian should be the main language of instruction in schools in Ukraine and whether teaching Ukrainian should be mandatory.[25] Ukrainian speakers supported both proposals (66 per cent and 75 per cent), although it is surprising that there was not a much greater consensus.[26] Only 33 per cent of Russian speakers supported Ukrainian as the main language of education, but a majority (55 per cent) believed it should be obligatory at school. The real linguistic fault line was revealed when responses by region were tabulated. As was predictable, respondents living in central and western Ukraine were more supportive of Ukrainian language use than those in eastern and southern areas.[27]

Demands have been made by Crimea, the Donbas and other eastern oblasts to grant Russian the status of a state language alongside Ukrainian. Dominique Arel depicts this demand the following way: 'The politics of anxiety among Russophones is colliding with the politics of identity among nationally-conscious Ukrainians, for whom it is a question of principle that Ukrainian be used in public offices in all regions of Ukraine.'[28] In turn, Roman Solchanyk has pointed to the broader agenda behind this demand: 'demands for upgrading the status of Russian to that of a state language are typically accompanied by calls for dual Ukrainian–Russian citizenship, a federated structure for Ukraine, a higher degree of integration within the Commonwealth of Independent States (CIS), and closer ties with Russia.'[29] Solchanyk held that fears of Ukrainiszation were unfounded. For example, between 1988 and 1992 the proportion of schoolchildren taught in Ukrainian increased by just 2 per cent, and in the Crimea there was not a single Ukrainian school to serve the half a million Ukrainians (26 per cent of the region's population). In a bizarre twist, then, the Law on National Minorities in Ukraine of 25 June 1992 guaranteeing all minorities cultural autonomy and linguistic rights was not used by the Ukrainian-speaking minority in the Crimea to obtain extended educational facilities.

Religious and regional differences

Differences in the ethnic make-up and attitudes of the inhabitants of western and eastern Ukraine are crucial to an understanding of whether a national identity exists. The historian Orest Subtelny highlighted the contrast between the western part of the country, which was more agrarian and backward and where the Ukrainian language was dominant, and the eastern part, associated with modernising, industrial, urban life.[30] Another view is, however, that it is western Ukraine that is the more modern part when political and national factors are considered. The west had begun to construct a civil society already under the Austrian empire whereas Russian oppression retarded political development in western Ukraine. Thus, political differences were inherent long before independence.

Bohdan Kravchenko referred to Galicia in western Ukraine as the country's Piedmont and described how its population of 5.4 million – of the total of 10 million living in western Ukraine – drove the independence movement prior to 1991.[31] To be sure, electoral studies have shown that western Ukraine is itself not politically homogeneous and that, for example, Volhynia, long ruled by Moscow, is considerably less radical than Galicia, where grass-roots political organisations existed before the First World War.[32] For reasons of parsimony, I treat western Ukraine as a politically homogeneous region and ask what underlies the distinctive political behaviour on the part of the inhabitants here.

Religious differences are the first factor to consider.[33] Vasyl Markus asserted that 'Eastern Christianity in its two-denominational manifestations – Orthodox and Catholic – has become the national religion in the Ukraine, differentiating the native society from past and present dominating nationalities and/or state powers, whether Polish, Russian (at least in the case of the Uniates) or Austro-Hungarian.' He reported that 'The Russian Orthodox hierarchy never achieved the desired results in the "Orthodoxization" (*Opravoslavlennya*) of the Western Ukraine' even though the Uniate Catholic church of the eastern rite was banned and suppressed for most of the Soviet period.[34] But for centuries the Uniate church had also constituted a barrier against the polonisation of Galicia. Even where Ukrainians spoke Polish, according to Valentyn Moroz, 'they remained Ukrainians as long as they belonged to the Ukrainian religion and Church.'[35] Polish promotion of Roman Catholicism through the Union of Brest in 1596 sought to create an imperial–feudal national identity – *natione Polonus, gente Ruthenus*. But the Uniate church did not become the instrument of conversion that Poles had expected.

It was the Orthodox church, which had set up its own hierarchy in Ukraine in 1620 under the patronage of Constantinople but which was incorporated into the patriarchate of Moscow in 1686, that became more influential in defining national identity – if only to russify it considerably. Historically the Orthodox hierarchy did not embrace the Ukrainian national cause. It was difficult to identify an ethnic boundary separating Russia from Ukraine because of membership of this Russian Orthodox church. This was part of the reasoning behind Alexander Solzhenitsyn's belief that only an oblast-by-oblast referendum on union with Russia or Ukraine could resolve this identity question.

In 1921 the establishment of the Ukrainian autocephalous church finally produced a 'nationalist' national church. Markus wrote: 'The autocephalous church has been, in its substance, politically nationalist, and ideologically anti-Russian and anti-authoritarian, while the Russian church remained Russian nationalist and imperial.'[36] The latter, not unexpectedly, received preferential treatment in the Soviet period and continued to pursue 'orthodoxisation' by seeking to eliminate Latin influences in the rite of the autocephalous church. Stalin banned this church altogether in 1930 but it continued to operate as a silent underground church.

While the Greek-rite Uniate Catholic church and the autocephalous Orthodox church may have more theological affinity with Roman Catholicism and Russian Orthodoxy respectively than with each other, the fact is that they are regarded by Ukrainians living in western and eastern regions as their respective historic and national churches. Indeed, the membership of both the Uniate and the autocephalous Orthodox churches has been almost exclusively Ukrainian.

Religious faith alone does not fully explain regional differences within Ukraine. In another context, Conor Cruise O'Brien wrote about the process of decoupling national identity and nationalism from religion, which he claimed began with the anti-clerical French nationalism of Napoleonic times.[37] In the case of Ukraine, specific patterns of colonisation of its regions, the varying degree of experiments with constitutional development under rival empires, different social and economic interaction with neighbouring states, distinct in- and out-migration trends, as well as the rise of secular anti-Polish or anti-Russian forms of nationalism, have all been factors. The fact that western Ukraine first became a part of the Russian empire in 1939 while the eastern lands were a full colony for over 300 years cannot be overstated. It was only after 1945 that Russian settlement of Galicia and Transcarpathia began in earnest, whereas eastern regions and Crimea – won by Russians in eighteenth-century wars against the Turks – are widely viewed by Russians as part of the *rodina* or motherland. Overcoming this regional cleavage is pivotal to the construction of a state-wide national identity. David Marples echoes the view of many specialists, therefore, in arguing that 'much will depend on the raising of Ukrainian national consciousness in Eastern Ukraine' where the large Russian minority lives.[38]

Self-images and stereotypes

Surveys of Russians 'stranded' in non-Russian republics when the USSR collapsed can prove inconclusive. As many as 11 million Russians were living in Ukraine at the time of the 1989 census. When, before Ukrainian independence, they were asked whether they would migrate to Russia and whether they expected mass Russian out-migration in the near future, Russian respondents in western Ukraine gave inconsistent answers (as did their counterparts in Estonia and Latvia): While 44 per cent said they intended to stay in Ukraine, 41 per cent thought mass Russian migration was likely.[39]

Russians and Ukrainians display a low level of ethnic schism when measured by such factors as racial, linguistic and cultural differentiation. But different regional political cultures have not been easy to set aside. Many in the west express open dislike of 'Moskals', a disparaging term for Russians. A comparative survey of respondents in L'viv, Kiev and Simferopol conducted in 1992 revealed predictable regional differences in such attitudes. It found that L'viv respondents stood out in the attitudes they harboured towards Russians: over 45 per cent tended to assign Russians negative attributes and, related to this, 86 per cent reported that a majority of their friends were fellow Ukrainians. In Kiev the russophobe attitude was still relatively common (38 per cent), as was the rate of intra-ethnic friendships (82 per cent). Conversely, 'Self-approval ratings (Ukrainians on Ukrainians; Russians on Russians) were relatively high across the board' at over 70 per cent. Paradoxically, perhaps, self-identity seemed stronger among Ukrainians than among Russians: 'The differences between Ukrainian self- and other-stereotyping thus tended to be much more marked in general than that of Russians, who were more inclined to attribute similar characteristics to both themselves and Ukrainians.' One final item from the three-city survey data bearing on national identity was reactions to the assertion 'I should like to live in Ukraine and not in Russia.' Most Ukrainians in L'viv and Kiev fully agreed with the statement (86 per cent in both places). While 72 per cent of Russians living in the capital fully agreed, only 39 per cent of them in L'viv did so. In the Crimean city of Simferopol, 53 per cent of Ukrainians fully agreed and another 17 per cent agreed, while only 32 per cent of Russians agreed or strongly agreed. The much-touted distinctive political culture of Crimea was substantiated by these results.

Aside from Crimea, the Donbass region of eastern Ukraine has occasionally flexed its political muscle. A massive coalminers' strike was staged in June 1993, and eastern oblasts have seemed more sensitive to deteriorating economic conditions. Whereas 45 per cent of respondents in the eight western oblasts were not at all satisfied with Ukraine's economic situation, the figure was 65 per cent in the three eastern oblasts.

Support for a market economy was highest in the west and in the capital, and lowest in central and eastern regions. President Kravchuk's own support displayed regional variations, too: 'almost 60 per cent of respondents in the east, as opposed to just over 30 per cent in the west, evaluated his performance negatively.'[41]

A survey comparing attitudes of inhabitants in the western city of L'viv with those in the eastern city of Donetsk also highlighted the existence of different political orientations. L'viv respondents considered themselves more politically radical than their Donetsk counterparts did. On a ten-point scale ranging from very negative (0) to very positive (10), the L'viv sample assessed communists very unfavourably: 1.8, compared to a 5.2 rating given by Donetsk respondents. The assessment of Ukrainian nationalists was just the reverse: 5.64 for L'viv and 1.42 for Donetsk. As expected, Russians were more liked in the latter city (9.29) than in L'viv (6.26). The greatest difference in political views was on the issue of Ukraine's future: whereas 62 per cent of L'viv respondents agreed that Ukraine should remain a totally independent country, only 13 per cent of the Donetsk sample agreed. By contrast, 57 per cent of the latter preferred Ukraine to become part of a greater federation that included Russia, whereas only 5 per cent in L'viv approved of such a future.[42]

How third parties view Ukrainians and Russians can also help indicate the distinctiveness of the two national identities. Gitelman's survey of Jewish émigrés found, for example, a significantly higher rating accorded to Russians than to Ukrainians. Jews' assessment of the latter group was a full point less favourable than for Russians on a seven-point scale.[43] Not much other research has been carried out on this topic, though we shall see below that Poles were generally more sympathetic to Ukrainians than to Russians.

The self-image and political activity of Ukrainians living outside Ukraine can also shed light on the issue of national identity. In neighbouring Poland, on the pretext of destroying the alleged terrorist Ukrainian Insurrectionary Organisation (UPA), Ukrainians in the Bieszczady area became targets of an aggressive resettlement campaign in 1947. Codenamed 'Akcja Wisła,' it aimed at driving Ukrainians from traditional areas of settlement and forcing them to resettle in western Poland.[44] When political liberalisation took place after 1956 and a Polish road to socialism was announced, Ukrainians wanted their own road to socialism as well. A Ukrainian-language newspaper began publication and the Ukrainian Social–Cultural Association was established. The greater tolerance of the Gomułka regime may have been evoked by the resilience of Ukrainian identity in the region. Similarly, with the birth of the Solidarity trade union in August 1980, the status of Ukrainians in Poland again became the subject of attention. While Solidarity's policy was to foster conciliatory attitudes in inter-ethnic relations, the Warsaw-based Ukrainian weekly *Nashe slovo* went further and gave a sympathetic appraisal of Ukrainian nationalist sentiment in the country in the 1930s, a subject that caused consternation and exacerbated anti-Solidarity views in the USSR. After the democratic breakthrough in 1989, Ukrainians in Poland have resumed political activity and set up the Union of Ukrainians in Poland.

A detailed study of Ukrainian political activity in the course of the Prague Spring was undertaken by Peter Potichnyj and Grey Hodnett. Although they numbered only 120,000, Ukrainians played an influential role in the liberalisation campaign in Czechoslovakia, again evoking a harsh response by Ukraine Communist leaders who felt particularly threatened by the activity of their compatriots. Ukrainian cultural and social organisations were revived, the two Ukrainian-language newspapers and the literary-cultural journal *Duklia* published works viewed as subversive by the Ukraine republic Communist Party, and the radio station near the Soviet border in Presov broadcast events of the Prague Spring in Ukrainian to the USSR. All these media accounts espoused an interpretation of Ukrainian history at odds with the official Soviet version. Major historical and cultural figures were rehabilitated, and revisionist views of national self-determination and federalism were offered.[45] In summary, Ukrainian national self-awareness was asserted in Eastern Europe whenever political conditions allowed.

Government policies

When in December 1991 more than 90 per cent of the Ukraine republic's electorate voted for independence, it was viewed as evidence that citizens had a clear sense of national identity and had been politically mobilised to act on that identity. Mykola Ryabchuk observed that even the efforts at creating a civil society in Ukraine in the 1980s were ultimately aimed at Russian imperialism and expressed a desire for an independent state.[46] Closer analysis of the referendum vote permits other interpretations, however. One writer contended that 'The motive for the vast majority who cast ballots in favour of a separate Ukrainian state was less romantic nationalism than practical economics. A Ukrainian state, leaders convinced them, held the promise of a better life.' As a result, 'the push for independence did not so much come from the grassroots as from among the ranks of ambitious leaders.'[47]

Shortly after independence, political forces regrouped in a way that brought ex-communists and democratic opposition dissidents together. Personified by the first president, Kravchuk, their major achievements have been consolidation of statehood and liberalisation of society. The October 1989 law on language, the October 1991 law on citizenship, and the June 1992 law on national minorities in Ukraine have provided non-Ukrainians with a broad panopoly of rights. Non-Ukrainian culture, language, religion, education and communications were to be protected and promoted in areas where minority groups were concentrated. The search for Ukrainian identity has not, then, been at the expense of other groups. Indeed, it could be argued that clarifying Ukrainian and minority identities has proved a positive-sum game.[48]

The election of Kuchma to the presidency in July 1994 signalled the installation of a non-nationalist élite into power. As a member of the former Soviet military-industrial establishment and as an ethnic Ukrainian from the eastern part of the country, the new president seemed 'well placed to transcend geographic and generational divides.'[49] His policy focused principally on economic reform. The series of elections to the Supreme Rada, or parliament, between April and November 1994 also indicated that identity politics were taking on secondary importance. Nationalist parties received only about 15 per cent of the votes, prompting one writer to conclude: 'Political parties preaching ethnic isolationism or nationalist extremism did not receive significant support in the elections. Moreover, the same polls that show an erosion of support for Ukrainian independence also show little identification with Russia.'[50] The enactment of laws helping to define identity shortly after independence seems to have defused both nationalist and reactive nationalist threats in the subsequent years.

Party platforms

The process of political party formation in independent Ukraine was delayed because, as Solchanyk observed, 'a coalition was cemented first and foremost by the common interest in defending the newly achieved independent statehood.' Most surprising, in his view, was 'This shift among an influential group of Rukh leaders toward becoming a kind of unofficial "presidential party"' which effectively split this organization.[51] Rukh's first chairman, Ivan Drach, accepted Kravchuk's good-faith pledge that 'We should be guided only by the interests of our independent state.' By contrast, presidential candidate Vyacheslav Chornovil believed that Rukh would be best served by playing a role as opposition critic. The Rukh schism over the wisdom of supporting Kravchuk and other 'sovereign communists' – former party members who supported Ukraine independence – allowed Chornovil, a long-time political prisoner in the communist era, to take over the party's leadership in December 1992.

Once statehoood seemed secure, these leaders began to present competing visions of Ukraine's future. Highly-publicised issues such as whether Ukraine should have a large standing army, a Black Sea navy and a nuclear deterrent were central in negotiations with Russia but, in addition, they involved the question of political self-definition, too. Membership of the CIS and the signing of an economic integration treaty with Russia revealed ambivalence among Ukraine leaders regarding the degree to which links with Russia remained desirable.

Two democratic blocs emerged to challenge Rukh on these and other issues. The Congress of National Democratic Forces (KNDS) was effectively Kravchuk's presidential party and supported a unitary state, a strong military and withdrawal from the CIS. The liberal-democratic New Ukraine worked with Chornovil to challenge Kravchuk but it supported closer economic relations with the Soviet successor states. Adapting Marxist categories to the new reality, the New Ukraine leader Volodymyr Filenko aptly noted how differences in the democratic camp concerned whether to assign priority to a national liberation struggle – that is, state-building – or to a bourgeois revolution – that is, market reforms.[52] As with the policy differences between Kuchma and his predecessor, New Ukraine supported a capitalist revolution as the way of consolidating statehood, while the KNDS was fixated on state-building tasks.

An ultra-nationalist organization with para-military formations is the Ukrainian National Assembly–Ukrainian National Self-Defence (UNA-UNSO), set up in 1990-91. Its motto is 'Force, Order, Prosperity' and its programme is the establishment of Kiev as the centre of a Slavic empire and of Eastern Orthodoxy. Russia would be reduced to the status of Ukraine's junior partner. UNA was led by Supreme Rada deputy Oleg Vitovich and UNSO, its paramilitary offshoot with about 3,000 members, by Dmitry Korchinsky.[53] While even more obscure groups calling themselves freedom fighters exist in Ukraine, their influence – like that of the nationalist movement generally – has waned in the mid-1990s.

Polish National Identity

Collective memory

Already in the fifteenth century Poland's ruling magnates became conscious of the country's international role as *antemurale christianitatis* – Roman Catholicism's easternmost bulwark. Over the next centuries, this Polish version of a manifest destiny or mission came to be interpreted in more secular and political terms. Poland was viewed as the outpost of European civilisation beyond which Russian and Asiatic culture began. As a country at the crossroads of Western and Eastern civilisations, Poland had to face threats from both the Teutonic Order and from Mongols, Tatars and Turks to the east. A specific philosophy emerged that became known as Sarmatism. The name originated in the ancient tribe that had lived on the banks of the Dniester river seven centuries before Christ. As inhabitants of proto-Slavonic lands, they had conquered local tribes and established themselves as rulers. Sarmatian ideology claimed a special mission for Poland – a shield protecting Christianity from paganism. The crowning glory of this historic mission occurred in 1683 when King Jan Sobieski defeated the Turkish armies outside Vienna, thereby saving Christian Europe from Islam.

The nobility, in particular, had invoked its supposed Sarmatian origins in order to take upon itself all the obligations associated with Poland's manifest mission. Sarmatians were heroic knights and defenders of the faith and the fatherland. The theory of the *szlachta*'s common ancestry contributed to the integration of the otherwise diverse ranks of the nobility and made other differentiating factors of the time, such as language spoken, religion practised, or wealth accumulated, unimportant. All noblemen enjoyed equal privileges and responsibilities, and that fact constituted *szlachta* democracy. The Latin word *Respublica* was employed by nobles to suggest this political system's descent fom the Roman republic. The Polish nobility was convinced of the superiority of its democratic, representative, republican-style system. The Polish Republican Commonwealth thus became identified with *szlachta* democracy. When compared with many of the absolutist, autocratic monarchical systems found elsewhere in Europe at the time, the nobility may have had reason to boast of its democracy.

The concept of *antemurale* and the Sarmatian mission continue to have relevance today as Polish political and intellectual leaders debate what the country's role in Europe in the twenty-first century should involve. Although couched in different language, advocates of Poland's speedy admission into organiszations such as the European Union (EU) and the North Atlantic Treaty Organisation (NATO) have in mind Poland's status as a bulwark of Western civilisation in the east – especially when they are reluctant to support the right of membership of such organisations to Poland's eastern neighbours (notably, the Baltic states). The Sarmatian myth, then, is based on a patronising Polish view of alterity: Poles are *not* the peoples living on the other side of Catholicism's eastern rampart.[54]

Language and religion

There are no serious linguistic or religious divisions in present-day Poland. In particular, Polish identity today is frequently defined as being grounded in Roman Catholicism – perhaps an exaggerated and discriminatory claim but one that is understandable after decades of atheist propaganda under communism. However, surveys of public opinion conducted in the 1990s have shown an increasing number of respondents viewing the church (and also Jews) as exerting a disproportionate influence in politics. Other surveys suggest that respondents' views of what it means to be a Pole were not ethnically-grounded. In a poll in Autumn 1994, three of the top four answers referred to other criteria, such as speaking Polish (96 per cent), having Polish citizenship (92 per cent) and living in Poland (80 per cent). Eight-two per cent said that parents had to be Polish – presumably an ethnic ascription. But only slightly more than half of respondents (57 per cent) held that a Pole had to be a Catholic.

Parties that supported secular and even anti-religious visions of Poland – such as the Left Democratic Alliance (SLD), the Democratic Union (which shortly afterwards merged with another party to become Freedom Union, or UW), and the Union of Labour (UP) – emerged as the major parties after the parliamentary elections of September 1993. In the December 1995 presidential elections, it was again the representative of secular forces, Alexander Kwaśniewski, who defeated the candidate backed enthusiastically by the Catholic church, Lech Wałęsa. To be sure, the Peasants' Party (PSL) also performed well electorally in 1993, partly because it defended the Catholic ethos of rural Poland. But, significantly, it was the most secular of the peasant parties. Both the Vatican and the ecclesiastical hierarchy in Poland have lamented consumerist trends in the country since market reform was introduced. They are a long way from sharing nineteenth-century poet Adam Mickiewicz's depiction of the Polish nation as Christ on the cross, suffering for others. Ironically, then, they would agree that Catholicism is no longer such a defining feature of Poland.

Regional integration

If there are two Polands (as there are two Ukraines), then they are an urban and rural Poland. The extent of identification with the church is one feature of this chasm but, ultimately, rural and urban Polands represent more of an economic divide than anything else. The cleavage has little direct bearing on identity politics, however.

Purely regional – as opposed to ethnic – differences in Poland are less significant than other cleavages. To be sure, since the early 1970s the former ruling Polish United Workers' Party (PZPR) had seemed to give privileged status to Silesia, largely because of the disproportionate influence of its party bosses, such as Edward Gierek and Zdzisław Grudzień. Not surprisingly, when political space was opened up Silesian organisations were quickly established, for example, the Upper Silesian Union and the Movement for an Autonomous Silesia. Subscribing to a regionalist ideology stressing a 'Europe of nations' rather than a secessionist-driven goal of a 'Europe of national states', Silesia has been portrayed as a bridge linking eastern and western Europe. A 'Schlesien-Śląsk–Sleszko Forum' was established to co-ordinate and promote the interests of Silesians located in Germany, the Czech Republic and Poland.

The Gdańsk region has not only served as the home of the Solidarity trade union but, in recent years, it has been the base for neo-liberal leadership and entrepreneurship, as in the case of the now defunct Liberal-Democratic Congress (KLD). The Warsaw region, with its influx of Western investors and consultants, has a distinct, more Western-oriented political culture, as capital cities throughout the world tend to have. Poorer agrarian regions such as Siedlce display increasing frustration with economic reforms that leave them behind. Before the 5 per cent threshold was introduced (see below), some deputies were elected to the Sejm on regional tickets in 1991, for example, Podhale and Wielkopolska. A Kashub-Pomeranian was sent to the Senate that year, too. Generally, however, such differences play a marginal role in undermining the strong sense of Polish identity, fashioning distinct psyches, or affecting political mobilisation across the country.

Limited ethnic politics exist as well, though not at all on the scale of Ukraine or most other countries in the region. The Ministry of Culture and Art claims to subsidise some 120 schools teaching in the language of Poland's minorities.[55] About half of the forty or so minority associations registered in the country consists of German groups. They are mostly based in provinces bordering on the reunited Federal Republic, where the vast majority of people of German ancestry lives. As a measure intended to institutionalise minority representation in national politics, beginning with the 1993 parliamentary elections a new electoral law relieved parties of national minorities from having to reach the newly-imposed 5 per cent threshold for obtaining Sejm representation. As a result, the German coalition won four seats in the Sejm (it won nine in 1991), to go with one in the Senate. While western Poland has generally voted for leftist candidates in elections held in the 1990s, districts with a large German population have supported more conservative candidates such as Wałęsa.

The most influential German organisation is the Social and Cultural Association of the German minority in Silesia. German Chancellor Helmut Kohl's visit to Poland in July 1995 confirmed the Polish government's acceptance of Germany's role as an unofficial patron of Silesians.[56] Largely as a result of extending more autonomy to the German minority, the Polish population from the eastern provinces transplanted to the recovered territories after the war, though it remains a majority in this region, has felt threatened by these developments.

Ukrainian, Lithuanian and Belarusan minority associations are concentrated in areas of ethnic settlement like the Bieszczady, Suwałszczyzna and Białostockie provinces respectively. In the 1993 elections, Belarusans lost their only legislative seat, while Ukrainians and Lithuanians have not elected deputies to parliament.

Jewish cultural associations were formed in the 1990s, among them a veterans' organisation. While a number of Jews have been elected to the Sejm, they have been members of national parties, such as the UW, rather than any specifically Jewish party. Much has been written about whether Polish national identity encompasses the small Jewish population and whether, as in Russia and elsewhere in the region, assimilationist forces have been so strong as to blur Jewish identity. In terms of alterity, a posited Jewish identity has, at times and for certain segments of society, been critical in sharpening Polish self-identity, as is well known. Since the democratic breakthrough, however, efforts have been made by leaders of both groups to make the ethnic Pole–Polish Jew distinction anachronistic and irrelevant.

Self-images and stereotypes

When we examine Polish respondents' perceptions of other nations, we find considerable changes in ranking in the period between 1975 and December 1989. In terms of trust Poles had in other nations, Americans rose from fifth to first place during this interval, effectively exchanging places with Russians. The greatest single change, however, was in the trust Poles declared in Germans: from being ranked twenty-first in 1975 and also in 1987, Germans became Poles' fourth most-trusted nation in 1989 (after Americans, Italians and Hungarians). As Renata Siemieńska, the author of the study, concludes, 'Results of the Polish research confirm the hypothesis formulated elsewhere that above all trust is extended to those nations which achieved economic successes.'[57]

A different data set tells us more about the likes and dislikes of Poles. In 1991, 68 per cent of respondents expressed a like of Americans and only 1 per cent a dislike. The scores, in descending order, for other nations were: French 61 per cent and 2 per cent, Italians 59 per cent and 1 per cent, English 50 per cent and 3 per cent, and Hungarians 44 per cent and 4 per cent. The most disliked nations were: Gypsies 9 per cent sympathetic and 47 per cent antipathetic, Ukrainians 9 per cent and 38 per cent, Arabs 7 per cent and 32 per cent, Russians 16 per cent and 32 per cent, Romanians 17 per cent and 29 per cent, and Germans 23 per cent and 34 per cent (a marked contrast to Siemieńska's 1989 finding). Attitudes to Jews were mixed, with 17 per cent expressing a liking and 19 per cent a disliking.

Aleksandra Jasińska-Kania correlated such preferences with reasons given for them and observed: 'the wealth of a nation, Catholicism and wartime allies exerted the strongest relative influence on Poles' likes when other factors were controlled.' Her factor analysis revealed further that there were internally-consistent sets of attitudes towards four nationality groups: (1) those making up advanced capitalist economies and liberal democracies (such as the US, England, France), which received the highest set of scores; (2) those perceived as ethnically most different groups from Poles (Chinese, Gypsies, Arabs and to a lesser extent Jews), which received mixed evaluations; (3) those in the post-communist countries (Russia, Belarus, Lithuania and Slovakia), which were generally negative; and, (4) two neighbours (Germany and Ukraine) with whom historical conflict remained imprinted in people's minds and who were very negatively assessed.[58]

The value of such surveys is how evaluations of the cultural make-up of other nations says something about respondents' own sense of national identity.[59] The trivial but inescapable conclusion deriving from both data sets presented here is that Poles want very much to be like Americans and they want to avoid resembling Russians (occasionally referred to disparagingly as 'Mongols' or 'Asiatics'), Ukrainians, Gypsies and, to varying degrees, other Slavic and East European nations. It suggests a deprecatory self-image – the impossible desire to escape Slav and East European identity – that may cause trouble for Poland's political leaders. It also dampens chances of regional co-operation, a problem noted by EU and NATO leaders.

Governmental policies

As with economic reform, Poland's first non-communist governments were quick to carry out far-reaching political and legal reforms, including areas involving relations between Poles and other nations. Except for Lithuania, treaties with all Poland's neighbours were concluded before the SLD victory in September 1993. As early as July 1990, the Sejm Commission on National and Ethnic Minorities put forward a draft version of articles to a new constiution that would provide constitutional enshrinement of minority rights. No new constitution has been adopted, but the proposed article 24 of a 1995 draft was designed to expand minority rights.

The Solidarity government's promotion of multiculturalism was evidenced in other ways. The Bureau for Cultures of National Minorities was created in 1992 to support minority cultures, which included about one-half million Germans, 300,000 Ukrainians, 250,000 Belarusans, 25,000 Lithuanians, Slovaks and Gypsies and 15,000 Jews. The policy was especially concerned with promoting closer relations with German and Jewish communities, which had been the victims of past discrimination. A Council for Polish–Jewish relations was set up to give advice to the president. When President Wałęsa seemed to delay in speaking out against anti-Semitic comments made by a cleric close to him, as a protest two members of the Council tendered their resignations in July 1995. The fact that the resignations had some political significance and were directed at Wałęsa's unseemly silence, rather than a *faux pas* committed by the SLD government, indicated the value now placed on improving Polish–Jewish relations.[60]

In July 1990 the Polish Senate gave a strong endorsement for Ukraine's proclamation of sovereignty, and in the following month it passed a resolution condemning the so-called 'Wisła operation' which the Polish communist government had launched at the end of the war against alleged 'Ukrainian fascist bands' operating in the country. In March 1991 the Polish parliament also recognised the Uniate Catholic church which had been banned after the war./

Relations with the Belarusan community were also improved by the post-communist governments. In May 1992 a treaty of friendship and co-operation was signed between Belarus and Poland, but disagreements remained. In 1994 Orthodox Metropolitan Filaret criticised the proselytising role of Polish priests in Belarus, even though there was evidence that they were precisely those most committed to promoting Belarusan – as opposed to Russian – culture.[61] Even if the Metropolitan's charges were justified, they reflected on the mission assigned to itself by the Polish Roman Catholic church, rather than one crafted by the post-communist government. Relations with Belarus deteriorated rapidly in 1996 when the hardline Russophile President Alexander Lukashenka cracked down on opposition groups and took aim at Polish political leaders (Solidarity head Marian Krzaklewski) who expressed support for the Belarusan opposition.

If identity politics continue to play a role in democratic Poland, it is not because they are fanned by nationalist-oriented governments. So far the electorate has repeatedly rejected politicians' striving to make use of nationalist ideology. In Poland as elsewhere in Central Europe, identity politics operate at a different level. As Adam Gwiazda has observed in the case of Poland, 'The most difficult problem facing both ethnic citizens and national minorities is not "institutionalising" the rights of national minorities but in overcoming the persistent mutual prejudices and "divisions" between those groups.'[62] From Mazowiecki to Cimoszewicz, Polish governments have contributed to the relegation of nationality politics from a systemic to an individual-level problem.

Party platforms

It is surprising how weakly represented the nationalist current is in Polish politics. The two largest nationalist parties have been the Christian National Union (ZChN) and the Confederation for an Independent Poland (KPN). The first emphasised nationalist, religious, interventionist policies but was devastated in the 1993 parliamentary elections. The KPN is anti-communist and anti-Russian while supporting law-and-order, anti-corruption programmes. Led by the ultra-nationalist Leszek Moczulski, it salvaged 22 seats in 1993, making it effectively the only conservative (and sole nationalist) party in the Sejm. A Patriotic Bloc was formed in 1996 to prepare for the Sejm elections scheduled for 1997, but opinion polls in late 1996 showed two non-nationalist parties (the SLD and the recently-formed Solidarity Electoral Action, or AWS) leading the way. Two other parties which failed to secure 5 per cent of the vote in the 1993 elections are noteworthy in the nationalist context. The Liberal Democratic Congress (KLD), headed by one-time Prime Minister Jan Krzysztof Bielecki, advocated extreme *laissez-faire*, supply-side policies. By contrast, the Movement for the Republic (RdR) of another former Prime Minister, Jan Olszewski, pressed for far-reaching de-communisation. His creation of the Movement for Poland's Reconstruction (ROP) in 1996 was an effort to parlay his image as a nationalist. A third group formed just before the 1993 elections as a presidential party, the Non-Party Bloc in Support of Reform (BBWR), obtained only 16 seats despite Wałęsa's open endorsement of it. In their own ways these parties appealed to differing notions of national identity – the Pole as successful entrepreneur, the Pole as anti-communist and Russophobe, the Pole as Piłsudskiite and devout Catholic. The fact that they were marginalised in 1993 and were trailing in opinion polls in 1996 suggests that such partial identities do not provide sufficient appeal to the Polish electorate today.

The left-wing SLD, in power since 1993, has insisted that it will not commit the mistake of its communist party predecessor in sacrificing national interests to 'internationalist' ones. But the SLD is far from nationalist and has sought to match the achievements of the pre-1993 governments in granting wider rights to minorities while continuing to promote greater integration with Western Europe. From its inception, Social Democracy of the Republic of Poland (SDRP), the core party in the SLD alliance, declared its commitment to minority rights. Article 5 of the party's declaration at its founding congress in January 1990 stated: 'The rights of minorities should be guaranteed in all areas: political, cultural, religious and national.'[63] In February 1995 the Oleksy government signed an international convention on the rights of national and ethnic minorities. Just as significantly, there was no turn to more nationalist discourse in the SLD effort to gain votes for its presidential candidate in November 1995. On the contrary, the emphasis on integration with Europe was as strong as under Mazowiecki or Hanna Suchocka. Nevertheless, the Polish communist party's legacy of ignoring minority groups remained ingrained among many non-Poles and, in the 1995 presidential elections, the majority of the non-Polish population in eastern Poland and Silesia voted against Kwaśniewski.

The failure of nationalist movements to attract large followings can be understood as revealing the unproblematic nature of national identity in Poland. The question of what it means to be Polish does not inform electoral politics in the 1990s. To be sure, the inevitable appearance of groups of skinheads, and the brief emergence of an ultra-nationalist peasant self-defence league, have marred the otherwise steady growth of a civic, as opposed to ethnic, form of nationalism. But they have been so transparently the exception underscoring the rule.

Conclusion

At the beginning of this chapter, I hypothesised that defining national identity after communism would be a less tortuous process in Poland than in Ukraine. Historical and social conditions have favoured the retention of a Polish national identity *despite* partitions and communist rule, whereas they have sparked greater disagreement over the notion in Ukraine *because* of partitions and communist rule. While that view has largely been substantiated, it has not always been consistent with traditional self-images. In Ukraine political movements have been preoccupied with state-building since independence. In terms of priorities, the search for historical identity and the general process of nation-building now rank below state-consolidation. The perception of a Ukrainian nationalism that compels the country to hold on to a nuclear arsenal is inaccurate, then. State-building and nation-building are interrelated but they are not isomorphic processes and need separate treatment. The sensitivity shown to minorities in Ukraine so far suggests that a form of statism, rather than nationalism, is the end goal of today's leaders.

For Poles, national identity has largely been a given since the fall of communism; arguably, it was a given even in the communist period. But popular images circulating in the West of Poles as necessarily Catholics are misleading and are not shared by large sections of Polish society. With the influx of new immigrant groups – Vietnamese, Palestinians, citizens of many parts of the former Soviet Union – Poles find it easier to recognise traditional minorities such as Ukrainians, Germans and Jews as 'natural' components of their state. It would be an exaggeration to speak of a multinational Polish national identity, but it has become less ethnically exclusivist than in the 1930s or 1950s.

In both countries, exclusivist approaches to national identity have not been victorious. Sceptics might argue that it is the effort to make a good impression on the West that make these states adopt liberal minority-rights regimes. Nevertheless, there are no overt symptoms of national paranoia, though some of the survey data suggest that ethnic schisms sometimes lie not far below the surface.

Returning to Bloom's psychological account of identity enhancement, let me propose that political independence has not generated a significantly greater sense of well-being. But this failure clearly owes more to economic problems faced by the transition to the market than to anxiety about identity. To be sure, identifying with America as Poles do, and with Europe as western Ukrainians do, may exacerbate identity diffusion when Eastern European reality remains so remote from these preferred models. When citizens become aware that state actions provide little benefit to them, shared identity may eventually break down. Violations of minority rights, discrimination and ethnic conflict then become more likely.

Notes

1. See the special issue, 'Nationalism and National Identity After Communism', *Journal of Area Studies*, 1994, no.4. On Ukraine see the article by Taras Kuzio; on Poland by Frances Millard. See also Roman Szporluk (ed.), *National Identity and Ethnicity in Russia and the New States of Eurasia* (Armonk, NY: M.E. Sharpe, 1994).
2. See Peter J. Potichnyj (ed.), *Poland and Ukraine: Past and Present* (Edmonton: Canadian Institute of Ukrainian Studies, 1980).
3. James Rosenau, *Turbulence in World Politics* (Princeton, NJ: Princeton University Press, 1990), chapter 16.
4. Dankwart Rustow, *A World of Nations: Problems of Political Modernization* (Washington, DC: Brookings Insittution, 1967), p.41.
5. Earl Jeffrey Richards, 'European Literature and the Labyrinth of National Images: Literary Nationalism and the Limits of Enlightenment', unpublished manuscript, New Orleans, August 1991, chapter 1.
6. Samuel P. Huntington, *American Politics: The Promise of Disharmony* (Cambridge, MA: Harvard University Press, 1981), p.63; see also Seymour Martin Lipset, *The First New Nation: The United States in Historical and Comparative Perspective* (New York: Basic Books, 1993).
7. George C. Lodge, 'Introduction', in George C. Lodge and Ezra F. Vogel (eds), *Ideology and National Competitiveness* (Boston, MA: Harvard Business School Press, 1987).
8. William Bloom, *Personal Identity, National Identity and International Relations* (Cambridge: Cambridge University Press, 1993), p.52.
9. Ibid., p.61
10. Ibid., p.50.
11. Ibid., p.114.
12. Gregory Gleason, 'Nationalism and Ideology', *The Russian Review*, 1991.
13. Mark von. Hagen, 'Does Ukraine Have a History?', *Slavic Review* **54**, no.3 (Fall 1995), pp.658–73. Also relevant here is Steven Velychenko, *Shaping Identity in Eastern Europe and Russia: Soviet and Polish Accounts of Ukrainian History, 1914–1991* (New York: St. Martin's Press, 1993).
14. Roman Szporluk, 'The Ukraine and Russia', in Robert Conquest (ed.), *The Last*

Empire: Nationality and the Soviet Future (Stanford, CA: Hoover Institution Press, 1986), pp.160–61.

15. Ibid., p.164.
16. Thomas Masaryk, *The New Europe: The Slav Standpoint*, edited by W. Preston-Warren and William B. Weist (Lewisburg, PA: Bucknell University Press, 1972), pp.119–20.
17. Szporluk, 'The Ukraine and Russia', pp.172–3.
18. Arnold Toynbee, *A Study of History*, vol.8 (London: Oxford University Press, 1954), p.536.
19. While Toynbee did not consider this, linguistic scholars would even argue that Dante was a supra-nationalist, for 'Dante was adapting examples of Old French narrative fo Italian': Richards, 'European Literature and the Labyrinth', p.67.
20. Walker Connor, 'Nation-Building or Nation-Destroying?', *World Politics* 24, no.3 (April 1972), p.338.
21. See the special issue on Rybalka in *Journal of Ukrainian Studies* 7, no.1 (1982).
22. Vladimir A. Zamlinskii, Ivan F. Kuras and Larisa A. Nagornaya, *Osushchestvlenie leninskoi natsional'noi politiki* (Kiev: Vysha shkola, 1987), pp.10, 212. This volume was unique even for its time in the number of references to non-Soviet sources, including writers especially harsh on Soviet nationality policy such as Yaroslav Bilinsky, Hélène Carrère d'Encausse and Hugh Seton-Watson.
23. Jaroslaw Martyniuk, 'Attitudes Towards Language in Ukraine', *RFE/FL Research Report* 1, no.37 (18 September 1992), p.69.
24. Zvi Gitelman, 'Are Nations Merging in the USSR?', *Problems of Communism*, Spring 1984, p.38.
25. The best study of this subject is by Dominique Arel, 'Language Politics in Independent Ukraine: Towards One or Two State Languages?', *Nationalities Papers* 23, no.3 (September 1995), pp.597–622.
26. Compare, for example, the overwhelming support given by francophones for French as the main – and, at times, sole – language of education in Quebec: Donat Taddeo and Raymond Taras, *Le Débat linguistique au Québec* (Montéal: Presses de l'Université de Montréal, 1987).
27. Martyniuk, 'Attitudes Towards Language', p.70.
28. Arel, 'Language Politics', p.616.
29. Roman Solchanyk, 'The Politics of Language in Ukraine', *RFE/RL Research Report* 2, no.10 (5 March 1993), p.2.
30. Orest Subtelny, *Ukraine: A History* (Toronto: University of Toronto Press, 1994).
31. Bohdan Kravchenko, 'Ukraine: The Politics of Independence', in Ian Bremmer and Raymond Taras (eds), *Nations and Politics in the Soviet Successor States* (Cambridge: Cambridge University Press, 1993), especially pp.79–80. See also Taras Kuzio and Andrew Wilson, *Ukraine: Perestroika to Independence* (Basingstoke: Macmillan, 1994); Mykola Ryabchouk, 'Political, Not Ethnic, Identity Will Unite Ukraine', *Meeting Report*, Kennan Institute for Advanced Russian Studies XII, no.11 (1995).
32. See Sarah Birch, 'Electoral Behavior in Western Ukraine in National Elections and Referendums, 1989–91', *Europe–Asia Studies* 47, no.7 (November 1995), p.1166.
33. See Stephen K. Batalden, *Seeking God: The Recovery of Religious Identity in Orthodox Russia, Ukraine, and Georgia* (DeKalb: Northern Illinois University Press, 1993).
34. Vasyl Markus, *Religion and Nationalism in Soviet Ukraine After 1945* (Cambridge, MA: Ukrainian Studies Fund, Harvard University, 1985), pp.101, 112.
35. Valentyn Moroz, 'Khronika oporu', in *Chronicle of Resistance in Ukraine* (Baltimore,

MD, 1970); quoted in Markus, *Religion and Nationalism*, p.103.

36. Markus, *Religion and Nationalism*, p.61.
37. Conor Cruise O'Brien, 'The Wrath of Ages', *Foreign Affairs* **72**, no.5 (November/ December 1993), p.144; see also his *God Land: Reflections on Religion and Nationalism* (Cambridge, MA: Harvard University Press, 1988).
38. David R. Marples, *Ukraine Under Perestroika: Ecology, Economics and the Workers' Revolt* (New York: St. Martin's Press, 1991), p.221; see also Bohdan Krawchenko, *Social Change and National Consciousness in Twentieth-Century Ukraine* (London: Macmillan, 1985).
39. Klaus Segbers, 'Migration and Refugee Movements from the USSR: Causes and Prospects', *Report on the USSR* **3**, no.46 (1991), pp.6–14.
40. Ian Bremmer, 'The Politics of Ethnicity: Russians in the New Ukraine', *Europe–Asia Studies* **46**, no.2 (1994), pp.274, 278.
41. Kathleen Mihalisko, 'Ukrainians and Their Leaders at a Time of Crisis', *RFE/RL Research Report* **2**, no.31 (30 July 1993), p.60.
42. The survey was carried out by the University of Michigan and the Ministry of Education of Ukraine. The total sample was 821 (391 from L'viv and 430 from Donetsk). I am grateful to Andrew Wilson for supplying me with results to the 191 survey questions.
43. Gitelman, 'Are Nations Merging in the USSR?', p.46.
44. See Potichnyj, *Poland and Ukraine.*
45. Grey Hodnett and Peter Potichnyj, *The Ukraine and the Czechoslovak Crisis*, Occasional Paper No.6, Department of Political Science, Australian National University, Canberra, 1970.
46. Mykola Ryabchuk, 'Civil Society and National Emancipation: The Ukrainian Case', in Zbigniew Rau (ed.), *The Reemergence of Civil Society in Eastern Europe and the Soviet Union* (Boulder, CO: Westview, 1991), p.102.
47. Chrystyna Lapychak, 'Ukraine's Troubled Rebirth', *Current History*, October 1993, p.337.
48. See a minority-by-minority account in Susan Stewart, 'Ukraine's Policy Toward its Ethnic Minorities', *RFE/RL Research Report* **2**, no.36 (10 September 1993), pp.55–62.
49. Adrian Karatnycky, 'Ukraine at the Crossroads', *Journal of Democracy* **6**, no.1 (January 1995), p.128.
50. Ibid., p.129.
51. Roman Solchanyk, 'Ukraine: Political Reform and Political Change', *RFE/RL Research Report* **1**, no.21 (22 May 1992), p.1.
52. Roman Solchanyk and Taras Kuzio, 'Democratic Political Blocs in Ukraine', *RFE/RL Research Report* **2**, no.16 (16 April 1993), p.16.
53. See Vasily Andreev, 'Ukrainian Nationalism: Ambitions and Reality', Jamestown Foundation *Prism* **II**, part 1 (August 1996); Jamestown Foundation <brdcast–jamestown.org>
54. The single best English-language summary of the evolution of a national identity in Poland is Aleksandra Jasinska-Kania, 'National Identity and Image of World Society: The Polish Case', *International Social Science Journal* **XXXIV**, no.1 (1982), pp.93–112.
55. See Stanisław Podemski, 'Prawo mniejszości', *Polityka*, 23 October 1993, p.8.
56. Silesians are a clearly distinguishable group, possessing a German background; but one Polish politician remarked in 1995 that, given Germany's present citizenship law,

which extends citizenship to anyone who has a grandparent of German origin, millions of Poles (not to mention members of other Central European nations) could also be regarded as German. Given the migratory movement it could set off, it did not seem in either Germany's or Poland's interest to follow this conception of *Deutschvolk*.

57. Renata Siemieńska, 'Zaufanie Polaków do innych narodów w okresie politycznych i ekonomicznych przemian', in Aleksandra Jasińska-Kania (ed.), *Bliscy i dalecy*, vol.2 (Warsaw: Uniwersytet Warszawski, Instytut Socjologii, 1992), pp.208–9.
58. Aleksandra Jasińska-Kania, 'Zmiany postaw Polaków wobec różnych narodów i państw', in Jasińska-Kania, *Bliscy i dalecy*, pp.220, 231–2. This volume contains additional chapters on Poles' attitudes to Russians, Germans and Jews. See my summary of relevant data in *Consolidating Democracy in Poland* (Boulder, CO: Westview, 1995), pp.92–4.
59. Peter Weinreich, 'National and Ethnic Identities: Theoretical Concepts in Practice', *Innovation in Social Science Research* **4**, no.1 (1991).
60. The two members were Marian Turski and Krystyna Kersten. Jerzy Wiatr has noted how, in the 1993 Polish parliamentary elections, the most transparently anti-Semitic electoral alliance compri sing the Polish National Commonwealth (PWN) and the Polish National Party (PSN) received just 0.11 per cent of valid votes cast. Another anti-Semitic group, calling itself 'The Fatherland – List of Poland' (OjLP), received 0.12 per cent. We may infer from this that there is negligible support for an anti-Semitic form of Polish nationalism. See Jerzy J. Wiatr, 'Powrót do historii: nacjonalizmy w erze postkomunistycznej', in Jerzy J. Wiatr, *Co nam zostało z tych lat? szkice i polemiki* (Toruń: Wyd. Adam Marszałek, 1995), p.84, n.18.
61. Iwona Kabzińska, 'The Polish Population in Belarus: Ethnic Identity' (paper presented at the V World Congress of Central and East European Studies, Warsaw, Poland, 9 August 1995). See Chapter 9 of this volume.
62. Adam Gwiazda, 'Poland's Policy Towards its National Minorities', *Nationalities Papers* **22**, no.2 (Fall 1994), p.439.
63. 'Deklaracja Socjaldemokrac ji Rzeczypospolitej Polskiej uchwalona przez Kongres Założycielski w dniu 28.01.1990 r.', in *Programy partii i ugrupowań parlamentarnych 1989–1991*, vol.1 (Warsaw: ISP PAN, 1995), p.96.

6 A New Interpretation of Ethnicity in Central and Eastern Europe

Małgorzata Budyta-Budzyńska

The late Ernest Gellner, a leading analyst of nationality and ethnicity in recent times, applied historical and sociological analysis to nationalist phenomena, and argued that there is a necessary connection between nationalism and 'modernity'. According to him, the modern, liberal economy requires a market larger than local ones, therefore it establishes such a national market by combining local ones. The modern economy requires a powerful, centralised state and the state, in turn, requires 'the homogeneous cultural branding of its flock' (Gellner 1983, p.140), for greater efficiency and cohesion. The development of capitalism is easier and quicker in the case of homogeneous structures of organisation and the same patterns of culture. These requirements coincide in part with people's subjective needs. The rapid social changes which industrialisation, mobility, high technology and rapid communications bring about lead to the loss of individual identity. Ordinary people lose their ties with family and their local environment, and begin to feel the need for a new identity on a higher level. The promulgation of a national identity via nationalist doctrines and movements can help them to 'locate' themselves. Thus nationalism is both psychologically and socially functional: it aids individual fulfilment and social solidarity.[1] Gellner shows how industrial development influenced the creation of nations and in consequence the creation of nationalism, and vice versa: nationalism, by creating nations, stimulated economic development. According to Gellner, in the major transition from feudalism to capitalism, nationalism was the tool for the creation of nations.

It can be asked whether nationalism can help to establish capitalism in Central and Eastern Europe in the last decade of the twentieth century. What can be the role of nationalism, national ideas and ethnicity in Poland, in the current transformation?

In this chapter I will try to answer these questions. I shall not portray all the possible functions of nationalism, but rather focus on its special role in the process of modernisation of the country.

When the modernisations of different countries in the nineteenth and twentieth centuries are compared, it should be remembered that the face of contemporary capitalism is completely different from that of its nineteenth-century predecessor. At present, there is a radically different structure of the market from that of a century ago. This causes the role of nationalism to be completely different.

Here I will formulate the thesis of 'selective incorporation', examining this phenomenon in two cases: the Russian Federation and the southwestern part of Poland.

Selective Incorporation as a Possible Method of Modernisation

The economic differentiations between regions of a country often lead to its division. The rich regions do not want to share their wealth with the poor and do not want to finance this development. They often want to decide for themselves about the trade, natural resources and raw materials of their land without waiting for the decision of central government.

Demands for greater economic and political autonomy are often backed by ethnic and historical differentiations, for example in Italy (Northern League), Spain (the Basque country, Catalonia) and Canada (Quebec). They are also supported by general tendencies: decentralisation of state power and regionalisation. In many cases, it is difficult to say whether economic and political interests rationalised ethnic interests, or if the opposite was the case.

Ethnic, historical and economic differentiations were the causes of the divisions of Yugoslavia, Czechoslovakia and the Soviet Union. They may also become causes of the division of the Russian Federation. The leaders of the autonomous republics, national and autonomous regions, who are usually Russians, often want to break with Moscow because they do not want to share the profits from natural resources with the central authorities.[2] They want to decide for themselves matters of trade with Japan, South Korea and China. Their aspirations are obviously backed by the local, ethnic people, but also by ethnic Russians who live there.[3] In March 1992, during a referendum in Tatarstan, more than half of the people opted for sovereignty, even though ethnic Tatar people make up less than a half of the population of the republic. This means that a part of the Russian inhabitants supported the aspirations for independence. Tatarstan, rich in oil resources, declared independence in October 1991.

Siberia and the Far East Region established direct contacts with Japan, South Korea and Hong Kong, in matters dealing with mining of natural resources and trade in second-hand cars.[4] Some regions established barter relations concerning the mining of oil and gas (Zajączkowski,1993).

The demands for autonomy were often justified by artificially created ethnic and historical differentiations. For example, Russians from Primorskii *krai* claim that they are a different category of Russians from Russians from Moscow. On the Sakhalin peninsula, the Russian *nomenklatura* hired American ethnologists to explore the Russians' 'ethnicity'. In the Chakas autonomous *oblast* Chakasian people demanded that their land and natural resources be recognised as exclusive property of the Chakasian people, but in the republic they make up only 11 per cent of the whole population. The local government decided to recognise all inhabitants, mainly Russians, as constituting the Chakasian nation. Russians agreed with this.[5] Ethnicity, which was introduced in a very artificial way, became a justification for the separation of rich regions from poor. This problem became so acute that President Yeltsin decided to introduce special economic sanctions against those who stopped paying taxes to the central government.[6]

In the 1970s, during the transformation in Spain, Portugal and Latin America, various interest groups and lobbies pressed the relevant government for changes. In Russia, there were no traditional interest groups. The managers of major state enterprises and the leaders of local government bodies began to play the role of interest groups. In this way, the old economic and political *nomenklatura* began to transform itself into a new class of businessmen and entrepreneurs.

Another example of regionalisation is the plan for the creation of regions in the western part of Poland. There are to be three regions: Pomerania, Nysa and Silesia.

The process of regionalisation is the most advanced in Silesia[7] because the idea of autonomy has deep roots there. For many centuries, when Silesia did not belong to Poland, the upper strata of society became Germanised, while the lower strata preserved the Silesian culture and language. Nationality became rather a matter of choice, as in other European borderlands, for example, with Danish–German or French–German. Silesia was a typical borderland territory with a broad spectrum of national attitudes, ranging from radical German, Polish or Silesian chauvinism to indifferentism or acceptance of universal European culture. One single universal and national culture was not possible in this region. Some scholars assert that here the nation-building process is not finished yet: socialism merely put it on hold. After the First World War, Silesians protested against the incorporation of all of Silesia into Germany. They organised three uprisings in 1919, 1920 and in 1921, and in this way triggered change. Eventually, one-third of Silesia was incorporated into the Polish state, preserving a certain degree of independence: its own budget and a Silesian parliament.

After the Second World War, Silesian autonomy was abolished. Many indigenous people emigrated to Germany and many Poles from the eastern territories settled here. An ethnic mixture was created, often leading to social conflicts between 'locals' and 'aliens' (Ossowski,1984). Indigenous inhabitants were branded by Poles coming from the eastern territories as Germans, and Silesians called Poles from the east Russians or Ukrainians. After the Second World War, the traditional conflict between Silesia and Zagłębie Dąbrowskie was also revived. Before the war, Silesian territory was closed to the migration of workers from Zagłębie, but after the war many workers from Zagłębie arrived and settled there. According to Silesians, Zagłębie provided a political and economic *'nomenklatura'*; the leaders of the party and the managers of the coal-mines came mainly from 'Red Zagłębie'. This led, of course, to antagonisms between *'gorol'* and *'hanys'*.[8] Origin is the main factor which differentiates inhabitants in Silesia, as sociologists who carried out a survey here found (Błasiak, 1992; Szczepański, 1992a). In addition, for four decades Silesia provided 50 per cent of Poland's GNP, but only part of it returned and was reinvested there. Silesia was treated by the central government as an internal colony (similar to Moscow's treatment of its Asian territories).

After the collapse of communism, the leaders of Silesia began to realise that something had to change. They began to set up cultural organisations and economic associations and to demand more autonomy for the Silesian region. At present, there are many different political and social organisations and associations: Polish, German and Silesian, such as *Niemiecka Wspólnota Robocza – Pojednanie i Przyszłość*[9] (the German Working Community – Reconciliation and the Future); Związek Górnośląska Chrześcijańska Demokracja (Upper Silesian Christian Democracy).[11] All of these invoke, to a greater or lesser degree, Silesian autonomy before the Second World War.[12]

Until recently, the most significant organisation was the Silesian Union (Związek Górnośląski). Many of its members were leaders of local governments. In 1989, at the beginning of its activity, it was a cultural organisation supported by the local Catholic church. Its leaders wanted to defend Silesian culture and customs against Poles and Germans, against Polonisation and Germanisation. After 1991, the Silesian Union changed its goals and has tried to organise a supranational region consisting of parts of Polish, Czech, Moravian and German territories. The leaders of the Union began to establish the infrastructure of the future region. They created economic institutions such as local banks (Górnośląski Bank Gospodarczy), a Silesian Foundation (Fundacja Górnośląska), a Silesian Economic Association (Górnośląskie Towarzystwo Gospodarcze), a film production company (Antena Górnośląska), and local publishing houses (Górnośląska Oficyna Wydawnicza). They also established a new territorial 'entity', the Association of Silesian Villages (Związek Gmin Górnośląskich), including Polish and Moravian villages. For the purpose of intellectual legitimisation of the regionalisation projects, Silesian leaders founded a Centre of Cultural Inheritance of Silesia (Centrum Dziedzictwa Kulturowego Górnego Śląska' and a Silesian Foundation. It is characteristic that every one of these organisations and associations has the adjective 'Silesian' in its name.

Many people claim that these proposals can be the first step towards the reinstatement of Greater Silesia,[13] and in consequence a step towards the slow and stealthy incorporation of this region into Germany. The leaders of Silesia do not conceal that they want to realise two goals: firstly, like other local organisations, they strive for decentralisation of central power. Secondly, they want to create a supranational region and in this way make a quicker entrance into Western economic structures, without waiting for other regions of Poland.[14]

It is interesting that most inhabitants of Silesia do not share these aspirations. According to scholars from the Silesian University, who carried out surveys concerning regionalisation, the idea of autonomy is little known and has a weak following. In the province of Katowice, for example, where indigenous inhabitants make up only a little over 30 per cent of the whole population of the region, 30 per cent of respondents agreed with a certain degree of economic autonomy, but at the same time one in four was against it. Respondents who wanted political autonomy for Silesia made up only 3.5 per cent (Szczepański,1992a; Błasiak,1992). The ideas of autonomy and regionalisation have not taken deep root in individual and group awareness. This means that the legitimisation of aspirations to autonomy through an appeal to public opinion is not possible. Firstly, it seems to be rather a spring-board for local leaders to cross local borders and become leaders of a supra-national region. The best example was a scandal having to do with the establishment of a German consulate in Katowice[15] and the proposal for joining the province of Katowice to the Association of European Regions without consulting the central government.[16]

Secondly, this is a method for quicker modernisation of the region and its entry into the world economic system. It is interesting that regionalisation is often justified by reference to historical and ethnic differentiation. In Poland, ethnically an almost homogeneous state, this justification sounds rather artificial. It is true that Silesia is the most separate and distinct region in Poland, but far more than one half of its inhabitants are ethnic Poles.

It seems that support for Silesian autonomy has weakened further in recent times. The organisations that backed this idea (the Upper Silesian Union and the Movement for Silesian Autonomy) lost in the general election of 1993 and did not manage to return any of their candidates to parliament. From this time, they have become almost invisible on the local and state political scene. Some commentators believe that this is only temporary, however.

The above observations do not concern the other part of Silesia, the province of Opole (the Movement for Silesian Autonomy and the Upper Silesian Union are most active in one part of Silesia, mainly in Katowice and Gliwice). In Opole, the German National Minority is relatively strong. During general elections in this region the German Minority received the largest numbers of votes. In 1991, they obtained seven seats in parliament and in 1993 five seats. Almost every fifth inhabitant of this province voted for the German National Minority, while only 3 per cent of inhabitants of the provinces of Katowice and Gliwice voted for the Movement for Silesian Autonomy and the Upper Silesian Union.

Some leaders of the German minority in Poland believe that the process of German unification has started but has not finished. It has not included all German territories, they say, and sooner or later the leaders of the German Federal Republic will demand a return of their brethren in Poland. In July 1995, during his visit in Poland, Chancellor Helmut Kohl met the leaders of the German minority and warned them against too high ambitions and desires. It seems that German rulers are busy with their own problems of unification and are not keen to interfere in Polish internal matters, even those that concern the German national minority.

Regionalisation can be further reinforced by increasing differentiations between so-called Poland A and Poland B. Since the inter-war period this division has existed and was not suppressed during the communist era. Recently it has become more visible. According to a recent survey by the Research Institute on the Market Economy, the western part of Poland and Warsaw, Kraków and Gdańsk – so-called Poland A – are very quickly moving ahead of Poland B – the so-called Eastern Wall and this division is getting deeper.[17]

The possible process of 'selective incorporation' has so far been described on the regional level. A similar phenomenon can be observed taking place on the national level.

All the Central and Eastern European countries wish to belong to the European Union and world economic structures. For these reasons, they established the Visegrad group and the Central European Initiative as pressure groups. These could have united the countries of this region and pressed Western governments to accept Central and East European countries as members of the European Union, and as groups could be more effective than any country acting alone.

This opinion was not shared by Czech leaders. They did not believe in the success of the Central European Initiative and have been trying to join the European Union on their own. They claim that the Czech Republic is the most developed country among Central European states and has recorded the most spectacular successes in economic transformation. For these reasons, it should not wait for others but try to join the world economic system alone. Furthermore, the incorporation of one small country would be easier than of the whole group. The Czech prime minister Václav Klaus is an adherent of the idea of 'selective incorporation' on the national level.

Spain, which presided over the European Union in 1995, protested against separate and individual admission of eastern countries into the Union. Madrid, and other less wealthy Western countries, is afraid that the more speedy admission of the Czech Republic or Hungary will cause Spain and others to share the Union's assistance funds with new eastern partners. The leaders of Spain also admit that incorporation of the whole group will be more difficult and will demand a change in the structure of the Union. For these reasons, Spanish politicians are strongly against the 'selective incorporation' of Central and East European countries.

Conclusion

Regionalisation is a method of decentralisation of central power and realisation of the idea of local government. It can make society more active and can be a method for 'selective incorporation' into Western economic structures and in consequence a method for more rapid modernisation.

The post-communist countries want to modernise and join the world economy. But regionalisation and quicker entrance of the wealthier regions into the world economic system can lead to the division of countries. In this case, poor regions may remain on the economic periphery of the world system.

In this chapter, I have described one possible role of nationalism and ethnicity in the process of modernisation of a country. 'Selective incorporation' can be a way of faster development, and 'fabricated' ethnicity can be used to justify the division of the country into poor and wealthy regions. This phenomenon is further reinforced by the more general tendency towards regionalisation and decentralisation of central administrative power. One may ask whether the splitting of countries will be a necessary outcome of regionalisation. It seems that the answer is no. Regionalisation may, however, lead to the appearance in Poland of two levels of ethnic identification, one involving *Heimat* (or, as Ossowski call it, *'private homeland'*), and a higher level connected with *Vaterland* (what Ossowski called *'ideological homeland'*)[18].

Finally, let me return to the question posed at the beginning: what can be the role of nationalism in Poland in the process of transformation? Is it the same role that nationalism played in Western Europe in the nineteenth century? At that time, it was an integrated ideology. It helped to established larger national markets. It was, as Gellner stated, the answer to the challenge of industrialisation and the rise of social entropy. When the old, feudal social structures broke down and people began to feel alone, it gave them new identification – national identity – and integrated them into a new community – the nation.[19]

In the last decade of the twentieth century in Central and Eastern Europe, it seems that nationalism plays a completely different role than in the West in the nineteenth century. At the present time, except for the initial period, it does not join, but divides, and often divides where no real ethnic distinctions are present.

Last, but not least, nationalism need not become a negative phenomenon in the next stage of transformation. During the modernisation of Japan, nationalism was the main factor promoting changes. The transformation of the Japanese economy took place in the name of the glory of Japan and of the Japanese nation. Economic state nationalism turned out to be a very useful tool for the modernisation of the country. It played the role of substitute for the Western Protestant ethic, persuading people to work hard and delay consumption for national glory (rather than for personal salvation). This was also the official state ideology that justified state intervention in the economy. It was an 'open' nationalism, ready to adopt the best of 'alien' solutions and patterns.

References

Błasiak, W. (1992), 'Społeczne źrodła mobilizacji i demonopolizacji regionalnej i lokalnej zbiorowości Górnego Śląska i Zagłębia Dąbrowskiego', mimeograph, Katowice.

Deutsch, Karl (1953), *Nationalism and Social Communication* (Cambridge, MA: Harvard University Press).

Gellner, Ernest (1983), *Nations and Nationalism* (Oxford: Basil Blackwell).

Kedourie, Elie (1966), *Nationalism* (London: Hutchinson).

Lerner, Daniel (1964), *The Passing of Traditional Society* (Glencoe, IL: Free Press, 1958).).

Ossowski, S. (1984), *O ojczyźnie i narodzie* (About Homeland and Nation) (Warsaw: Państwowe Wydawnictwo Naukowe).

Report of the Institute of Investigation of Market Economy (Warsaw, September 1994).

Szczepański, M.S. (1992a), *Regionalizm górnośląski w społecznej świadomości* (Silesian Regionalism in Social Awareness), mimeo, Katowice.

—— (1992b), *Pokusy nowoczesności – polskie dylematy rozwojowe* (Temptations of Modernity: Polish Dilemmas of Development (Katowice: AMP).

Zajączkowski, W. (1993), *Czy Rosja przetrwa do 2000 roku?* (Will Russia Survive until the Year 2000?).

7 Working-Class Nationalism among Polish Migrants in the Ruhr Region

John J. Kulczycki

The Polish-speaking population that migrated to the Ruhr region before the First World War developed a nationalism that had a working-class character. We can distinguish working-class nationalism from other forms of nationalism by its distinctive conceptions of the nation and of the national interest, and by its responses to calls for national solidarity across class divisions and for working-class solidarity across national divisions. Both in theory and in practice, working-class nationalism sets itself apart and takes on specific features.

The character of the Polish migration to the Ruhr, which reached massive proportions from the later half of the 1890s, provided a fertile environment for the growth and development of working-class nationalism.[2] The overwhelming majority of migrants came from lower economic strata of Prussian Poland, and most of them took up work in the mines of the Ruhr, where they only rarely advanced to supervisory positions. Thus, in the Ruhr region, they formed a largely homogeneous working-class population. Characteristically, after its formation in 1902, the Polish Trade Union (Zjednoczenie Zawodowe Polskie or ZZP) became the most important organisation in the Polish community in the Ruhr, and this working-class institution provided the basis for the expression of Polish nationalism in that region.

Furthermore, the vast majority of the migrants came to the Ruhr with only a regional or local identity,[3] and as a result of this, they developed a national identity at least partly removed from the direct influence of the large landowners, clergy, intelligentsia, and nascent bourgeoisie, who had shaped Polish national identity in the homeland. At the same time, the migrants came into direct, daily contact with the German working class and its labour movement, of which they formed a part. The interests that the migrants shared with the native German workers, as well as the conflicts that separated them, gave rise to an ethno-class consciousness among the migrants that had no equivalent in the homeland.[4] We see this most clearly in the relations of the migrants with the Polish national leadership.

Conflicts with the Polish National Leadership

The Polish national movement in Prussia had its centre in the province of Poznań. The province elected most of the Polish deputies who formed the Polish Circles that sat in the German Reichstag and the Prussian Landtag and, as such, officially represented the Polish minority of Germany. The Polish migrants in the Ruhr nowhere constituted a sufficiently large portion of the population to elect their own representatives. Therefore they looked to these deputies as their titular national leaders. Nevertheless, activists in the Polish community in the Ruhr early on recognised a conflict of interest with this leadership.

In 1897 Polish migrants in the Ruhr undertook to establish a local electoral organisation to designate which candidates Poles should vote for in parliamentary elections. When a provisional committee met delegates of Polish associations in the Ruhr on 12 December 1897 in Bochum to approve the organisation's statutes, a miner, Jan Wilkowski, objected to a clause that would have subordinated the new organisation to the Polish Central Electoral Committee in Poznań. He argued that the homeland's Polish deputies represented the interests alone of employers and were even hostile towards emigrant Polish workers. Nevertheless, the others present accepted the national necessity of this tie with Polish political structures in the homeland.[5] But the Polish Main Electoral Committee for Westphalia, the Rhineland and neighbouring provinces, elected that afternoon by a popular assembly of between 1,600 and 1,800, frequently ignored the directives of the Central Electoral Committee when it endorsed candidates for Polish voters.[6]

The warning that Polish deputies cared little about Polish workers seemed justified when in 1902 the Polish delegation in the Reichstag voted for the government's tariff bill which favoured agricultural interests, particularly those of large landowners, who formed an important part of the Polish national leadership in the homeland. The response of migrants in the Ruhr reflected the working-class character of their nationalism..

At a public meeting in Alstaden in January 1903, one of the main speakers was a miner named Tomasz Kubiak, who was an activist in the Union of Poles in Germany (Związek Polaków w Niemczech or ZPwN) – a nationalist organisation founded in the Ruhr in 1894 to unite all Poles living in the German provinces. Its statute expressly forbade 'party conflicts and attacks against particular social strata'.[7] Yet Kubiak began his speech by criticising the Polish Circle in the Reichstag for its position which, he asserted, contradicted its claim to be a friend of workers. Otherwise his speech had a strong Polish nationalist accent in addressing such topics as official efforts to Germanise the Poles, local examples of unhappy marriages between Poles and German women, the importance of thrift to accumulate capital for the purchase of a farm in the homeland, and buying only Polish newspapers.[8] Those assembled identified the interests of the Polish nation in these areas with those of the working class: the first of four resolutions passed unanimously at the meeting's conclusion denounced those who had voted for the tariff, that is, members of the titular leadership of the Polish nation, as 'enemies of the Poles'. Also criticised were those who sold Polish land to the Colonisation Commission, sought to Germanise Poles, and did not educate their children in the Polish language.[9]

In 1909 a controversy again arose over a vote in the Reichstag, which pitted the economic interests of the Polish miners of the Ruhr against the political interests of the Polish national movement. This occurred when the Polish Circle provided the margin of victory for the opposition in rejecting a tax proposal of the Bülow government, which ultimately led to Bülow's resignation in July 1909.[10] Bülow's proposal would have imposed an inheritance tax that affected only the wealthy. The Polish Circle then voted for the opposition's tax package that included an increase in indirect taxes on items of necessity, which had the effect of raising the cost of living.

In defence of their actions, Polish deputies touted their contribution to the overthrow of Bülow's government, whose anti-Polish policies had exceeded in severity and extent those of any previous government. Nevertheless, the tax increases set off a storm of protest and provided Polish socialists with an opportunity to denounce the policies of the Polish Circle as favouring the interests of the wealthy over those of the working classes.[11]

The Polish Trade Union in the Ruhr (ZZP) criticised socialists for supporting Bülow and even accused them of hoping he would 'pass still more laws discriminating against Polish unions'.[12] But the ZZP also opposed the position taken by the Polish Circle on the tax increase and did not let the matter rest even after other Polish critics of the Polish Circle rose in its defence in the name of national solidarity. At a conference in November 1909, the ZZP passed a resolution calling for the participation of a representative of the working class in the Polish parliamentary delegations. Moreover, it demanded that 'in matters relating to workers, the Polish Circle consult with representatives of workers before taking a final decision.'[13]

Nearly two years later, the wound was still festering. In seeming contradiction to earlier demands, a meeting of the central directorate and the executive committee of the board of supervisors of the ZZP decided on 29 October 1911 that a paid union official elected as a parliamentary deputy would have to resign his union office because, as a member of the Polish Circle, he would be bound by its rule of unanimity, and some of its decisions harmed the working class, which hindered the union's organisational efforts.[14] In December 1911 in Berlin a meeting with the full board of supervisors at first confirmed this decision, but the personal intervention of the Polish deputy Wojciech Korfanty persuaded them to reconsider the matter and repeal the decision by a margin of a single vote.

The relentlessness with which ZZP leaders maintained their opposition to the tax policy of the Polish Circle and the bitterness stemming from the difference of opinion with the Polish nationalist movement in the homeland even led to a court case. Among the staunchest defenders of the Polish Circle in this matter was the Polish deputy Wiktor Kulerski, publisher of the *Gazeta Grudziądzka* (Grudziądz Gazette), the most widely circulated and rabidly nationalist Polish newspaper in Germany and the homeland's most popular paper in the Ruhr.[15] After the leader of the Miners' Section of the ZZP, Franciszek Mańkowski, criticised the Polish Circle and the defenders of its tax policy in 1911, Kulerski used his newspaper to launch a personal attack on the union leader. Kulerski also criticised the Polish union's co-operation with the socialist-oriented *Alter Verband* in the labour movement in the Ruhr. He printed thousands of fliers critical of Mańkowski for the general assembly of the Miners' Section in Dortmund in March 1911 in the hope of preventing his re-election as head of the Miners' Section.

Kulerski's charges made for a stormy session of the general assembly. While the parliamentary deputies Jan Brejski and Stanisław Nowicki took part as guests, Kulerski's agent in the Ruhr, Stanisław Kunz, was denied admittance. Nor did the criticism have the effect Kulerski sought: the assembly re-elected Mańkowski by a nearly unanimous vote and passed a resolution sharply critical of the *Gazeta Grudziądzka*. For his part, Mańkowski sued Kulerski and Kunz for libel and thus kept the dispute alive until the court ruled in Mańkowski's favour in June 1912.[16]

These incidents indicate that the Polish national identity that developed among the Polish migrants in the Ruhr had a strong working-class content. They and their leaders equated working-class interests with the interests of the Polish nation. They proved willing to challenge the leadership of the Polish national movement in Germany in spite of appeals to national solidarity when that leadership went against working-class interests. Additional evidence of the working-class character of Polish nationalism in the Ruhr lies in the relations between the Polish migrants and the German miners in the Ruhr.

Solidarity with the German Working Class

In 1889, when a mass strike broke out among coal-miners in the Ruhr, the Polish-speaking migrants among them were still too few in number and too poorly organised for the native miners to pay much attention to them during the strike. Yet, although none of the migrants assumed any leadership role, the available evidence indicates that they generally acted in solidarity with their fellow workers and in some areas proved even more militant than their German counterparts.[17]

Although most of the migrants had not yet developed a consciousness of their national identity by 1889, their behaviour did not change after the formation in 1902 of the most important expression of that identity, the Polish Trade Union. When a strike began in late 1904, which led to the massive miners' strike of 1905, the ZZP took a leading part in supporting the workers against management, even though relatively few migrants worked at the mine where the strike began.[18] As a result, the Polish union received representation equal to that of the major German unions in the Commission of Seven that led the strike.

During the strike, the ZZP had the support of the leadership of the Polish national movement in Prussian Poland. Yet, they tended to view the conflict differently. The ZZP and the striking Polish and German miners looked to the benevolent intervention of the Prussian government for an improvement in their working conditions. Polish nationalists in the homeland were more likely to regard Polish participation in the strike as part of a continuing Polish–German conflict and to see the Prussian government as the enemy.[19]

Polish participation in the labour movement in the Ruhr following the 1905 strike further illustrated the differences between the Polish leaders in the Ruhr and in Poznań. Whereas the German Christian trade union, the *Gewerkverein*, broke with the coalition that led the 1905 strike, the ZZP continued to co-operate with the German socialist-oriented union, the *Alter Verband*. When this co-operation culminated in the 1912 strike, which the *Gewerkverein* vehemently opposed and the *Alter Verband* and the ZZP supported, conservative elements in the Polish national movement condemned the leadership of the ZZP.[20] The ZZP took their accusations seriously enough to convoke a joint meeting in Berlin of its central executive board, its board of supervisors, the boards of the union's sections, and its district secretaries.[21] At this meeting the ZZP formally concluded that the leadership of the Miners' Section had acted properly and was not under the influence of any German trade union – a repudiation of those who saw it as acting at the behest of the *Alter Verband*.

Conclusion

The Polish migrants in the Ruhr had a commitment to both their class and their nation. For them, no contradiction existed in their loyalties. Their nationalism differed from the Polish nationalism in the homeland in its recognition that class interests divided the Polish nation and in its identification of the national interest with the interests of the working class. Therefore they saw no weakening of their national loyalties in opposing the class interests of the leadership of the Polish national movement in the homeland, even in the face of appeals to the principle of national solidarity.

The Polish migrants' open identification of the national interest with working-class interests enabled them to participate in major mass movements, such as the strikes in the Ruhr, that overcame the national divisions among workers to promote their common interests, despite the criticism of part of the leadership of the Polish national movement. Both in theory and in practice the migrants developed a nationalism based upon an ethno-class consciousness that derived from their particular situation in the Ruhr. The key element in the development of their working-class nationalism was the existence, in the Polish Trade Union, of an institution with mass support that represented

128   *John J. Kulczycki*

both the national and the class interests of the Polish workers in the Ruhr.

As demonstrated in the case of the Polish migrants in the Ruhr, working-class nationalism has a greater propensity than other forms of nationalism to recognise the clash of class interests within the nation, notwithstanding appeals to national solidarity. At the same time, it shows a greater flexibility in its willingness to join in a class-based mass movement irrespective of national differences, without at the same time abandoning its national separateness.

Notes

1. The presentation of this paper and the research on which it is based were made possible in part by the generous financial assistance of the International Research and Exchanges Board (IREX), the Campus Research Board of the University of Illinois at Chicago, and the Joint Committee on Eastern Europe of the American Council of Learned Societies and the Social Science Research Council, financed in part by the Ford Foundation and the National Endowment for the Humanities, which also provided a grant for research in Poland.
2. The most important works on the history of the Polish migrants in the Ruhr region are as follows: Christoph Klessmann, *Polnische Bergarbeiter im Ruhrgebiet, 1870–1945: Soziale Integration und nationale Subkultur einer Minderheit in der deutschen Industriefesellschaft* (Göttingen: Vandenhoeck & Ruprecht, 1978); Jerzy Kozłowski, *Rozwój organizacji społeczno-narodowych wychodźstwa polskiego w Niemczech w latach 1880–1914* (Wrocław: Ossolineum, 1987); Krystyna Murzynowska, *Polskie wychodźstwo zarobkowe w Zagłebiu Ruhry w latach 1880–1914* (Wrocław: Ossolineum, 1972); Valentina-Maria Stefanski, *Zum Prozess der Emanzipation und Integration von Außenseitern: Polnische Arbeitsmigration im Ruhrgebiet* (Dortmund: Forschungsstelle Ostmitteleuropa an der Universität Dortmund, 1984). See also John J. Kulczycki, *The Foreign Worker and the German Labor Movement: Xenophobia and Solidarity in the Coal Fields of the Ruhr, 1871–1914* (Oxford and Providence, RI: Berg, 1994).
3. Murzynowska, *Polskie wychodźstwo*, pp.68, 76. On the strength of these regional identities see John J. Kulczycki, 'Uwarunkowania świadomości narodowej polskich górników w Zagłębiu Ruhry przed I-ą wojną światową' (unpublished paper presented at the XV Powszechny Zjazd Historyków Polskich, Gdańsk, 19–21 September 1994), pp.3–7.
4. Yoav Peled, *Class and Ethnicity in the Pale: The Political Economy of Jewish Workers' Nationalism in Late Imperial Russia* (New York: St. Martin's Press, 1989), used the term 'ethno-class consciousness' in another context. On working-class nationalism see John Breuilly, *Nationalism and the State*, 2nd edn (Chicago: University of Chicago Press, 1994), pp.36–44, which explained the origin of working-class nationalism primarily in terms of communal conflict over scarce resources but did not deal extensively with its manifestations or its differentiating characteristics.

5. Klessmann, *Polnische Bergarbeiter im Ruhrgebiet*, p.125; Kozłowski, *Rozwój organizacji społeczno-narodowych*, p.159.
6. Murzynowska, *Polskie wychodźstwo zarobkowe*, pp.189–92; Klessmann, *Polnische Bergarbeiter im Ruhrgebiet*, pp.126–7.
7. Klessmann, *Polnische Bergarbeiter im Ruhrgebiet*, p.101; Murzynowska, *Polskie wychodźstwo zarobkowe*, p.97.
8. Nordrhein-Westfälisches Hauptstaatsarchiv Düsseldorf (HSTAD), Regierungsbezirk Düsseldorf (RD) Präs 871, ff.33–35, copy of police report on meeting, 18 January 1903; Kozłowski, *Rozwój organizacji społeczno-narodowych*, p.187, identified the speaker Tomasz Kubiak as a chairman of the ZPwN.
9. HSTAD, RD Präs 871, ff.33, 33–35, copy of police report on meeting, 18 January 1903.
10. Zygmunt Hemmerling, *Posłowie polscy w parlamencie Rzeszy niemieckiej i sejmie pruskim (1907–1914)* (Warsaw: Ludowa Spółdzielnia Wydawnicza, 1968), pp.230–45.
11. J. Adamek, 'Die Kampfesweise der polnischen Reichsfraktion', *Die neue Zeit* **XXVII**, no.2 (1909), pp.772–82; Julian Marchlewski, 'Gorzałka a patriotyzm Koła Polskiego w Berlinie', in Julian Marchlewski, *Pisma wybrane*, vol.II (Warsaw: Książka i Wiedza, 1956), pp.401–9.
12. Adamek, 'Die Kampfesweise der polnischen Reichsfraktion', pp.773–6.
13. Marian Orzechowski, *Narodowa demokracja na Górnym Śląsku (do 1919 roku)* (Wrocław: Ossolineum, 1965), pp.240–42.
14. Franciszek Mańkowski, 'Historja Z.Z.P.', in *Ćwierć wieku pracy dla Narodu i Robotnika* (Poznań: Nakładem Zarządu Centralnego Zjedn. Polskiego, 1927), pp.102–3.
15. Jerzy Marczewski, *Narodowa Demokracja w Poznańskiem 1900–1914* (Warsaw: Państwowe Wydawnictwo Naukowe, 1967), pp.295–7. On the *Gazeta Grudziądzka* see Tadeusz Cieślak, '"Gazeta Grudziądzka" 1894–1918. Fenomen wydawniczy', *Studia i materiały do dziejów Wielkopolski i Pomorza* **III**, no.2 (1957), pp.175–88; according to Klessmann, *Polnische Bergarbeiter im Ruhrgebiet*, p.282, this newspaper accounted for over half of the Polish newspapers received in the Dortmund postal district in 1909 and 1911; Johannes Altkemper, *Deutschtum und Polentum in politisch-konfessioneller Bedeutung* (Leipzig: Duncker & Humblot, 1910), p.233, referred to it as one of the most widely-read Polish newspapers in the Ruhr, 'which at least equals the *Wiarus Polski* in radicalism and in malicious tone'. A German socialist opponent of the Polish national movement also acknowledged the influence of the newspaper in the Ruhr: Julius Bruhns, 'Polenfrage und Sozialdemokratie', *Die neue Zeit* **XXVI** (1908), p.762.
16. Staatsarchiv Münster, Oberpräsidium 5365, Königl. Polizei-Präsident, Bochum, 7 April 1911; Archiwum Państwowe Miasta Poznania i Województwa Poznańskiego, Prezydium Policji 6639, press clippings, ff.30, 32, 39–40, 42; Murzynowska, *Polskie wychodźstwo zarobkowe*, p.251; Mańkowski, 'Historja Z.Z.P.', pp.99, 107.
17. See John J. Kulczycki, 'Polish Migrants in the Ruhr Region and the Great Coal Miners' Strike of 1889', in Jerzy Topolski, Witold Molik and Krzysztof Makowski (eds), *Ideologie, poglądy, mity w dziejach Polski i Europy XIX i XX wieku: Studia historyczne* (Poznań: Wydawnictwo Naukowe Uniwersytetu im. Adama Mickiewicza, 1991), pp.165–77; Kulczycki, *The Foreign Worker*, pp.50–70.
18. Kulczycki, *The Foreign Worker*, pp.154–203.
19. See a long article sympathetic to the strike in *Oredownik* (Advocate), 24 January 1905, no.19; excerpts reprinted in Witold Jakóbczyk, *Wielkopolska (1851–1914): Wybór źródeł* (Wrocław: Ossolineum, 1954), pp.74–6.

20. *Dziennik Poznański*, no.84, 13 April 1912, in German translation, *Gesammtüberblick über die polnische Tagesliteratur*, no.16, 23 April 1912, pp.353–5.
21. *Kurjer Poznański*, no.89, 19 April 1912, in German translation, *Gesammtüberblick über die polnische Tagesliteratur*, no.17, 30 April 1912, p.397; *Wiarus Polski*, no.90, 19 April 1912, in German translation, *Uebersetzungen aus westfälischen und anderen polnischen Zeitungen*, no.17, 26 April 1912, pp.183–4; see also a summary in Mańkowski, 'Historja Z.Z.P.', pp.107–8.

8 Poles in the Newly Independent States of Lithuania, Belarus and Ukraine

Z. Anthony Kruszewski

This case study deals with the somewhat unexpected revival of the Polish communities to the east of the present border of Poland – the 'Polonia in the East'.

'Polonia' – the Polish minority in the newly independent republics of Belarus, Lithuania and Ukraine – is a residue of the 1386–1795 Polish–Lithuanian Commonwealth, which included the territories now encompassing Latvia, Lithuania, Belarus and two-thirds of modern Ukraine;[1] 46 per cent of the pre-1939 Polish Republic's territory is also included in that area.

Poles in the Russian empire were reduced from a ruling group to a subject and oppressed minority by tsarist punitive policies following the two nineteenth-century Polish uprisings in 1831 and 1863; others experienced even more horrible treatment in the 1917–22 Bolshevik revolution and War Communism that followed, the Stalinist terror of 1936–38, (including the post-1936 mass deportations to Kazakhstan and the interior of the USSR), and post-Second World War population transfers.

In the USSR, Polish inter-war autonomous regions, with their Polish schools, theatrers and cultural activities,[2] were completely destroyed by the Stalinist terror. In pre-war independent Lithuania, Polish schools and cultural activities were permitted and were re-activated after the Second World War after Lithuania's incorporation into the USSR. This large Polish minority, one to two million strong, has been rapidly losing its native language. Until the *glasnost'* breakthrough, the Polish minority, along with the Jews and the Germans in the USSR, were the largest minorities singled out for mass assimilation.

The collapse of the communist system in 1991 and the achievement of independence of the Baltic republics, Belarus and Ukraine brought about the revival of socio-cultural activities and the quest for national identity among the titular nations of these republics, and also among the minorities. These developments have been only sporadically discussed in the West although they are an expected phenomenon resulting from the independence of those republics.

The Poles have lived within what used to be the borders of the USSR at least since the thirteenth and fourteenth centuries and are mostly the descendants of the Polish colonisation waves triggered by the Polish–Lithuanian Union of 1386. Recent research suggests, however, the presence of Polish colonies in Lithuania and Rus' prior to the thirteenth century.[3] Those Poles were in all likelihood the descendants of prisoners of war captured by the Lithuanians and the Ruthenians in numerous wars pre-dating the union. The union was supposed to prevent wars between the parties in order to face the challenge of a new common enemy, who appeared on the coast of the Baltic in 1228 – the Teutonic Knights. The subsequent Polish colonisation of the areas in question hence followed a much earlier wave of Polish settlement. The large-scale migration of Polish peasants and nobility, who received land grants from the Polish rulers, resulted in a considerable and marked transformation of many parts of that territory.[4]

Their numbers grew in spite of the demographic setbacks after each war and the ensuing depopulation. The Polish population peak was reached towards the end of the eighteenth century – during the partitions of Poland between her three rapacious neighbours – Russia, Prussia and Austria. Russia received the bulk of the territory of the Polish–Lithuanian Commonwealth, which existed from 1386 until 1772. The nineteenth-century Polish uprisings (especially those of 1830 and 1863) were very severely and brutally suppressed by the tsarist government. The reprisals undertaken by the victors were of great importance for the future status of the Polish population. Confiscated Polish landed estates were allocated to Russian generals or sold to the Russian upper classes, and those changes in land ownership have markedly altered the position of the Polish community.[5] Although the small size peasant holdings were not greatly affected (the peasants generally did not participate in those uprisings *en masse*), there were notable exceptions. The dispossession of many vast Polish land holdings irrevocably turned the balance of power in the countryside in favour of the Russians.

Finally, the Bolshevik revolution not only eliminated all remaining Polish estates but also affected the Polish peasants during the collectivisation campaigns. Most of the land still owned by the Poles was but a fraction of the original holdings given by the Polish kings (and native aristocrats) to the Polish settlers of the period between the fourteenth and seventeenth centuries. Loss of land effectively undercut the Polish position in the borderlands and effectively closed that chapter of history by terminating Polish political and social domination in those territories. It is estimated that there were over 5 million Poles in the borderlands before the Bolshevik revolution. With their political and social power gone, there was to occur the first exodus of upper classes from the borderlands (in Polish- 'Kresy') towards other ethnic parts of Poland.[6]

The Bolshevik revolution was followed in November 1918 by the re-establishment of an independent Poland. As a result of the Polish–Soviet war of 1919–21, areas which are now known as Western Belarus and Western Ukraine were allocated to Poland under the Treaty of Riga of 1921. Under that treaty a transfer of over 1.2 million Poles from the USSR was authorised and completed. A drastic reduction of the size of the Polish population in the areas east of the border that the treaty had established, and that had become part of the USSR, left only 863,300 Poles there in 1931.[7] Educated Poles, generally, but especially the former petty nobility, bourgeoisie and middle class, left for the new Poland. While this strengthened the Polish presence in the 'Kresy' area left to Poland, it irrevocably weakened the strength of the Polish communities in the USSR.

A complete socio-political restructuring of that community by the new Soviet government followed. Besides industrialisation and collectivisation of agriculture, there was also an attempt to build the new Polish–Soviet intelligentsia of worker and peasant origin to replace the educated classes that had left for Poland.

Autonomous Polish areas were established in line with Leninist nationality principles. One such area was in the Ukrainian SSR, in the Zhitomir province to the west of that city; the town of Dolbych/Markhlevsk became a centre and was named the Markhlevski Polish Autonomous District (*raion*). The second autonomous district was west of Minsk, the capital of the Belorussian SSR, with the town of Koydanov/Dzerzhinsk as its centre, and called the Dzerzhinski Polish Autonomous District (located just a few miles east of the 1921–39 Polish–Soviet border).[8] Being purely Polish, those two regions warranted such a political-administrative treatment, although the Polish minority was to be found all over the Ukrainian and Belorussian republics and in some parts of the Russian republic (RSFSR).

In implementing the Leninist nationality principles, two institutions of higher education for the training of the teachers were established, in Kiev and Minsk respectively. Those capital cities also boasted Polish theatres and other socio-cultural organisations. A fully developed Polish primary and secondary school system was set up in localities where there were at least ten Polish-speaking pupils. A Polish-language daily '*Młot*' (Hammer) was published in Minsk in the 1920s.[9]

These measures were aimed at creating a new communist-oriented Polish intelligentsia in the USSR. However, the overwhelming proportion (over 80 per cent) of the Polish minority in the USSR until 1939 was peasant in origin. It was to be remoulded socially and economically, not very differently from all other segments of Soviet society. Anti-Polish bias existed in reaction to centuries-old Polish socio-political domination of the areas described, but it was officially frowned upon. The initial post-revolutionary terror was directed, ironically enough, by Felix Dzerzhinski, a Polish nobleman and close friend and associate of Lenin, primarily against the remnants of the former leading classes.

This policy towards minorities was to change during the Stalinist purges and terror against society at large in the 1930s. By 1936 both of the Polish Autonomous regions were abolished and the larger part of the Polish community was either expelled or forcibly resettled in Kazakhstan[10] or in the interior of the Russian republic. All its socio-cultural institutions and organisations were closed by 1939.

The Ribbentrop–Molotov Pact of 23 August 1939, which divided Poland between the USSR and nazi Germany, brought into the USSR not only Ukrainians and Belorussians but also some 3,500,000 – 4,200,000 Poles as well.[11] The range of figures suggests the difficulty of assessing the exact size of the Polish community. The first one is based on a religious criterion – the Roman Catholic faith (the prevailing measure of national identification in those areas of pre-1939 Poland) according to the 1931 Polish census. While the census was subject to manipulation by the Polish authorities – the Belorussian and the Ukrainian citizens of pre-1939 Poland often feared being classified as non-Poles – it would be realistic to extrapolate from this and accept a figure of 3,800,000 as the size of the Polish community in the pre-1939 Eastern Poland that had been annexed by the USSR.[12] That figure was increased by the inclusion of the Białystok area within the 1939 Soviet borders and the influx of refugees from the nazi-ruled part of Poland. The sizeable Polish communities in Lithuania, Latvia and the Romanian provinces annexed in 1940 by the USSR have also to be added. Hence we arrive at the possible minimum of over five million (plus 0.9 million from the old Polonia),

250,000 in Lithuania, 60,000 in Latvia, 65,000 in Romania, 3,000 in Estonia,[13] and an undetermined number of refugees from the nazi-occupied part of Poland (possibly 100,000–200,000).

The Polish minority in the annexed eastern Polish 'Kresy' was able to retain many of its schools and cultural organisations (although obviously communised in form and context) until the nazi attack on the Soviet Union in June 1941. But it was severely reduced by a series of deportations in 1940 and 1941 that affected at least 1.2 million Poles in the areas annexed by the USSR in 1939, that is, some 32 per cent of the total.[14] Although it is impossible to assess precisely the numerical scale of the deportations and the death toll which followed in Siberia, the interior of Russia and the Central Asian republics, it is generally accepted that at least half of them died there. Those losses associated with prison terror, executions and wholesale deportations of various professional groups thus account *in toto* for at least 12 per cent of the pre-1939 Polish population of eastern Poland occupied by the Soviets.

As a result, in percentage terms those losses equal the losses inflicted on the Poles under the nazi occupation (about three million deaths out of the 24 million population).[15] Whereas the latter have been fully documented by scholars since the Second World War, the losses of the eastern Poles caused by the Stalinist terror were, until 1988, documented only in the West. The collapse of Communism in Poland in 1989 created the opportunity to document the history of the deportations, the Katyń forest massacre, and the status of the former Soviet Polonia.

As if devastation at the hands of the Soviet authorities were not tragic enough, eastern Polish territories also suffered losses at the hands of the nazis who occupied the area for three years (1941–44). Hence the Polish Kresy were brutalised by both totalitarian oppressors of the Second World War – the nazis and the Stalinists. Furthermore, instead of liberation, that community was subjected to the ultimate disaster – loss of their homes after the Second World War. By 1958 population transfers had affected some three million Eastern Poles.

The initial wave of transfers from the territories of the Lithuanian, Ukrainian and Belorussian republics from 1944 to 1947 affected over 1.7 Poles who were resettled in the Western Territories of Poland newly acquired from Germany under the Potsdam Treaty of 1 August 1945. The migration forced by the westward shift of Soviet borders, which were now to include 46 per cent of the pre-1939 territory of the Second Polish Republic, caused tragic human hardships. It split many families as the older generation often opted to stay and try to save their homes, while the children were more inclined to move within Poland's new

borders. The difficulty of making such a harrowing decision is documented by the fact that the number of those initially registered for the
transfer was larger by 50 per cent than the number of people who
actually left for Poland.[16]

The people who opted for transfer also in practice lost contact with
their families who remained within the USSR, as the new border – the
Curzon Line – became an almost inpenetrable boundary until the advent
of *glasnost'* in the late 1980s. The 1,200 km.-long new Polish–Soviet
border had until 1989 only two road crossings and three railroad ones.[17]

In spite of the losses caused by Stalinst and nazi terror and the
population transfers, according to the 1989 census at least 750,000 Poles,
but probably at least twice that number, live in Lithuania and Belarus,
mostly in the areas that formed the pre-1939 territory of the Polish state.
Because of violent Polish–Ukrainian nationalist confrontations, almost all
the Poles from West Ukrainian areas fled to Central Poland before 1944
or were transferred out after the Second World War.[18] Hence, the Poles
living today in Ukraine are the tragic remnants of the pre-1939 Soviet
Polonia, who somehow escaped the 1936 expulsion to Siberia and Kazakhstan. They now live east of the pre-war Polish–Soviet border in the
Zhitomir, Vynnitsa and Khmelnitsy *oblasts* (as shown in a Soviet ethnographic atlas published in 1962). By contrast, the distribution of the
Polish minority in Lithuania and Belarus is still, curiously enough, reminiscent of the pre-World War II situation, in spite of the post-war
population transfers: the Poles still live in a stretch of territory from the
border city of Grodno to Daugavpils on the Dvina in Latvia.[19]

The Polish population of the former USSR is overwhelmingly rural,
except for a large urban concentration in Vilnius (Wilno) of over
100,000 Poles, who form some 19 per cent of the city's population.
Ironically enough, it almost equals numerically the pre-war Polish population of Wilno, which was 126,000.[20] The only other sizeable Polish
urban population is that of Grodno, Lida, Lviv (Lwów) and Zhitomir
(the last city was within the pre-1939 borders of the USSR).

The total number of Poles in the USSR had officially decreased from
1.38 million in 1959 to 1.1 million by 1989.[21] However, those figures
result from manipulation and pressure, especially *vis-à-vis* the 'undesir-
able' minorities. This was documented by the fact that the last issue of
the Soviet encyclopedia did not even provide specific data and the *oblast*
distribution of the Polish community in its major area of present settlement in the Belorussian SSR – as if to hide the fact that the area around
Grodno and Lida (the two major cities) is still overwhelmingly Polish.[22]

Accurate data finally began to be published in the Polish press after

1989. The area of Grodno was shown in the above-mentioned Soviet encyclopedia as being more Polish than the area west of the 'Curzon Line', that is, inside Poland. Yet the border was supposedly an ethnographic one.[23] Such an admission, implied by the Soviet map, questions the rationale used for the 1945 Polish–Soviet border and it corroborated data reported in the school atlas published in Poland in the 1930s by Professor E. Romer, a world-famous Polish geographer.[24]

There were very few post-Second World War descriptions of the Soviet Polonia, in either Soviet or Polish sources. The paucity of the Soviet sources did suggest Soviet uneasiness about the fate of the Poles in the USSR. After 1989 the Polish government broke the silence over the fate of the Soviet Poles.[25] The beginning of a veritable flood of contacts, discussions and publications can be dated from the visit of General Wojciech Jaruzelski to Vilnius/Wilno after his meeting with the Soviet leader Mikhail Gorbachev in 1986. By contrast, Polish communists not only encouraged but propagandised and very often subsidised contacts with the 'Polonians' in the West. That attitude had always been denounced by Polish and 'Polonian' leaders in Western countries as hypocritical, given the neglect shown to the Soviet Poles. Since 1989 that duplicity has ended.[26]

Now, for the first time in half a century, Poles from the east are coming in large numbers to Poland to study at Polish universities,[27] (they had always been excluded from Soviet–Polish student and scholar exchanges), visit their families and come *en masse* as tourists or shoppers. Likewise, Poles can now visit Poland's new neighbours – areas that were largely out of bounds to them since the end of the Second World War. The sudden influx of visitors – some 7 million entered Poland from the east in 1993 – and travel in both directions resulted in the opening of new highway border crossings – two with Lithuania, four with Belarus, and a promise of more to come. This new cross-border traffic has become a mass phenomenon. Subsequently, a series of agreements has been signed that were also intended to guarantee the protection and flourishing of the Polish cultural heritage in the former Polish eastern territories.

In spite of the drastic new political changes, the fate and very survival of the Poles in the east as a group is still under threat. While forming the second largest international Polonia, these Poles still largely suffer the results of past discrimination. The Polish autonomous districts were not reactivated in the former Soviet areas, nor until *glasnost'* were Polish schools, theatres or organisations allowed outside Lithuania and the Lviv area of Ukraine.[28]

The Polish minority, like the Jews and Germans, was a million-plus community in the Soviet Union subjected to 'de-nationalisation'. Those three groups were the only communities of their size that did not profit from Soviet 'federalism' and were denied political autonomy. Of the three groups, the Poles arguably fared the worst of all at the hands of the Soviet government. After 1958, the Poles were not allowed to migrate to Poland, while Jews and Germans were allowed to exit.

Poles in the former USSR had the *lowest percentage* of native language speakers from among *all* large Soviet nationality groups (15 per cent).[29] This figure may have been tainted to a degree, but it illustrates the fate of the Polish community within the former USSR. The almost total lack of schooling in the Polish language was considered to be the overriding element in the rapidly progressing de-nationalisation of the Poles in the former USSR. The nearly total *indifference* of the Polish communist regime to the subject until a few years before the collapse of Communism largely deprived the Poles in the USSR of even such meagre support as educational materials in the Polish language.

That situation was described as critical in the Polish press of the late 1980s. The policy reversal by the Polish government after 1988 allowed new initiatives to be undertaken to rescue the Soviet Polonia from Russification and rapid assimilation. The summer of 1989 witnessed a first – the visit by Polish scholars from the USSR to the Third Meeting of Scholars of Polish Extraction held in Warsaw, and the appearance of Poles from the USSR at Polish universities. A political taboo had been finally broken and an open Polish–Soviet dialogue on those issues had begun.[30]

The rebuilding of Polish cultural life in the former Eastern Polish area began in earnest after the collapse of communism. The rebuilding has been receiving impetus from the Lithuanian Poles who have been both providing their experience and sharing some educational materials with Poles in other areas. But in some other regions (for example in Belarus and Western Ukraine), local authorities still often try to prevent the revival of Polish culture by delaying permits for the opening of Polish schools, clubs or socio-cultural organisations. Attempts have been made to deny the very existence of the Polish community. The argument is advanced that those in question are not Polish but Lithuanians, Belarusians or Ukrainians who happen to speak Polish.[31]

In Belarus attempts are still being made to deny the existence of Polish ethnic areas that were in the past officially re-classified as non-Polish ones. Pressure is applied to prevent the opening of Polish language classes, which by law require a minimum of ten students. Administrative pressure is often used to scare away the parents of the tenth child. Nevertheless some 300 Polish language classes do exist now in Belarusian schools.

The reopening of Polish-language church services in Roman Catholic parishes, which were previously destroyed, is proceeding rapidly. Recent research has pointed to the existence of over 800 Roman Catholic parishes (over 450 in Ukraine and over 350 in Belarus) re-established through the relentless efforts of local Poles. Since 1991 the Vatican has re-established the Catholic Church hierarchy in the east destroyed during Soviet rule (1917–91). Because of past history, however, it still serves mostly the Polish minority (except in Lithuania).

Generally the quest to re-establish local parishes of the Catholic church is by far the most effective weapon in the rebuilding of Polish spiritual and socio-cultural life in the former Polish borderlands and beyond. This is largely because of the time-honoured equation, a Pole = a Catholic, which is the perspective of Belarusians and Ukrainians. Religious activity is apparently seen as less of a challenge and more 'neutral' in the eyes of local leaders in these countries. The rebuilding and reorganisation of the Catholic parishes is often linked with the reopening of churches, some of considerable cultural and historic value that date back to the sixteenth century. It helps parishioners to obtain permits when their petitions are couched in the language of cultural preservation of buildings, formerly used as warehouses or falling into disrepair and ruin. In such cases the repairs are done spontaneously by the community. The rebuilding is often achieved in a relatively short time considering the universal shortage of building materials in the former USSR. All such materials and labour are usually spontaneously donated. Reports of such an activity suggest the existence of vast untapped human and material resources that are being used in the interest of rebuilding communities.

The slow but steady growth of organised Polish Catholic life is obviously hampered by a serious shortage of Polish-language parish priests. There were at the time of the collapse of communism only 70 local Polish-speaking priests, some in their seventies and eighties. The others – an overwhelming proportion – were trained in the only remaining seminars: Kaunas Catholic seminary where the Lithuanian language of instruction is used, and the Riga Catholic Seminary using Russian.[32] Most new priests serving newly reopened Polish parishes are graduates of the Riga seminary, even if they are of Latvian or German nationality. They study Polish and German – the two other languages of Soviet Roman Catholics (apart from Lithuanian) during their course of study in the seminary. Additionally, some 100-150 priests have been sent from Poland with the approval of Poland's eastern neighbours.

In the Kaunas seminary the compulsory fluency in the Lithuanian language, an educational requirement applicable to all students, although useful and helpful in the training of future priests for the Lithuanian parishes, had become a barrier for students of other nationalities. A growing conflict also emerged over the reintroduction of Polish in the reopened Lithuanian and Belarusian parishes. For example, in 1989 St. Stanislaus Cathedral in Vilnius was returned to church use but no Polish masses were allowed and Poles were advised to worship in other outlying churches.[33]

The lack of Polish-language priests, who were mostly killed during the Stalinist terror, emigrated to Poland in the 1940s, or simply died a natural death in the intervening forty-odd years, became a major obstacle to re-establishing Polish religious and cultural life. In spite of those problems, we still witness a relatively rapid rebirth of Polish life, which had been largely suppressed through administrative measures shortly after the liberation of the area from the nazis towards the end of the Second World War.

The role of the church parish in the reorganisation of Polish life cannot be overestimated. It had traditionally functioned as the pillar of such activity, which constituted one of the reasons for its destruction at the hands of the communist security authorities in the 1940s, and it remains the reason for the current nationality struggle reappearing openly in those areas.[34]

The struggle over liturgical language is waged within the Catholic Church among Lithuanians, Poles and Belarusians. The Poles in Belarus and Ukraine who now largely speak Ukrainian or Belarusian at home generally insist on liturgy in Polish and hence are perceived as Poles by their neighbours.

Thus we observe the growing role of the Catholic Church in Polish national revival in the old 'Kresy'; it functions as an anchor of all the other cultural and educational activities in the villages. Conversely, the reopening of Polish-language schools and cultural organisations is almost impossible without reopening the church and reintroducing Polish language services. The lack of Polish language priests was remedied with the help of the Catholic hierarchy in Poland, which delegated priests from Poland to serve in the territories in question.

In that context the well-publicised 1988 pastoral visit of the Polish Primate, Józef Cardinal Glemp, to Belarus (where he engaged in an extensive visitation of the Polish parishes) was historic and momentous.

He was the first Polish head of the Catholic Church in 50 years to be allowed to make such a visit. He also held meetings with the local Orthodox Church leaders, the first and only such high level ecumenical meetings between Catholics and Orthodox ever! Here lies their historical importance since they were obviously approved at the highest Soviet governmental level at the time. Cardinal Glemp's interview carried in *Literaturnaya gazeta* was also a first in the history of the Russian-language press.[35]

The connection between the 'de-nationalisation' of the Soviet Poles and the lack of Polish-language schools has been stressed above. The increase in the scale of Polish language use in Belarus and Ukraine, now about 15 per cent, could not have been achieved without the rebuilding of Polish schools. Yet that issue has several potentially explosive dimensions. Different attitudes towards minorities can be found at various levels of government in the newly independent states. Pitting various nationalities against each other can be a method of preserving their respective linguistic spheres of influence. Unfortunately, it coincides with the 'divide and rule' syndrome of past Soviet nationality policy.[36]

The other aspect negatively affecting learning Polish (as explained to this author during research trips to Lithuania, Belarus and Ukraine in 1992–94) is that use of the Belarusian language in the schools, especially in the cities, was previously suppressed. Use of Ukrainian in Kiev, Kharkiv and the Donbass region was severely restricted by the in-migration of Russians as well as by administrative restrictions. Any further growth of the Polish language undoubtedly creates problems for Belarusian and Ukrainian officials, who perceive a minority language being revived at the expense of their own. Such feelings have already brought forth a long-ignored language conflict between Lithuanians and Poles in the Vilnius area, which is still bitterly debated in the Polish and Lithuanian-language press and radio. A private Polish university, unaccredited and unrecognised by the Lithuanian authorities, has operated in Vilnius since 1992. Books describing past tensions in the early 1940s have also appeared.[37] But Polish-language schools now function freely and are increasing in number in Lithuania (see Appendix 1).

Whereas Polish school systems in Lithuania do enable the Polish minority to maintain its language and culture in spite of some tensions and conflicts with the Lithuanian government, Polish schools in neighbouring Belarus and Ukraine do not provide the same opportunities for Poles. There are fewer than a half a dozen Polish-language schools in Ukraine and only three or four in Belarus (plus some 300 Polish language classes). Only an appropriate extension of schooling in Polish can enable Poles there to re-learn their language, extinguished under Soviet rule (some 80 per cent or more speak only Belorusian and Ukrainian or Russian). Addressing this problem is crucial if Polish minorities there are to continue to survive.

Unfortunately, the re-emergence of ethnic and linguistic conflicts and tensions is spreading. While the collapse of communism has undoubtedly allowed many discriminatory practices *vis-à-vis* the Polish minority in the former USSR to be redressed, it also has reopened many inter-ethnic conflicts and issues, hitherto carefully hidden from public view. There is an air of urgency in the attempts now being made to arrive at inter-ethnic accommodation in order to avoid the tragic nationalisms of the past which divided ethnic groups in the area, exacted a human toll and brought misery and reciprocal hatred.

The revival of organised Polish cultural, religious and educational life represents a normalisation of policies after nearly half a century. It is a great opportunity and challenge for the Polish, Belarusian and Ukrainian nations. Likewise most of the discussions going on in mass media and organisations are generally far less nationalistic and emotionally charged. The success of the Polish-language radio programme in Vilnius in its first 3 years of existence (listened to by 40 per cent of that city's population) bodes well for the future. That channel also broadcasts in Lithuanian and Russian.

There is, however, still a tendency to revive old historical grievances, especially between Poles and the many Lithuanians who consider General Zeligowski's occupation of Vilnius in 1920 to have been illegal. For its part the Polish side remembers the clashes between the Polish Underground Home Army (1941–44) and the Lithuanian nazi-organised police and army units which participated. Likewise they remember Lithuania's support of the Soviet march on Warsaw in 1920. Lithuanians respond that in both cases they were protecting their national identity.

The post-communist tensions between the two nationalities centre also on the privatisation of land, a mainstay for the Polish minority's existence. The issue is complicated by the Lithuanian refusal to honour pre-Second World War Polish deeds and documents in the Vilnius area.

Generally the role of the old Polish–Lithuanian Commonwealth is viewed negatively by Lithuanian, Belarusian and Ukrainian historians, who blame it for the loss of their national identity and for the Polonisation of their elites. That issue has to be resolved by future historians.

The positive diplomatic stand of Poland – accepting present borders, not giving any support to separatism of the Polish minority and eschewing any territorial claims whatsoever – will undoubtedly remove the tensions in time. These positions are based on the premise that those nations need one another in full partnership. Once European standards are implemented fully for the Polish minority (and other minorities throughout the region), guaranteeing cultural, economic and linguistic rights, tensions are bound to disappear between neighbouring countries.

It remains to be seen whether present and future generations can avoid the nationalistic pitfalls of their forefathers and thereby contribute to a historic breakthrough in an area of Europe which in the past was not known for such tolerance. Some old prejudices are being resurrected because the Wilno (Vilnius) Poles, ironically enough, by reason of their Slavic linguistic background, sided initially with the Russians against the Lithuanians fighting for national independence. The predominantly Polish Vilnius rural and Salcininkai districts voted 57 per cent and 53 per cent respectively for Lithuanian independence in the plebiscite held in February of 1991.[38] The same regions, however, voted for the Polish Party by 63 per cent and 56 per cent respectively in local elections in March 1995.

There are no Polish parties yet in Belarus and Ukraine and it is doubtful whether there will be because of the Poles' geographical dispersion. But in all three newly-independent republics (Lithuania, Belarus and Ukraine), the Polish minority has re-established strong and extensive central organisations and dozens of specialised cultural organisations and newspapers. Hence a basic foundation for the future existence of those minorities has been laid. A great deal will depend on the speedy rebuilding of their élites, hence the argument in favour of the Polish university in Vilnius. Although hundreds of Poles from these countries study in Poland, a considerable percentage does not want to return home after graduation, owing to vastly higher standards of living found in Poland. That issue poses a potential threat to the development of the 'Polonia in the East' in the future. Lithuanian Poles studying at Lithuanian universities and colleges do, however, comprise 2.3 per cent of the total student population (or 1,146 students).[39]

As I have noted, inter-ethnic relations, especially between the majority population and the minority, are still often driven by past grievances, in spite of the passage of half a century. Are we, then, in for more of the same historical misunderstandings? Or will the opportunity be seized to close the sordid chapters of nationalist tragedies for the sake of a better joint future for Poles, Lithuanians, Ukrainians and Belarusians – without any thought of national domination over each other? The present generation can fashion a better future for all people who love that part of Europe, so steeped in the past.

Appendix

The Polish minority in Lithuania: general data

The Polish population is over 250,000 strong, or 7 per cent of the Lithuanian population. Poles comprise 19 per cent of the population of the capital, Vilnius, and form a majority of the population of the Vilnius rural and Salcininkai regions: 63 and 81 per cent respectively; in the Sviencienis region, it is 29 per cent and in Trakai 24 per cent.

There are 128 schools in Lithuania teaching Polish to 11,000 pupils, and the number is growing; a new Polish school was recently completed in Vilnius. Twenty-four other institutions are also teaching Polish on weekend courses. In 1990/91 484 pupils received instruction in Polish in high schools, some of which in Vilnius are technical or pre-medical; in the same year, 1,146 Poles were studying at Lithuanian colleges and universities, and since 1989 others have been attending Polish universities. Vilnius Pedagogical Institute offers Polish Language and Literature on the curriculum. The number of Polish college graduates has been growing since the 1970s: in the past twenty years it has expanded by a factor of 4.5, but Poles are still last in educational terms among the minorities of Lithuania.

Some thirteen Polish organisations have been formed since 1988, and ten newspapers and journals appear in Polish. Warsaw television is being re-transmitted in Vilnius and the surrounding areas inhabited by Poles. Moreover, Lithuanian television and radio have daily information programmes and a special Sunday television programme in the Polish language.

The Polish minority in Belarus: general data

The Polish minority officially comprises over 400,000, or 4 per cent of the population of Belarus, but those figures are probably only half of the genuine ones. There were no Polish schools allowed from 1947/48, and some 300 Polish language classes are now in the process of formation, although none has its own building: they have to make use of various buildings. Dozens of organisations uniting Poles have been formed: for example, the Central Union of Poles in Belarus, with headquarters in Grodno, where a Polish House has been built for them by the Polish 'Wspólnota' organisation in Warsaw, and the Polish Scientific Association in Minsk. Some 350 Roman Catholic churches have been offering services in Polish. The Union of Poles plans to construct four buildings for Polish schools in Grodno, Lida, Baranowicze and Slonim.

The Polish minority in Ukraine: general data

The Polish minority comprises some 250,000, or 0.5 per cent of the Ukrainian population. Those figures, based on the 1989 Soviet census, should probably be doubled. At present there are only two Polish secondary schools (with their own buildings, in Lviv), and a number of Polish language classes or schools in the process of formation (for example, Gorodok in Podolia). Dozens of Polish organisations are being formed. The Union of Poles in Ukraine, with headquarters in Lviv, has 27 branches all over western and central Ukraine. Some 450 Roman Catholic churches offer services in Polish. The position of the Polish minority varies greatly between western Ukraine, where there are many Polish–Ukrainian tensions, and central Ukraine, outside the pre-Second World War Polish boundaries, where Polish–Ukrainian relations are relatively good. It is there that some two-thirds of the Poles live. In western Ukraine, the Polish population numbers 70,000–80,000, with fewer than 20,000 in Lviv.

Sources: Author's 1992–94 field research in those three states.

Notes

A somewhat different version of this chapter appeared as 'The Revival of the Polish Diaspora in Lithuania, Belarus and Ukraine', *Polish Review* XLI, no.3 (1996), pp.293–308.

1. Heinz Quirin and Werener Trillmich, *Westermanns Atlas zur Weltgeschichte* (Braunschweig: Georg Westermann Verlag, 1963), p.139.
2. *Rocznik polityczny i gospodarczy 1936* (Warsaw: P.A.T., 1936), p.1160.
3. T. Manteufel (ed.), *Historia Polski*, vol I–IV (Warsaw: Państwowe Wydawnictwo Naukowe, 1958–84), p.562.
4. Ibid., pp.589–93.
5. A. Lewicki and J. Friedberg, *Zarys Historii Polski* (London: S.Z.P.Z. Publishers, 1947), pp.317–22.
6. *Mały Rocznik Statystyczny 1939* (Warsaw: G.U.S., 1939), p.52, table 18.
7. *Rocznik polityczny i gospodarczy 1936*, p.1160.
8. Ibid.
9. *Encyklopedia Popularna PWN*, 11th edn (Warsaw: Państwowe Wydawnictwo Naukowe, 1985), p.476.
10. Krajowa Agencja Informacyjna, 'Kazachstan: Przesiedlency i ich Potomkowie', no. 11/1478, 14–20 March 1989; 'Polacy w Kazachstanie', *Dziennik Związkowy*

146 Z. Anthony Kruszewski

(Chicago), 14–15 July 1878. Note also that Ambassador Yuli Kvitinski, a Soviet Pole and a Soviet negotiator on nuclear disarmament, is by his own admission the son of an engineer who in the 1930s 'emigrated' to Siberia.

11. Z.A. Kruszewski, *The Oder–Neisse Boundary and Poland's Modernization: The Socioeconomic and Political Impact* (New York: Praeger, 1972), pp.49–53.
12. Ibid.
13. *Rocznik polityczny i gospodarczy 1936*, p.1160.
14. Julian Siedlecki, *Losy Polaków w ZSSR w latach 1939–1986* (London: Gryf, 1988); Jan T. Gross, *Revolution from Abroad* (Princeton, NJ: Princeton University Press, 1988).
15. *Mały Słownik Historii Polski* (Warsaw: Wydawnictwo Państwowe, 1967), pp.478–9; *Wielka Encyklopedia Powszechna PWN. Polska* (Warsaw: Państwowe Wydawnictwo Naukowe, 1967), pp.67–72.
16. Kruszewski, *The Oder'Neisse Boundary*, pp.13–14, 49–53.
17. Z.A. Kruszewski, 'Border Problem Solving in the Communist World: A Case Study of Some European Boundaries', in Oscar J. Martinez (ed.), *Across Boundaries* (El Paso: Texas Western Press, 1986), pp.191–200.
18. Kruszewski, *The Oder'Neisse Boundary*, pp.51–3.
19. *Atlas narodov mira* (Moscow: Akademiya nauk SSSR, 1964), p.16.
20. *Mały Rocznik Statystyczny 1939*, p.38, table 33.
21. *Great Soviet Encyclopedia*, vol.31 (New York: Macmillan, 1983), p.246.
22. Ibid., vol.3, p.613.
23. *Atlas narodov mira*, p.16.
24. E. Romer, *Powszechny Atlas Geograficzny* (Lwów: Książnica Atlas, 1934), p.56.
25. Krajowa Agencja Informacyjna, 'O zmianach programowych i strukturalnych towarzystwa "Polonia"', no. 17/1484, 25 April–1 May 1989.
26. In 1993–94, 284 from Belarus, 232 from Lithuania, 40 from Latvia; 75 from Russia; 61 from Kazakhstan, and 418 from Ukraine.
27. Krajowa Agencja Informacyjna, 'O zmianach programowych i strukturalnych'.
28. Two Polish schools were also allowed to open in the Lviv (Lwów) area: see 'Przebudzenie', *Polityka*, no.30 (1682), 29 July 1989, p.12.
29. *Słownik Geografii ZSSR* (Warsaw: Wydawnictwo Państwowe, 1974), p.714.
30. Krajowa Agencja Informacyjna, 'Polonia Radziecka – Naturalnym Pomostem między Polską a ZSSR', no.8/1473, 21–7 February 1989; ibid., no.6/1473, 7–13 February 1989.
31. *Przegląd Wiadomości Agencyjnych*, no.188/1989, quoted in 'Po 1 zjeździe Związku Polaków na Litwie', *Nowy Dziennik* (New York), 22 June 1989, p.4. See also Sergei Matunin, 'Border Controversy about Vilnius/Wilno/Vilna Area', *Nationalities Papers* (forthcoming).
32. P. Lida, 'Parafie Rzymskokatolickie na Białorusi i Ukrainie w 1988 Roku – Obsada Personalna', *Zeszyty Historyczne* **88** (Paris, 1989), pp.1233–44.
33. Ibid., p.140.
34. Ibid., p.143.
35. That pastoral visit had been very extensively covered in the Polish press, which also reprinted his interview given to *Literaturnaya gazeta*.
36. In Lithuania, Poles are blamed for often preferring to study in Russian rather than in Lithuanian schools (when not attending Polish ones).
37. P. Lossowski, *Litwa a Sprawy Polskie 1939–1940* (Warsaw: Państwowe Wydawnictwo Naukowe, 1985); K. Podlaski, *Białorusini, Litwini, Ukraincy* (Białystok:

Versus, 1990); M. Iwanów, *Pierwszy Naród Ukarany: Polacy w Związku Radzieckim 1921–1939* (Wrocław: Państwowe Wydawnictwo Naukowe, 1991); T. Gawin, *Ojcowizna* (Grodno and Lublin: Fundacja im. T. Goniewicza, 1992); *Mniejszości Polskie i Polonia w ZSSR* (Wrocław: Ossolineum, 1992); J. Ochmański, *Historia Litwy*, 3rd edn (Wrocław: Ossolineum, 1990); W. Wresinski (ed.), *Polska. Polacy. Mniejszości Narodowe* (Wrocław: Ossolineum, 1992).

38. Lithuanian Information Center news release, Brooklyn, New York, 10 February 1991.

39. Severinas Vaitiekus, 'Wiedza i spuscizna ojców', *Forum Polonijne* (Warsaw), 1995, no.3, pp.14–15.

9 The Ethnic Identity of the Polish Population in Belarus: A Research Note

Iwona Kabzińska

In this note I present the results of field studies carried out in the years 1992–94 among the indigenous Polish peasant population living in several villages in the districts of Grodno and Minsk of western Belarus.

First of all, the studies permitted the identification of local criteria for ethnic or national self-definition, with the most important role ascribed to religion. According to the prevalent stereotype still existing among the local Poles, Polish nationality is closely identified with Catholicism, while the Russians, Belarusians and Ukrainians are considered to be exclusively of Russian Orthodox denomination. All three non-Polish nationalities, as well as some other nationals of the former USSR, are, more often than not, defined by the local Poles using the term 'Ruskii'. 'Russian faith' has the meaning of 'Orthodox faith' while Catholicism is generally defined as 'the Polish faith'.

Most of the informants' responses make it clear that they conceive of religion as synonymous with national identity. 'I am Catholic means I am Polish' was the most common answer to the question about one's nationality. Or: 'I am Polish because I attend the Catholic church'; and, 'here, for us, Polish means Catholic'. The same manner of thinking can be deduced from the terms in which the local Poles talk about intermarriages: in such cases one of the spouses is expected to change religion. According to common opinion the Catholic partner who turns Orthodox 'becomes Russian' and, if it is the Orthodox side who turns Catholic, he or she 'becomes Polish'. It is clear, then, that changing of religion is perceived as entailing an automatic change of national identity.

It is remarkable that not only the Poles but also the Russians and

Belarusians tend to identify 'Polish' with 'Catholic'. It seems improbable to them that any Belarusian could be Catholic. Here the stereotype neglects reality since there used to be groups of Catholic Belarusians in these ethnically and religiously mixed areas, which has been demonstrated by historical documents. One of the informants claimed that any person of Belarusian ethnicity would turn Catholic only under pressure.

It is also noteworthy that Russians who attend the Polish (that is, Catholic) church are defined by the Poles as a kind of intermediate category between the 'real Catholics' and non-Catholic groups. It is said that they pray together with the Poles but they have their own ways of crossing themselves, confessing and so forth.

The term 'Polish–Catholic' was used by my informants mainly when they were directly asked to declare their nationality. In more open-ended discourses (usually biographies of individuals and families), particular categories of people were usually defined by the terms 'our people' and 'us', as opposed to 'them', 'the strangers', 'alien people', or even 'stray people', 'newcomers' and the like. These categories denote and emphasise the differences between people born in the locality and their descendants (no matter where they actually live now), and the newcomers who arrived after 1945. Also, Jewish people who used to live in particular villages before the Second World War are defined as 'our people'. That reveals the importance of territorial, local ties for the local classification of people. The term 'our people' is close to that of 'local people' and sometimes the two terms are applied interchangeably. In other cases they serve to denote ethnic identity.

Older people tend to define as Polish all those persons who were born on the pre-war Polish Eastern Borderland (that is, original Polish citizens). It is also important to have Polish ancestors. On the other hand, knowledge of one's genealogy and family roots, and also Polish national history and cultural traditions, is rather meagre. The cultural transmission among the Polish population in the former USSR was interrupted and limited after 1945. The only tradition that has remained was the Catholic faith and, to some extent, the language, although this was usually limited to the religious sphere. Command of the Polish language among the population with Polish national identity is not extensive, mainly restricted to religious purposes. Older people think that it is every Pole's duty to know his native language but the young generation does not consider it indispensable even if one defines oneself as Polish.

The problem of the liturgical language in the Catholic church in Belarus is a complicated one. Besides Polish, Russian and Belarusian are used by the clergy as well since there are also Russian- and

Belarusian-speaking Catholics. Most of the local Poles do not approve of this practice, considering it as threatening the preservation of their national identity. Priests try to undermine the 'Catholic equals Polish' stereotype and to replace the notion of 'Polish church' with that of 'universal church'. If we assume that such changes in Church practice turn out to be meaningful, the probable future base of the ethnic or national self-definition of the Polish population in Belarus is put into question.

Another important subject of my research was the impact on integration of local communities by the changing social and political system. Communities re-integrate, even if temporarily, around the reconstruction of local churches or resuming possession of former church buildings. Here again the Church appears as a 'bastion of Polish nationality'.

The situation of the Polish minority in the former Polish Eastern territories has recently been affected by the demarcation of the border between the two, now independent states, Lithuania and Belarus. The state border has weakened contacts between Poles now living on opposite sides and this may undermine the unity of the group. The inhabitants of the borderland, being now citizens of two separate states, find themselves under the influence of two different political, economic and linguistic spheres. They have to turn to new social networks within the country in which they live and to break their previous ties.

A further research topic is an examination of the categories recognised by the Poles inhabiting the former Polish Eastern territories – now Belarus and Lithuania: namely, Poles from Belarus, Poles from Lithuania, Poles from Poland, 'the American Poles' and so on. In addition, there are various locally-defined categories, classified according to their supposed loyalty to Polish nationality. In vernacular terms they are called 'The Poles with the Russian bow', 'perekurshchyki' – people loyal to every power; 'the Judases' who served the Soviet authorities against their countrymen; 'the Kalmuks' that is, the Poles who have changed their Catholic faith; and, finally, 'zakarenyonnye' – the Poles who remained faithful to their nationality under all circumstances. Each of those categories has presumably its own way of defining nationality, national identity, and so on. Moreover, it seems important to conduct research beyond the group of the 'church Poles' found among the strongly religious peasant population and the activists of the Polish Association in Belarus, and to turn attention to the intelligentsia, youth, the urban population, people formerly active in the Communist Party and, above all, people with Polish background who have lost their Polish identity and no longer acknowledge their Polish roots.

10 Nationalism as an Expression of Social Conflicts in Contemporary Poland

Marcin Kula and Marcin Zaremba

The language of nationalism does not seem to be the prevailing mode of expression of social conflicts in Poland. One of the present authors (M. Zaremba) participated in 1994 in a study conducted by the ARC Marketing and Social Research Agency for Local Democracy Development Foundation in Miastko, Słupsk province. The province is among the regions of greatest unemployment in Poland, reaching 35 per cent at the time of the study. The crash of PGRs (State Farms) had several consequences for local institutions connected with agriculture and for the only local factory.

It is no surprise, then, that unemployment was the most important local problem identified by respondents. One of them noted how 'the factory was closed down and people were left out of work'. Another respondent, unemployed for some time, recollected: 'When I lost my job and I went on relief I was weighed down with fear [...] I was ashamed that I had become unemployed. I hoped that nobody noticed that I was unemployed. That was humiliating.'

A climate of increasing frustration and discontent and continuous conflicts broke out in Miastko in 1993 and a Committee for the Defence of the Rights of the Unemployed was formed. The expiry of unemployment and maternity benefits was the catalyst for this. The conflict was resolved only after the town hall had been occupied and the government stepped in.

Difficulties in finding a new job and focusing on one's own problems conspired to destroy social bonds in Miastko and undermine the sense of community. Almost every respondent repeated: 'Everyone is concerned only with his own situation and problems. People notice only their own yards and families.' Such an outlook generated, in the opinion of respondents, widespread alcoholism and drug addiction among young people. Most respondents did not regard unemployment as the result of objective economic processes. A pervasive belief was that the PGRs did not have to collapse, but 'someone' went out of their way to make them crash. What is interesting is that there were no accusations against ethnically 'alien' people, which is a crucial point to our argument. We should stress that Miastko is inhabited by relatively large groups of Ukrainians and people of German origin. Organisations representing these inhabitants are very active, but their members did not complain of ethnic hostility.

This is all the more surprising since some discord and conflict between Polish and Ukrainian people had taken place in Miastko in the past. The last significant conflict emerged in 1993, involving a building purchased by the Ukrainian community from the Roman Catholic church with money collected by the Greek Catholic parish. Roman Catholics set up a committee to hold on to that building and the chapel inside. Eventually the potential for conflict dissipated because the change of ownership was approved by the church authorities.

We have reported the situation in Miastko as an example of what had been happening in other, equally unknown small towns. As another example, let us refer to the ethnic-religious quarrel that took place in Przemyśl, itself a major regional centre. The conflict there had been (and to some extent, still is) analogous, because it was triggered by a transfer of a former Roman Catholic church building to the Greek Catholic community. The episode took on broader proportions than in Miastko: public feeling ran high and the matter left considerable tension between the two religious and ethnic communities. In contrast to Miastko, this dispute gained national attention and even broader resonance. The Pope himself became involved in the matter during his pilgrimage to Poland in 1991. But even his support for the transfer of the building did not remove the tension. It will probably last for a long time but unlike the case of Miastko, it does not seem to be influenced exclusively by recent social changes. The antagonism between Poles and Ukrainians in the region is of long standing and is stimulated by historical memories and the symbolic importance of the issue. In addition, the fact that many Ukrainians, from across the frontier, come here to trade is a reason for prejudice against the Ukrainian community. These people appear to be poor and vulnerable but, along with these characteristics, they supposedly become richer and richer as a result of trade and also alleged criminal activity. The wrath of the citizens of Przemyśl is thus turned against the Ukrainians. Despite this, there is no sign that nationalism is a significant factor in the matter.

[A more nationalist backlash against deteriorating social conditions was the pogrom against the Gypsies that took place in Mława in June 1991. Even if, fortunately, it did not take human life, this was a 'classical' pogrom. It was started by a car crash caused by one Gypsy. Quickly an angry mob destroyed everything that was Gypsy and within reach. This hatred was fuelled by signs of wealth within the targeted community. Credence was lent to the belief that the Gypsies were rich, possessing luxurious cars and houses, while Poles by contrast, were poor. In addition, it was often alleged that the Gypsies had become rich in illegal ways.⌡

[Accepting that the case of the Mława pogrom may be an illustration of the expression of social conflict through nationalistic means, we wish to stress that this is a relatively rare example of the spontaneous emergence of such a causal link in Polish society. We can also point to skinheads and other similar movements, and also to right-wing groups, which drew the connection between economic hardship and ethnic rivalry, although using different methods. Such groups are, however, relatively weak in Poland./ Poor job prospects for young people surely contributes to an increase in the number of skinheads and of other right-wing groups. By contrast, the phenomena are not easily or fully explained by reference to ethnic hatred alone.

The fact that social protest can become an incitement to nationalist assertions is made clear by considering two political movements acting in the policy arena. Both movements are concerned with defending the interests of social groups, but they differ in many other ways and are not comparable. The two are NSZZ 'Solidarność' (Independent Self-governing Trade Union 'Solidarity') and Andrzej Lepper's 'Samoobrona' ('Self-defence').

[In 'Solidarność's demonstrations a recurring theme that first appeared in the 1980s but continues to reappear is the need to save the country from the communists, who were connected to an alien power. During a demonstration in the centre of Warsaw in February 1994, chants and banners called for the post-communist government to go to Moscow.⌡ They reviled the communists and stressed that 'Poland will rise again'. They claimed the country was fit only for Poles ('Poland for Poles'). Nationalist slogans were promoted especially by trade union members from the tractor factory outside Warsaw. They also appeared during other 'Solidarność' rallies or those organised by its branches. The charge of 'national betrayal' was often directed at the top state leaders including President Wałęsa. On 26 May 1995 red paint was sprayed on the walls of the Office of the Council of Ministers and clearly chauvinistic slogans painted. These actions, at least, were condemned by the Council of Trade Unions.

More typical of a nationalist movement is 'Samoobrona', which interprets social claims in nationalist categories. The organisation brings together farmers, state farm workers and small town inhabitants who have lost their position in society as a result of social changes. The most famous 'Samoobrona' demonstration took place in summer 1993 in Praszka (Częstochowa province) – that is, in a commune where the only industrial plant that previously produced parts for Soviet trucks was shut down. One-third of employees was left out of work and in most cases with no right to unemployment benefits.

In 'Samoobrona' rallies the slogan 'We want work' alternates with the slogan 'Poland for Poles'. The organisation calls for pursuing 'truly Polish' policy and its adherents like to be called 'true Poles'. It sympathises with extreme political groups that emphasise chauvinistic slogans. It opposes the new institutions of capitalism, above all banks which demand that farmers pay off their debts, plus the World Bank and the International Monetary Fund. 'Samoobrona' condemns the new economic system, characterising it as ignoring Poland's needs, or more simply as being anti-Polish. 'Samoobrona' attacks the privatisation of formerly state-owned property, particularly when it is bought by foreigners. Western consultants, for example, the Harvard economist Jeffrey Sachs, are vilified as malignant alien influences on Poland.

Since these movements are both characterised by a nationalist backlash to social change, we need to ascertain how many people support them and how strong their nationalist rhetoric is. With regard to NSZZ 'Solidarność' the answers are not simple. In spite of the steady decrease of the power and influence of the union, it remains a potent force. Generally, nationalist rhetoric does not dominate union discourse. During the wave of protests and strikes in spring 1994, discourse about social and political conflict and a critique of the structure of the economy seemed predominant. By contrast, 'Samoobrona' can be characterised as at best a negligible group. Its actions are spectacular and consequently it obtains much publicity. For example, in Praszka the mayor was wheeled out of town in a wheelbarrow after being wheeled around the market square. The mayor then resigned his post under the pressure of the crowd of unemployed. Police had to clear the area to enable the deputy minister of finance to leave the building where negotiations were being conducted. Symbolically, the wheelbarrow stood chained to a tree in front of the town hall – ready to be used again. The demonstrators stood guard under a banner with the words: 'Betrayed – sold – deceived – we persist!' In a subsequent incident in Kobylnica near Słupsk in August 1994, the receiver for farm debt was spanked on his naked buttocks and shaved bald, apparently to the accompaniment of shouts of 'Jewish Ukrainian' and 'Carve a Star of David' on his head! It is obvious that such actions have wide resonance but 'Samoobrona' has not attained any significant position in Polish politics to date. On the other hand, there is little jingoism associated with promoting Polish-owned companies. There are no signs of opposition to the employment of foreigners – legally or more often illegally. However, the scale of this employment is not great at present, and criticism of it might appear if it were to increase markedly. Similarly there are few exhortations to buy Polish goods, though sometimes one can find advertising which emphasises the Polish origin of a product. During the election campaign of 1993 the Catholic Election Committee "Ojczyna" ('Fatherland') handed out Polish fruit and 'Hortex' juices to passers-by and announced: 'By buying Polish products you can actively support the struggle against unemployment. Eat excellent Polish apples and vote for the excellent politicians of 'Ojczyzna''. In the same campaign the Liberal-Democratic Congress, though very different in political terms from the previous group, also promoted Polish products and services and employed the campaign slogan 'Buy Polish products'.

Such actions towards the promotion of Polish production remain very limited and perfunctory; the political establishment lends it weak support. People normally prefer to buy Western goods whenever possible. Furthermore, some actions taken in Poland in the name of fairness would not be acceptable in countries considerably richer than Poland. During one of the Pope's visits to Poland the question arose whether he should use a tested and safe Polish helicopter or another kind. Many countries would have used such an opportunity for advertising the quality of their own product especially if it involved a choice between increasing exports or stopping local production altogether. Nevertheless, the Polish body overseeing preparations for the visit ordered a Western helicopter.

Government contracts also give no marked preference to Polish-owned companies. For example, the printing of new banknotes to replace the old ones was entrusted to a foreign printing firm, even though there were good reasons to award the contract to the State Precious Papers Printingshop. The voice of Polish producers in this case was ignored. Another example comes from Warsaw: the city authorities contracted with a company having a substantial amount of American capital to create pay parking in the centre of Warsaw – as if they could not collect money themselves.

The weakness of indigenous occupational groups in struggling against foreign competition is also surprising. Farmers obtained some compensation for imported food after long and hard efforts, but only for particular goods and for a short time. Workers in agriculture-related industry opposed importing used machines from the West. Fishermen fought against foreign competitors by blocking all Polish ports for one day. Arms manufacturers tried to take advantage of the fact that their product – weapons – went hand-in-hand with the Polish vision of national security and independence. To sum up, the country did not align itself on the side of Polish production – no matter how much this might have been in the national interest.

Considering the foregoing account we are drawn to the conclusion that social claims and conflicts are expressed in present-day Poland in ways other than nationalist manifestations. Nationalism is confined to symbolic rather than material purposes. If this conclusion is true it is worth inquiring about the reasons for this. The issue is all the more interesting because the greater part of national dissent in the decade of the 1980s was expressed through nationalist discourse (though most often not of a chauvinistic character).

We have observed that manifestations of nationalism are relatively restrained in today's Poland. Even if sometimes news spreads around the world about some condemnable statement or action in Poland, such news is in fact rare; we cannot find many other actions like those in Mława or Przemyśl. Some research findings confirm that negative ethnic stereotypes still exist. A survey conducted by the Sopot Centre for Social Research in June 1995 asked the question: 'Should Poland be a country open to all foreigners?' While 46 per cent of respondents answered: 'Yes, it should be open to all', 15 per cent gave the answer: 'In general the country should be for Poles'.[1]

Extreme groups mentioned at the beginning of this chapter, as well as right-wing parties operating in the political arena which emphasise nationalist rhetoric, have achieved few successes. The weakness of nationalist rhetoric as an expression of social protest may be caused by some specific reasons or it may be a part of some larger-scale phenomenon. We can only suggest some of the most probable causes. One favourable circumstance is probably that since 1989 Poland has overcome limitations upon its national sovereignty. To be sure, nationalist rhetoric sometimes does occur even in conditions of full sovereignty:

even superpowers resort to this. Also the absence of serious ethnic differences, the narrowness of the economic gap between Poles and minorities, and the absence of conflicts with foreign countries are favourable conditions. Still, it was observed a long time ago that such phenomena as anti-Semitism without Jews can exist.

If the difficult social situation that the country has faced in the 1990s has not spawned any significant nationalistic rhetoric, there are four possible explanations for this: (1) in spite of everything, the situation is not severe enough to resort to such a discourse; (2) nationalist language as an expression of protest is discredited in Poland; (3) there are other ways to express dissatisfaction; and (4) the times have changed and so has the political language.

The first possibility is the most difficult to consider, for there is no reliable estimate of how many people need to live below the 'average level' for such nationalist language to emerge. The situation in Germany in the 1930s – when the number of unemployed reached a particular threshold – is not a good measuring-stick for today's Poland. We should take into consideration not only people's present situation, but also the outlooks for them. It is possible that many who are now lower in the social scale see bright or reasonable prospects for themselves. It is also likely that opinion leaders do not propose nationalist ideas and rhetoric as strongly as they used to. Perhaps they realise that taking such an approach back-fired in the past. Moreover, they may be more interested now in overall economic development. Furthermore, the nationalist conception and language are less and less popular in the West (which those groups look intently at) – even if this is a limited and temporary phenomenon. Also, in Poland many people who watch Western TV programmes, use Western products, and take part in the exchange of goods and ideas with the whole world arrive at the conclusion that the nationalist paradigm is an anachronism nowadays. We would attach the greatest importance to the last two factors mentioned above. In the period of communism the language of social protest was appropriated and ritualised by the regime. That is why nationalist rhetoric grew stronger over the years. The language of social protest is only now being reanimated. In the last years of communist rule, people dissatisfied for many different reasons arrived at the conclusion that they could struggle for a free Poland. Now we hear these same voices saying with sarcasm that they did not struggle for a free Poland just in order to gain it but to be hungry after all that. The language had to change.

In addition we have the last of the factors mentioned above: some nationalist rhetoric got worn out in specific Polish conditions; nothing lasts forever. Moreover, the retrospective view of our time is shorter now; we seem to find our roots not in the thousand-year history of Poland but, for many people, in the transformation at the end of the 1980s which was viewed as the beginning of a new era. Nationalist rhetoric was thus the language of the transition. The disappointment with the results of the transformation has made people seek other languages. The frustration that follows euphoria lowers the nation's self-esteem. Without it, as sociologists contend, it can be more difficult to emphasise the national quest. The new (or rather renewed) discourse is not nationalism, therefore, but the language of social protest. It often makes reference to the era of the Polish People's Republic (PRL). Then support was sought beyond that political system. Now, with a new form of government, part of society seeks support in the former PRL. Instead of an intensification of nationalist rhetoric there is a post-revolutionary tendency to restore the past. This is seen in a more positive assessment of the era of communism than was common not long ago and voting for the successors to the Polish United Workers' Party has rebounded. The presidential election of December 1995 offered further confirmation of this tendency. The future of nationalist discourse will surely be influenced by many different and unforeseeable factors. We can easily imagine that, for example, a more conflictual world order may revive it dramatically. In that case the optimism reflected in this chapter may turn out to be merely wishful thinking.

Note

1. *Rzeczpospolita*, 3 July 1995.

11 The Russians in Moldova: Political Orientations

Alla Skvortsova

The beginning of *perestroika* in the USSR spurred all of Soviet society to take an active part in political life. The leaders of the reconstruction announced democratisation as one of their main goals, gave comparative freedom to the mass media, made contacts with foreign countries easier, and helped in the creation of a number of 'informal' organisations. People who were previously quite indifferent to politics felt the wind of change and began to participate in political life, being inspired with new hopes. The initial division of Soviet society was between the advocates and adversaries of *perestroika* – 'democrats' and 'conservatives'. But when the first stage of restructuring – the destruction of the old order – dragged on, and while Soviet state leaders demonstrated an obvious inability to pass to the second, constructive stage, these two camps began to splinter into smaller ones reflecting the specific interests of different groups of the population. In the Soviet republics the process of division took place along nationality lines. The people who assumed leadership in the democratic movements in the republics were concerned first of all with nationality problems, although they attempted to conceal them under the cloak of democracy.

The contradictions accumulating in inter-ethnic relations could not help but manifest themselves in a situation where all was permitted, which was created by the fathers of *perestroika* in Moscow. And the fighters for national rebirth in the republics could invent nothing better than to use undemocratic methods in their struggle for national liberation. They considered the non-titular populations in the republics as the main threat to their goal of creating independent national states, and they mobilised members of their own ethnic community against 'migrants' or 'foreigners' so as to force the latter to leave their republics. It is understandable that in these circumstances the non-indigenous population had to defend its rights and oppose the political goals of the nationalists. Growing opposition between titular and non-titular nations in the republics turned the problem of inter-ethnic relations into one of the most acute and complicated within the USSR.

In recent years, many works have been published on the development of inter-ethnic relations in the Soviet and post-Soviet republics. Of special worth are the works of those authors who, as early, as the 1960s and 1970s, analysed Soviet nationality policy and nationality relations in the USSR, and predicted the collapse of the 'inviolable Union of the free republics'. I will mention some of the works which concern the events of the period of *perestroika* and after; some of these describe the processes occurring between 1988 and early 1991, when the USSR still existed.[1] The strength of these works lies in the discovery of the reasons for the crisis in ethnic relations in the USSR, and a description of their development. But they were very careful in making any prognoses; as noted, the Soviet Union was too complicated and fragile an organism, and the pace of change too rapid, to allow for any predictions.[2]

After the break-up of the USSR, researchers proceeded to study events in the separate Soviet republics, sometimes treating them in groups, mainly on the basis of their territorial contiguity (for instance, the Baltic republics, Central Asia, Transcaucasia). To be sure, territorial proximity and common geographical and geopolitical conditions in many cases resulted in common historical fates and common features in their modern development. Moldova did not fit into any of these groups, however, because of its peculiarities connected with its historical ties to Romania.[3] No other republic has a counterpart of a state of similar ethnic origin across the border. No other has been incorporated entirely into the other country. And no other republic has a significant political movement towards unification with another country which is eager to incorporate new territories.

The primary attention found in the scholarship was directed towards the problem of the formation of national independent states, while the problem of the new ethnic minorities was only touched on.[4] One of the dimensions of the ethnic minorities' problems that did attract the interest of researchers was the problem of the Russians in the Near Abroad.[5] This is understandable since the Russian population is present in every republic. Moreover, it forms, as a rule, the largest ethnic minority, yet its importance lies not only in the quantitative dimension. The influence of the 'Russian factor' in the republics' life is much greater than might be expected if the proportion of Russians in the republics alone is taken into account. There are other reasons for this. For several centuries Russian language and culture played an exceptionally important, even dominant, role in all the territories of the Russian Empire and the Soviet Union. The Russians considered themselves as the 'elder brother' and felt responsibility for the Union's fate. They were much more 'sovietised' than any other nationality in the USSR. They were the most modernised, urbanised sector of the population, separated from their historical homeland and ethnic roots as a result of migration. The Russian population in the republics became a nucleus around which other groups of the population that opposed the new nationalist movements galvanised, and the withdrawal of the republics from the USSR led to the destruction of the Soviet Union.

The movement of the Russian-speaking population was different in the various republics, and it acquired different organisational forms. But all fought for similar principles: equal rights for peoples regardless of their nationality in the use of languages in the social and educational spheres and in the mass media; a gradual and non-punitive transition to a monolingual system in the republics; citizenship for all inhabitants regardless of the length of their presence in the republics; the right to express their views, that is, assuring ethnic minorities of their democratic rights. But many Russians saw the preservation of the Soviet Union as the main guarantee of minority rights. Conversely, this is why Russians became a symbol of the anti-independence movement in the republics.

If for politicians Russians are a central issue in political games,[6] it seems that scholars more carefully analysed the real and potential consequences of the appearance of the new Russian minority population in the newly independent states. Scholars have suggested methods for their adaptation to the new conditions, made prognoses about their future status, assessed their impact on the internal development of the republics, and considered the latter's relations with Russia.[7] A survey conducted by Moscow ethnologists in spring 1993, intended to show the status and social-political orientations of the Russian minority in the national republics, is noteworthy. The survey's conclusions seem to be persuasive, in so far as they are based on hard empirical evidence.[8]

The Moscow team directed attention to the fate of the Russians in the former Soviet republics not because it was unprecedented in world history, but precisely because it was similar to the fates of representatives of other imperial nations in their former colonies (such as the French in Algeria). Although Russians could not be considered as an imperial nation, their case interests scholars as a good example for comparative analysis. It may contribute to finding practical solutions to the problems faced by the new ethnic minorities.[9] On the other hand, Russians in the

Newly Independent States continue to be perceived as bearers of Communist ideology and defenders of imperial power.[10] As the Western world is concerned about the possibility of the restoration of the Soviet Union and the communist regime, Western researchers seek to understand the political behaviour of this group of the republics' population. Some attempts of this kind have been undertaken with regard to the Russians in Moldova.[11] Writers from Moldova itself have published studies on the political orientation of the Russians in the republic as well. The main advantages of these works consist in the presentation of rich statistical material, in the view presented 'from within', and in the combination of scientific research methods with practical experience.[12] The authors of works on Russians in Moldova, both from within the republic and from outside it, consider the process observed in interethnic relations in Moldova during the past several years to be common to the other former Soviet republics.

In Moldova the nationalist movement was organised in the first half of 1988 and was represented by two organisations: the Democratic Movement in Support of Perestroika and the 'A. Mateevich' Literature and Music Club. The early programme announcements of these movements stressed that their activity conformed with the long-term interests of the development of socialist society, and was located within the framework of the Constitutions of the USSR and the Moldavian SSR.[13] The Russian-speaking intelligentsia in Kishinev, inspired by the promised *glasnost'* and 'democratisation', expressed interest in these organisations. Some of its representatives even joined the Democratic Movement, sharing the anxiety of the Movement's leaders about the survival of the Moldovan nation, language and culture, the neglect of ecological problems in the republic, and the imbalance in the economy.

But the first meetings of the Democratic Movement and the 'A. Mateevich' Club indicated that the main goal of these organisations was not simply the 'national revival' of the Moldovans within the framework of renewed socialism. Using this pretext they assigned the key positions in the leadership to ethnic Moldovans and simultaneously enforced the exclusion of non-Moldovans. The demand to declare the Moldovan language the official one recognised by law was a good method of accomplishing this task, since only a small number of the non-indigenous population were fluent in Moldovan.

In 1989, more than 500,000 Russians (13 per cent of the total population) lived in Moldova, in addition to about 400,000 members of other nationalities who considered Russian to be their native language. More than 200,000 Moldovans also considered Russian their mother tongue.[14]

Therefore, the majority of non-Moldovans (about 35 per cent of the whole population), and also Moldovans who considered Russian as their native language, were all 'Russian-speakers', or 'russophones'. Naturally, these people did not all want the linguistic situation in the republic to be changed abruptly, although they were not against giving Moldovan the status of official language. But they did demand the same status for Russian as well.[15] If the Democratic Movement's leaders were really interested in the development of democracy in Moldova, they would have considered the interests of the Russian-speaking population and would have searched for a compromise. But both the actions and the declarations of the leaders of the Moldovan nationalist movement testified against this.

Simultaneously, the Democratic Movement's leaders initiated an anti-Russian campaign not only in the language sphere, but in other important areas of social life. They explained the crisis in the republic's economy, environment, public health, culture and other fields as the result of the ill-intentioned goals of Moscow. Naturally, such declarations roused the ire of the Russians and Russian-speaking population, because behind the transparent allusions to 'the hand of Moscow' they saw a threat to their own fate: they were supposedly the fingers of this hand. The leaders of the nationalist organisations at meetings, attended first by hundreds and then thousands of people, as well as in the mass media, accused 'migrants' – meaning Russian-speakers – of responsibility for all the evils the Soviet regime had perpetrated in Moldova. Russian-speakers began to understand that these accusations would deprive them of the opportunity to take part in the reform process, and obviously also exclude them from being beneficiaries of the republic's sovereignty.

This predicament of the Russian minority was more or less repeated in every union republic, but in Moldova it had its own peculiarities, connected with the existence of Moldovans' ethnic counterparts across the border in Romania. Concurrent with the accusations levelled against Moscow's policies, the Democratic Movement demonstrated its pro-Romanian orientation. It advanced demands for language reform, including official status for the Moldovan language and recognising its identity with the Romanian one, and its transferring from the Cyrillic alphabet to the Latin. These demands became the main platform in the Democratic Movement's agenda, which already had lost the spirit and terminology of *perestroika*.[16] It revealed the real goal of the nationalist leadership: recognising the common identity of the Moldovan and Romanian language, culture and people so as to prepare for the political unification of Moldova with Romania. The fear of such a prospect – but not the unwillingness to accept the free functioning of the Moldovan language in the republic – became the principal motive in the subsequent political activity of the Russian population.

Some of the researchers studying political developments in Moldova have expressed their surprise at the high level of support for Moldova's withdrawal from the Soviet Union and the high level of 'reactive nationalism' that followed in the republic, which had been considered one with a history of inter-ethnic conciliation and harmony.[17] It can be suggested that the main reason for the unexpected level of inter-ethnic conflict in Moldova was determined by the fact that the nationalist movement viewed the republic's independence not as the final goal, but only as the stepping-stone on the way to political unification with Romania. It is well known that in the Baltic republics and in Ukraine, for example, a significant proportion of Russian-speakers voted in favour of these republics' independence before or just after the collapse of the Soviet Union. In Moldova such a referendum was conducted only in 1994, after the removal of the pro-Romanian forces from power structures and long after the break-up of the USSR, when there was no chance of its restoration. In such conditions independence was the single alternative to unification with Romania, and Russian-speakers participating in the referendum voted for a sovereign Republic of Moldova.[18]

During the struggle for the new language legislation the mobilisation of the nationalist and pro-Romanian forces in the republic continued, and the conclusive proof was the organisational unification of the Democratic Movement for the Support of Perestroika and the 'A. Mateevich' Club under the name of the Popular Front of Moldova.

Following publication of the demands for language reform, an anti-Russian campaign was launched in the mass media. Well-known Moldovan writers, poets and journalists began frequently to publish articles on the Russian 'migrants', who were compared with sewage, and who were blamed for turning Moldova into a rubbish pit. They argued that the only Russians who could be respected were those who lived in their own country.[19] Naturally, all non-Moldovans – both those who had come to the republic in recent decades and those whose ancestors had lived there for centuries – were offended by such articles. Groups of Russian-speaking citizens even addressed letters to the Procurator General with requests to stop inflaming inter-ethnic conflict by vilifying Russians. They argued that it was wrong to blame the Russian population for all the misfortunes in Moldova's economy, science, environment, culture and education, and that it offended people who had worked for Moldova's benefit for their entire life.[20] Anti-Russian actions on the part of the Popular Front of Moldova divided the whole of the republic's population into 'ours' and 'theirs', 'natives' and 'non-natives', first-class and second-class. Simultaneously there were attempts to provide special rights for Moldovans. It was reiterated that the future of Moldova could be decided only by Moldovans. When the republican Supreme Soviet discussed the question of Moldova's participation in the referendum on the fate of the USSR on 17 March 1991, leaders of the Popular Front proposed allowing only ethnic Moldovans to vote. As a result the non-indigenous population was denied basic civic rights.

In such conditions, for the Russians and Russian-speakers the notions of *perestroika*, ethnic nationalism and Russophobia became identical, so their attitude to *perestroika* became negative. The gradual worsening of their situation was attributed not merely to the anti-democratic positions of the Popular Front's leadership, but to *perestroika* itself, which had allowed nationalist forces to come to power.

The passive position of the republican Communist Party's leadership towards the anti-Russian attacks, and Gorbachev's own hypocritical position – on the one hand consisting of high-minded declarations about the need to improve inter-ethnic relations and to achieve real equality in the rights of all the nations and languages, and, on the other, countenancing the pseudo-democratic and nationalist forces in the Soviet republics – in practice strengthened this tendency. Step by step the Russian-speaking population, which had welcomed the ideas of *perestroika* with enthusiasm and had backed the process of economic reforms, renewal of the Communist Party and liberalisation of social and political life, began to cross over into opposition to the so-called 'democrats'. It was not wrong Soviet nationality policy that was seen as a reason for inter-ethnic tension in the republics, but the attempts to liberalise political life in the USSR.

The difference in the political programmes of the leaders of the Popular Front of Moldova and of the Russian-speaking population lay in different visions of *perestroika*'s aims. While the Russian-speakers considered that *perestroika* had to be the method for improving life within the framework of socialism and the USSR, the Popular Front wished to destroy the socialist system and secede from the Soviet Union. Indeed, most russophones did not support the conservative elements in the Communist Party, which did not want change at all, but believed in the prospects promised by 'renewed socialism with a human face' and supported the democratisation of Soviet society. It is not surprising that the founders of the Russian-speakers' political movement proclaimed these ideas as their political goals.

In January 1989, under the leadership of a group drawn from the scientific intelligentsia, a political organisation was formed which was supposed to defend the ethnic, cultural and political interests of the Russian-speaking population. It was named 'The "Unitate–Yedinstvo" International Movement for the Supporting of *Perestroika*', equivalent to the Intermovements of other republics at the time. Its name reflected the loose understanding of *perestroika* in Soviet society – both separatists and adherents to the Soviet Union regarded themselves as supporters of *perestroika*.

The 'Unitate–Yedinstvo' movement and the Councils of the Work Collectives and Strike Committees, founded in the summer of 1989, were the organisations which for a long time reflected the moods and aspirations of the Russians in Moldova. As colleagues have pointed out, these organisations of Russian speakers emerged as a phenomenon of 'reactive nationalism', that is, in response to the activity and propaganda of the Popular Front of Moldova[21] and as an attempt to defend themselves from the nationalists' attacks and their infringement of human rights.

During the first half of 1989 tension over the language problem gradually increased. Everyone realised that the proposed language law was not the final goal for the leaders of the Popular Front. They wished to stop the process of democratisation by permitting democracy only for Moldovans, to substitute for the Communist administrative–command system an ethnocratic government of the Moldovan bureaucracy, to force non-Moldovans to leave the republic, and to separate Moldova from the USSR. All these steps were a prerequisite for unification with Romania.

The 'Unitate–Yedinstvo' International Movement attempted to oppose these ideas with internationalist slogans. Participants in the meetings of 'Yedinstvo' demanded the recognition of two official languages in Moldova – Moldovan and Russian. They hoped to postpone a decision on the language problem until after a Plenum of the CPSU Central Committee (they believed that such questions could still be decided within the framework of the USSR), and displayed posters with such slogans as 'Our home is the USSR', 'We are the Soviet People', and '"No" to ethnic exclusiveness'.[22] The Movement formulated its political objectives in the terminology of *perestroika*: the destruction of the administrative-command system, the formation of new democratic structures within the socialist political system, guarantees for human rights. It stressed the importance of observing human rights regardless of nationality, thereby introducing for the first time into Soviet nationality policy the notion of the basic rights of all ethnic minorities, not only those of titular peoples in the union republics. It was emphasised that ethnic, linguistic and social prejudices had to be overcome in the name of progress of the USSR – the common Motherland.[23]

The Intermovement's ideology had widespread support in the non-titular population, but its main shortcoming consisted of an inability to advance new ideas and slogans, capable of attracting not only Russian-speakers but the indigenous population as well. What played the main role in its behaviour – the conservatism of its thinking, its aspiration to defend Russians from the harsh new reality, or a genuine devotion to socialism? Obviously, all these considerations and many other factors dictated the behaviour of the Russian-speaking population and its leaders. At that stage the attitude of russophones was characteristic not only for Moldova, but for other republics – for example, the Baltic states – as well. This was the Achilles' heel of the russophones' organisations. A political movement unable to elaborate new, attractive ideas is condemned to failure. The absence of new political values in the International Movement's programme significantly diminished the number of potential members and activists; the 'Yedinstvo' meetings never gathered more than a few thousand participants.

In spite of the obvious mistakes in ideology, 'Unitate–Yedinstvo' demonstrated strong organisational skills. The local organisations of the Intermovement were established in almost all towns and in the biggest industrial enterprises, and a number of well-attended meetings were held in Kishinev. They called for equal rights for all of Moldova's inhabitants, first of all the right to use their own language (meaning Russian primarily) in the educational system, at work and in the public service sector.

A clear illustration of the effective organisation of the International Movement was the all-republican political strike against the new language law, which took place in August–September 1989, and the rallies with thousands of protesters in Kishinev, Tiraspol and Comrat at the same time. Strikers from about 250 enterprises demanded two state languages – Russian and Moldavian – while the Popular Front of Moldova pressed for one – Romanian.[24] The position of the former group was not taken into consideration when on 31 August 1989 the Supreme Soviet of the Moldovan SSR adopted the new language law under pressure from crowds assembled by the leaders of the Popular Front of Moldova in the centre of Kishinev.

Although this law provided for a transition period of five years, made special arrangements for the districts populated by Gagauz, and recognised minorities' rights to obtain education in their own languages, its adoption was considered by the minorities themselves as a great failure. They were offended by the fact that none of their demands was recognised in the law. As far as they were concerned, therefore, the adoption of the law showed the minorities' inferior position in relation to the titular population.

The language law was a turning-point in the political development of the republic and a major victory for Moldovan nationalists. It split people into two groups – those who knew Moldovan, and those who did not – and gave different chances of social advancement to each. Such a result may be considered as a natural one. Among the relevant factors was the lower number of politically active Russians than of Moldovans. They used only legitimate methods of struggle and relied on the wisdom of local leaders, but they also accepted the interference of Moscow to defend them. Their programme was behind the times and had no constructive forward-looking elements. Intermovement proclaimed the slogans of *perestroika* when it had become clear that restructuring had collapsed. It defended the fortress of socialism and Soviet power when it had become clear that *perestroika* had been overtaken by fundamental change in the existing system.

However, in the course of this struggle a core group of political leaders of the Russian population of Moldova emerged. The leaders of the International Movement and the Council of the Workers' Collectives were elected in the republic Supreme Soviet in the spring of 1990 during the first free elections in the republic. Among the 370 elected members of parliament, 90 were firm supporters of the Popular Front and about 60 were staunch supporters of the internationalist bloc. The deputies from the International Movement, together with other Russian-speaking deputies, founded the 'Soviet Moldavia' faction, which became an important opposition group to the Popular Front. But the Popular Front succeeded in forming the 'Moldovan Bloc', uniting 65 per cent of all deputies, from among the radical deputies and deputies from the ethnic Moldovan *nomenklatura*. It won the struggle for power by exploiting the contradictory interests of ethnic–linguistic groups, which were themselves engendered by nationalists. They depicted the Russian-speaking deputies and all Russian-speakers as enemies of the Moldovans, fanned nationalist hysteria, and even resorted to direct physical violence against their opponents.[25] The initiatives of the 'Soviet Moldavia' faction were not passed and not a single candidate from this faction was appointed to ruling posts in the parliament. Russian-speaking deputies left parliament in protest at discrimination towards the parliamentary minority, but this did not change their situation. Their absence was used to elect the ruling body of parliament and to appoint the government without any discussion or compromise.

The 'Moldovan Bloc' insisted on the appointment of a pro-Romanian but under-qualified candidate, Mircea Druk, to the post of Prime Minister.[26] The new government, as with the ruling body of the parliament, consisted of a majority belonging to the Popular Front. During the discussion of candidates for different posts, leaders of the parliamentary majority demanded that they be Moldovan-speakers. This was only an excuse for selecting ethnic Moldovans, because deputies who were not Moldovans but knew the language nevertheless were not appointed. The conditions under which the top leadership of the republic was elected and the actual results of the elections left no doubt that in Moldova the policy of discrimination against ethnic minorities – that is, Russian-speaking people – was being implemented.

Other policies of the new state leaders corroborated this conclusion. The new parliament made changes to the state's symbols, bringing them closer to those of Romania. The new national flag that was approved was the Romanian 'tricolour' without its emblem, and the national anthem became 'Wake up, Romanian!'.[27] Russophobia became part of the state ideology along with exalting everything Romanian. In the mass media as well as in the speeches of state leaders, it was alleged that russophones in Moldova were 'strangers' and 'guests', and therefore they had no right to their own opinions, to defend their own interests or to criticise state policy.[28] Following proposals made by the Second Congress of the Popular Front of Moldova, large-scale renaming of cities, villages, streets, and institutions of education and culture was carried out. These changes were aimed not only at returning to traditional Moldovan symbols (most of which first emerged under Romanian rule), but at eliminating the names and symbols connected to the Russian past.[29]

The election of the new republican leadership was immediately followed by a purge in the state apparatus in which people of non-Moldovan nationalities and those considered not loyal were fired.[30] Simultaneously, Russian educational institutions were scaled back, Russian classes in schools and universities[31] were slashed and ethnic violence, directed against political opponents of the regime, including deputies and ordinary citizens (mostly those who did not speak Romanian[32]), was fanned.

Hence, it becomes obvious why the Russians and Russian-speaking population of Moldova sought to save the USSR. They wanted to preserve the country where they had not only not been discriminated against but, on the contrary, had reaped some advantages. Even later, when the

Soviet Union broke up, and the new union of republics, the Common-wealth of Independent States, turned out to be only a phantom, many russophones began to support the idea of an independent Moldovan state, but nostalgia for the former USSR remained very strong.

The political mood of Russian-speakers was best captured by the declaration of autonomous Gagauz and Dniester republics in August and September 1990. While they did not leave the Moldovan SSR, they both proclaimed their desire to remain part of the USSR, and even aspired to the status of union republic. Interestingly, many of the arguments made by Moldova in justifying its separation from the Soviet Union were made by Pridnestrov'e (Trans-Dniester) and Gagauzia in arguing for their own autonomy. After the secession of these regions political developments there began to differ strongly from those in Moldova, especially in ideology and politics, and they require a separate study.

The next great surge of political activity of the Russian population in Moldova was connected with Gorbachev's referendum of March 1991 on the future of the USSR. The republican parliament decided not to partici-pate in the referendum,[33] but voting centres were set up by some local Soviets, work collectives and public and political organisations; some were also set up for military units. During voting most of these centres were surrounded by pickets, who insulted those going to vote, threw stones and beat them, and blocked entry to the centres. Many of the voting centres for military units were ransacked and ballot-papers de-stroyed.[34] As a result, it is impossible to determine the exact number of those participating, nor, of course, of those who wished to participate in the referendum but could not do so. Voting turnout in Pridnestrov'e and Gagauzia, and support for the union there, was very high. According to the data of the Referendum Central Commission, a total of 943,000 people – about the entire Russian-speaking adult population – voted in Moldova, including 114,000 in Kishinev (one-fifth of inhabitants), and the overwhelming majority of them voted for the preservation of the Soviet Union.[35] The referendum persuasively demonstrated that Russian-speakers constituted an independent and strong political factor in Moldova. After the referendum, however, the political activity of the Russians began to wane.

The paradox of the situation in Moldova consists in the fact that the real policy towards the ethnic minorities was not reflected in the legisla-tion. Some Western analysts emphasise that the Moldovan government after 1991 (following the dismissal of Mircea Druk) 'was more accom-modating to minorities in general, and to Russian minority in particular' than in the other former Soviet republics. They drew such a conclusion from the fact that citizenship was granted by law to all who lived in Moldova before 23 June 1990 (the day of the declaration of the sovereignty of Moldova within the framework of the USSR). Language policy was supposedly liberal, education was supported in a variety of languages, and political representation was available for all sectors of the population.[36]

Indeed, after the proclamation of the independence of Moldova in August 1991, the republic's leadership took steps to demonstrate its concern for ethnic minorities. President Mircea Snegur attempted to convince the non-Moldovans that the new regime would reverse the state policy of cultural dominance by 'giving urgent priority to resolving ethnic grievances, establishing a system of guarantees for the observance of human rights, and developing the facilities for the cultural and linguistic expression of the ethnic communities'.[37] In early 1992 the government took some decisions on the development of the culture and education of the ethnic minorities, different for each of them. Earlier, ethnic cultural organisations of Russians, Ukrainians, Bulgarians, Jews and others were established by activists from these ethnic groups, all of whom stressed their non-political character. The 1992 decisions weakened the political clout of these ethnic groups by dividing them.

Certainly, if one were to judge by the laws and official declarations made by Moldova's leadership after the Moscow coup of August 1991, it would have seemed that it was indeed concerned about the rights of ethnic minorities. But it is necessary to take into consideration that not all Soviet traditions were eliminated in the Soviet successor states. One of them – to say one thing and to do another – remained. Creating an unbearable moral and psychological environment so as to force Russian-speakers out was one part of a two-track policy. The other was that the nationalist majority in parliament did not adopt discriminatory legislation because it was concerned about preserving a democratic image before international organisations and the Western world. However, the discriminatory decisions and acts adopted earlier were not reversed, even after significant changes had occurred in the parliament and in government leadership. To be sure, it is very difficult to prove that ethnic discrimination is encouraged. As one of the discussants in the Round table during the days of Russian culture held in Moldova at the end of 1993 stated, 'Outwardly all is legal but really you are squeezed out, bundled out. There occurs creeping, quiet discrimination.'[38]

Even though Moldova signed all international conventions on human rights after its independence, and although the republic's leaders promised non-conflictual development of inter-ethnic relations, the negative feelings of the Russian-speakers became apparent in attitudes on emigration. Opinion polls showed that in 1991 more than 60 per cent, and in 1992 80 per cent, of Russians were ready to leave Moldova, almost 70 per cent of them for Russia.[39] But few could actually leave because of financial problems and the cold reception awaiting them in Russia or Ukraine. There are no reliable date on emigration from Moldova based on emigrants' nationality, but the destination of emigrants can be used as evidence. Table 11.1 indicates that it was only Russians who moved to Russia and not only Ukrainians who left for Ukraine.

Table 11.1.   Out-migration from Moldova, 1990–94 (in thousands)

	Year				
	1990	*1991*	*1992*	*1993*	*1994*
Total number	162.7	149.2	130.7	94.6	83.2
To republics of the FSU	48.3	43.2	53.2	29.4	28.3
To Russia	25.4	22.1	25.3	16.7	18.7
To Ukraine	19.9	18.5	25.0	11.2	8.7

Source: Moldovan Ministry of Internal Affairs.[40]

Thus, among persons leaving Moldova for Russia in 1992, only 32 per cent were ethnic Russians.[41] Moreover, many emigrants did not register their departure owing to problems registering in their new places of residence, problems connected with changing citizenship, and so on. For this reason different sources may provide contradictory evidence. For example, according to the data of the Russian Federal Migration Administration, in 1992 more than 32,000 persons came from Moldova to Russia and, as was stated, many other arrivals were not registered.

In the period of the military conflict in Trans-Dniester, Russians on the right bank (that is, in Moldova proper) were very much afraid that they would pay for the failure of Moldova's troops in military action, and for the lives of Moldovans killed in the conflict. They hoped for the victory of Pridnestrov'e, but did not express their view openly. The nationalist mass media and even state leaders (including Prime Minister Valerii Muravskii) declared bluntly that right-bank Russians would answer for Pridnestrov'e's opposition.[42] The political activity of the Russian population in 1991–93 was manifested mainly in cultural issues, therefore: in the struggle against the closing of Russian schools, and for postponing language certification, required for all employees in January 1994.

It is not surprising that the political activity of the Russian population in Moldova decreased after the collapse of the USSR. The reasons for this were the aggressiveness of the nationalists, their efforts aimed at intimidating Russians, and the threat of civil war in the republic along ethnic lines.

Above all, however, the decrease in political activity of Russian-speakers was determined by the disappearance of the country which had been the common Motherland for them. The USSR, whose territorial integrity they supported, disappeared and they lost the reason for their common struggle. Despite Russia proclaiming itself as the successor to the Soviet Union, it failed to become that or even a common homeland for the former Soviet people. Despite their declarations, Moscow's rulers in practice abandoned all Russian-speakers and Russians outside Russia's borders. Russians, therefore, lost hope that Moscow would help. They were also more preoccupied with the economic problems of everyday life.

An increase in the political activeness of Russians and Russian-speakers was observed in early 1994, when the electoral campaign for the new parliament began. By then, the situation in the republic had changed significantly. In order to preclude a Russian backlash against the imminent language test, Prime Minister Andrei Sangheli postponed it to April 1994. In turn, President Mircea Snegur, aware of the low popularity of pro-Romanian political parties among much of the population, and being himself against the idea of unification with Romania, lent his support to the Agrarian–Democratic Party, whose programme affirmed the Moldovan language and the Moldovan nation as the bases for the existence of the independent Moldovan state. In order to win the votes of the minority population, at the beginning of the election campaign leaders of that party, together with the president, organised the 'Our Home is the Republic of Moldova' Congress. This proclaimed that all of Moldova's citizens have equal rights, regardless of their ethnicity, and that Moldova is a civic nation-state rather than an ethnic one.[43]

Minorities believed these long-anticipated announcements. In spite of nostalgia for the Soviet Union, given the unpredictable course of events in Russia they adopted the idea of independent Moldova as an alternative preferable to unification with Romania. But in the parliamentary elections of 27 February 1994 the majority of the Russian-speaking population, especially ethnic Russians, voted for candidates of the bloc formed by the 'Unitate–Yedinstvo' Movement for Equality (formerly the

International Movement) and for the Socialist Party (named the Socialist Bloc). This bloc received 22 per cent of the votes, while the Agrarian–Democratic Party, supported by the majority of Moldovans and by many Ukrainians and Bulgarians from the countryside, received 43 per cent. Two pro-Romanian parties surpassed the 4 per cent barrier and entered parliament, together accounting for 16 per cent of the votes.[44]

The main reason for the success of the candidates of the Socialist Bloc was their defence of human rights and, specifically, the rights of the ethnic minorities. The Bloc's pre-election list included people well known for their principled opposition to unification with Romania. Its programme included promises of closer integration of Moldova in the CIS, dual Moldovan–Russian citizenship, the status of a second state language for Russian, the abolition of language certification, and the preservation of socialist principles in education, culture, public health care and pensions.

The majority of the votes given to this bloc was in cities with a significant Russian-speaking population (see Table 11.2). Voting clearly took place along ethnic lines. Almost all of Gagauzia, which decided to participate in the elections virtually in the last days before the vote, gave its support to the bloc: 83.33 per cent in Comrat, 92.96 per cent in Vulcăneşti, 58.95 per cent in Basarabeasca, and 42.64 per cent in Ceadîr-Lunga. This list obtained many votes in the cities with a significant Ukrainian population: 65.79 per cent of all votes in Briceni, 65.49 per cent in Ocniţa, 47.62 per cent in Glodeni and 43.53 per cent in Donduşăni.[46] The bloc won 28 parliamentary seats and formed the Socialist Unity faction. The ethnic composition of the parliament included all main ethnic groups of the population, comprising 58 Moldovans, 17 Romanians, 13 Russians, 8 Ukrainians, 4 Bulgarians and 4 Gagauz.[47] Furthermore, the Socialist Unity faction was not merely an umbrella for

Table 11.2.   Support for the Socialist Bloc in the parliamentary elections of 1994 in the cities of Moldova.[45]

City	Percentage of Russian-speakers	Percentage of Votes for the Socialist Bloc
Chişinău	50.8	43.67
Bălţi	59.3	62.04
Cahul	50.8	61.75
Orhei	24.2	20.41
Soroca	37.7	32.32
Ungheni	31.9	31.84

minorities, for, along with 10 Russians, 5 Ukrainians, 1 Bulgarian and 2 Gagauz, its membership included 9 Moldovans.[48]

The Russian-speaking population demonstrated support for the independent state of Moldova during the referendum on the republic's future, called by President Snegur for 6 March 1994. With a turnout rate of 75 per cent, 95.4 per cent of voters expressed their wish to live in an independent Moldova.[49]

Some of the aspirations of the Russian population were fulfilled in the adoption of a new state nationality policy. Language certification was postponed for three years, its content was changed, and a smaller part of the population was required to pass it. Parliament ratified the agreement on the formation of the CIS and adopted a new Constitution of the independent Republic of Moldova, from which the notion of 'Romanian' was excluded. Steps to resolve the Dniester conflict were taken, and the question of Gagauz autonomy was solved by granting to Gagauzia a special autonomous status.

But other aspects of the policy on minorities remained controversial. Russian-speakers were disappointed with the Agrarian–Democratic Party because it did not raise the quota of representatives of the Russian population in state institutions. There were no Russians among the ministers, government officials or heads of local administration. In this way, Russians continued to be second-class citizens. In all state institutions and organisations concerned with education, culture and science, Moldovans formed an absolute majority both in leadership posts and at the level of ordinary employees. Non-Moldovans were not well-represented in big business, because this sector still depended on the state.[50] Moreover, the law on ethnic minorities in Moldova was not adopted, although several drafts had been debated. Therefore, the status of ethnic minorities in legislation and their legal rights remain unclear and insecure.

Not surprisingly, Russians continued to doubt the sincerity of the president and the Agrarians. After the parliamentary elections the political activeness of Russians fell, as is confirmed by the elections to the local state organs, when Russians – and citizens of other nationalities – did not come to the polling stations. For example, in Chişinău only 35 per cent of voters participated in the elections.[51] Pro-Romanian parties organised a student strike in the spring of 1995 that exacerbated tension in society, but Russian-speakers undertook no activity in response.

It seems likely that the political apathy of the Russian population will not continue. It demonstrated its potential for mobilisation at crucial moments, engaging in both constructive and defensive activity. After years of opposition to the idea of Moldovan independence it expressed loyalty to the new state and a readiness to participate in the process of transition. But Russian-speakers understood that the new minorities policy consisted more of declarations than of steps to engage them in state-building. They still feel threatened and marginalised in the Moldovan ethnic state not only because Russian-speakers have not yet learnt the Moldovan language but because social advancement in society depends in the first instance on ethnic identity. If the state treated them as equal citizens and provided opportunities for the realisation of their specific ethnic and political interests, Russians would use their skills to strengthen the independent Moldovan state. In other words, Russians' behaviour will depend on the level of democracy in Moldova. Russians have to reconcile themselves to the changes necessitated by the construction of an independent state in Moldova. But what could turn them into opposition again is the return to power of pro-Romanian political forces and their attempts to join Moldova to Romania. If on all other important questions the Russian population prefers to act within the legal framework, on the question of unification of Moldova with Romania Russians would employ other means as well. Therefore, inter-ethnic and civic stability in Moldova depends on the strengthening of democracy in an independent, democratic, multinational state and on preservation of existing borders.

Notes

1. Alexander J. Motyl (ed.), *Thinking Theoretically about Soviet Nationalities: History and Comparison in the Study of the USSR* (New York: Columbia University Press, 1992); Zvi Gitelman (ed.), *The Politics of Nationalities and the Erosion of the USSR* (Ann Arbor: University of Michigan, 1992); Alexander J. Motyl, *Will the Non-Russians Rebel?: State, Ethnicity and Stability in the USSR* (Ithaca, NY: Cornell University Press, 1987); Bohdan Nahaylo and Victor Swoboda, *Soviet Disunion* (New York: The Free Press, 1990).
2. Zvi Gitelman, *Development and Ethnicity in the Soviet Union: Post-Soviet Nations; Perspectives on the Demise of the USSR* (New York: Columbia University Press, 1992), p.238.
3. Charles King, 'Moldova and the New Bessarabian Question', *The World Today*, vol.49, no.7 (1993), pp.135–8.
4. Miron Rezun (ed.), *Nationalism and the Breakup of an Empire: Russia and its Periphery* (Westport, CT: Praeger, 1992); Ian Bremmer and Ray Taras (eds), *Nations and Politics in the Soviet Successor States* (Cambridge: Cambridge University Press, 1993); Michael Rywkin, *Moscow's Lost Empire* (Armonk, NY: M.E. Sharpe, 1994); Graham Smith (ed.), *The Nationalities Question in the Former Soviet Union*, 2nd edn (Cambridge: Cambridge University Press, 1995).
5. Hedrick Smith, *The New Russians* (New York: Random House, 1991); Anthony

Hyman, 'Russians Outside Russia', *The World Today*, vol.49, no.11 (1993), pp.205-8; Paul Kolstoe, *Russians in the Former Soviet Republics* (Bloomington, IN, and London: Indiana University Press, 1995).

6. Hyman, 'Russians Outside Russia', pp.205-6.
7. L.M. Drobiezhva, 'Russkie v novykh gosudarstvakh. Izmenenie sotsial'nykh rolei', in *Rossiya segodnya: trudnye poiski svobody* (Moscow, 1992); see also the articles in Vladimir Shlapentokh, Munir Sendich and Emil Payin (eds), *Russian Diaspora: Russian Minorities in the Former Soviet Republics* (Armonk, NY: M.E. Sharpe, 1994).
8. *Russkie v novom zarubezh'e. Srednyaya Aziya. Etnosotsiologicheskii ocherk* (Moscow, 1993), p.8.
9. Vladimir Shlapentokh and Munir Sendich, 'Preface', in Shlapentokh *et al.* (eds), *Russian Diaspora*, p.xix.
10. Neil Melvin, 'Russia and the Ethnopolitics of Kazakhstan', *The World Today*, vol.49, no.11 (1993), p.208.
11. Daria Fane, 'Moldova: Breaking Loose from Moscow', in Bremmer and Taras (eds), *Nations and Politics*, pp.121-56; Jeff Chinn and Steven D. Roper, 'Ethnic Mobilization and Reactive Nationalism: The Case of Moldova', *Nationalities Papers*, vol.23, no.2 (1995), pp.291-326.
12. Vladimir Solonar and Vladimir Bruter, 'Russians in Moldova', in Shlapentokh *et al.* (eds), *The New Russian Diaspora*, pp.72-90; A. Skvortsova, 'Russkie Moldovy: aspekty istorii i sovremennaya etnopoliticheskaya situatsiya', in *Russkie Moldovy: istoriya, yazyk, kul'tura* (Chişinău, 1994), pp.41-8.
13. V. Yefremov, 'Neformal'no o neformalakh', *Sovetskaya Moldaviya*, 28 July 1988.
14. *Itogi Vsesoyuznoi perepisi naseleniya 1989 goda po SSR Moldova*, t.1, kn.1, pp.92-5.
15. *Sovetskaya Moldaviya*, 9 December 1988. Dozens of citizens' and work collectives' letters were published in the newspapers *Sovetskaya Moldaviya* and *Vechernii Kishinev* during the year 1989.
16. V. Kalin, '"SOS" moldavskomu yazyku i kul'ture', *Sovetskaya Moldaviya*, 2 December 1988.
17. See William Crowther, 'The Politics of Mobilization: Nationalism and Reform in Soviet Moldavia', *Russian Review*, vol.50, no.2 (1991), pp.183-202.
18. Three-quarters of the voters turned out to vote, and 91 per cent of them supported the independent Moldovan state (*Vechernii Kishinev*, 10 March 1994).
19. *Sovetskaya Moldaviya*, 25 July 1988.
20. Ibid., 28 April 1989.
21. Chinn and Roper, 'Ethnic Mobilization and Reactive Nationalism', p.306.
22. *Istoricul 1989* (Chişinău, 1992), p.133; *Sovetskaya Moldaviya*, 25 April 1989.
23. *Rybnitskii metallurg*, 30 June 1989.
24. *Yedinstvo*, 11 October 1989.
25. Solonar and Bruter, 'Russians in Moldova', p.83.
26. A. Dashkevich, 'Eks-Prem'er: mysli vdogonku', *Sovetskaya Moldova*, 28 May 1991.
27. *Moldova Suverană*, 31 May 1992.
28. Ibid., 12 June 1992; *Sovetskaya Moldaviya*, 4 September 1990 and 6 June 1991.
29. *Sovetskaya Moldaviya*, 20 March and 14 August 1990; *Yedinstvo*, 15 July 1990; *Moldova Suverană*, 11 January 1991; *Kishinevskie novosti*, 14 June 1991.
30. *Sovetskaya Moldaviya*, 17 and 23 June 1990; *Sovetska Moldova*, 8 May, 23 July and 9 August 1991; *Yedinstvo*, 18 January 1991.
31. *Kishinevskie novosti*, 24 April, 3 and 31 July, 7 August and 4 September 1992, 17 April and 29 May 1993.

32. *Sovetskaya Moldaviya*, 24 March and 24 May 1990; *Dialog*, 3 April and 23 November 1990; *Yedinstvo*, 8 March 1991; *Sovetskaya Moldova*, 4 June 1991.
33. *Yedinstvo*, 8 and 31 March 1991.
34. Ibid., 31 March 1991.
35. Solonar and Bruter, 'Russians in Moldova', pp.79–80.
36. Chinn and Roper, 'Ethnic Mobilization and Reactive Nationalism', p.317.
37. *Moldova Suverană*, 11 September 1991.
38. *Kishinevskie novosti*, 4 December 1993.
39. T. Danii and Z. Gontsa, 'Russkie v Moldove', *Golos naroda*, 20 October 1992.
40. *Republica Moldova in cifre* (Chişinău: Departamentul Statisticei al Republicei Moldova, 1995), p.18.
41. *Kishinevskie novosti*, 23 April 1994.
42. In an address on the republican radio on 29 November 1991, the prime minister of Moldova, Valerii Muravskii, openly said that the population of the 'Dniester republic' should seriously consider participation in the referendum on that republic's independence, because expression of a wish to become independent of Moldova would provoke violence on the part of the titular population towards Russians and Ukrainians in the right bank territory.
43. *Zemlya i lyudi*, 12 February 1994.
44. *Vechernii Kishinev*, 17 March 1994.
45. *Electorala – 94. Ediţie dedicată* (Chişinău, 1994): *Dicţionar statistic al Republicei Moldova* (Chişinău: Departamentul Statisticei al Republicei Moldova, 1994).
46. *Electorala – 94.*
47. *Republica Moldova in cifre*, p.7.
48. I am grateful for these data to Valerii Opinka of the Centre for Information on Social Sciences, Academy of Sciences of Moldova.
49. *Nezavisimaya Moldova*, 12 March 1994.
50. *Russkoe slovo*, October 1994.
51. *Pamînt şi Oameni*, 6 May 1995.

12 National Development and Politics in the Finno-Ugric Republics of Russia

Yury P. Shabaev and I.L. Zherebtcov

Ethno-political problems have become an object of close attention of Russian social scientists. However, both the question of ethno-politics and the real opportunities for objective analysis of its occurrences and processes, have only recently become incorporated into the Russian scientific tradition. As a matter of fact, the definition of this science is still under discussion, but it is clear that 'ethno-politics has a border character because it occupies a sphere of interaction of ethnos with politics.'[1]

The Russian tradition of studying the political life of ethnic groups and communities, including the Finno-Ugric, is extremely scanty and a lot of what was published in social science and popular publications was highly disputable. Very often the greatest shortcoming in those publications was an absence of systematic analysis, an acceptance of political myths or political biases, and an emotional approach to the subject.

However, many foreign scholars often hold naive views concerning the development of the Finno-Ugric nations. For instance, some of them claimed that the development of literary languages of these nations was based on a linguistic construction that was a result of premeditated politics, 'planned by the same forces that wanted to exterminate all small nations and create a "Soviet person"'.[2] Or they charged that one of the dialects was selected to form a national language. We can also find that kind of reasoning about demographic processes and changes in the cultural appearance of the nations. Attempts to find malevolent intentions and to blame so-called 'Leninist nationality politics' are not only unjustified, but also cannot refute criticism for a simple reason. That is that although the first Bolshevik government was a government of intellectuals, the Bolshevik revolution brought the least socially advanced and educated strata of society to power and to rule over the country. These people were incapable of making long-term political projections and to foresee the results of actions taken by them.

As for theoretical paradigms found in nationality politics at that time, they were directed against the Russian nation and great power chauvinism. Some well-known statements of Lenin actually deny the equal value of national cultures and demand that closer attention be paid to the small nations. Though it is not fashionable to quote Lenin nowadays, we cite a passage from the draft programme of the RCP(b): 'It is necessary to increase help to the backward and weak nations by assisting independent organisations and educating workers and peasants ..., also by promoting the development of language and literature of oppressed and unequal nations.'[3]

Disturbing consequences for the fate of national cultures did result to some degree, but it relates primarily to the fact that social development was subordinated to ideology. Ideology became an insurmountable barrier for the free and independent development of the peoples of Russia.

We agree with the view of the distinguished American linguist Ron Wixman who considers that Soviet nationality policy was generally quite rational, logical, consistent over time, and even-handed for all nationalities because it was subordinated to the main goals and interests of the regime and was correlated with the functions of communist ideology and politics.[4]

Ideological motifs of the Soviet regime were the superiority of proletarian culture over bourgeois culture (often the traditional culture of peoples was considered to be bourgeois culture), extolling proletarian internationalism over bourgeois nationalism and, in the later Soviet period, the proclamation of a 'new historical community of people – the Soviet people', above any and all ethnic communities. These ideas defined all public life and were accepted by public opinion. Owing to this last fact, they did not encounter serious opposition, especially in the former Finno-Ugric autonomic republics. Current ideologues of national movements – those who attack the 'imperial' centre, accuse it of 'genocide' against their peoples, and assert the right of national self-determination – were not dissidents but quite loyal citizens in the Soviet period and did not oppose central power. What is more, many actions that produced ethnic erosion were carried out by local officials and representatives of the titular nationalities. This indicates that Soviet cultural values were more important for society than national values were.

Related to this, another belief professed by the modern ideologues of national movements, and also by a number of Western social scientists, is that Russian nationalism was an essential feature of Soviet nationality policy in general or, at least of some of its phases. The British political scientist Peter Duncan declared: 'By the end of Brezhnev's rule Russian nationalism had become an important component of the dominant ideology. It threatens awakenings of dissatisfaction of national minorities.'[5] Not only during the Brezhnev era, but also during and after *perestroika* when Russians found themselves in a vulnerable situation, especially those living in the other republics of the former Soviet Union, and in spite of numerous displays of russophobia and the efforts of Russian national-patriots, Russian nationalism has not been internalised by the majority of society. According to data compiled by the 'Public Opinion' research centre, only 23 per cent of Russians agree to some extent with the opinion that people of non-Russian nationality living in the Russian Federation are responsible for all the problems in Russia, while 67 per cent of Russians reject it in mild or categorical form.[6]

This lengthy introduction to the subject of our study is necessary because we must call attention to the historical and social background to the current situation of the Finno-Ugric peoples and the efforts to solve national problems through political reform. At the same time, we need to recognise the situation in which ethnic groups find themselves. As examples we mainly use data on two nations: Komi and Komi-Permiak. But the national problems of all eastern Finno-Ugric peoples are similar and we can learn about the conditions they all face.

According to census data from 1989, the total population of the Finno-Ugric nations of Russia is approximately 3.3 million. It is slightly more than 2 per cent of the population of the country, and this proportion remained unchanged for many decades although the rate of growth of individual nations varied. From 1897 to 1989 the population of Komi grew by 224.3 per cent, Mari – 78.9 per cent, Udmurt – 56.4 per cent, Komi-Permiaks – 45.2 per cent. As for Karelians and Mordva, their population is steadily following. Having their own national-state structure, the Volga-Permiak people have fluctuated from 23 per cent to 43 per cent of their state's total population. Karelians form just 10 per cent of the population of Karelia. Only Komi-Permiaks make up as much as 60 per cent of their district's population. The present ethnic situation of the eastern Finnish nations illustrates how over the last generation or two major changes have taken place. Some of these people became national minorities. For instance, between 1926 and 1989 the proportion of Komi fell from 92 per cent to 23 per cent; between 1934 and 1989 the Mordva were reduced from 38 per cent to 32.5 per cent, the Udmurt from 78.5 per cent in 1926 to 30.9 per cent in 1989, and the Mari from 80 per cent in 1926 to 43 per cent in 1989. During that time an extremely rural ethos was rapidly transformed into an urban one. For example, in 1926 only 3 per cent of Komi lived in cities but in 1989 half of Komi was town-dwellers. Besides the fact that urban culture is alien to predominantly rural ethnic communities, when they migrate to towns they usually make up a minority of the population (Komi represent 15 per cent of the urban population of the Komi Republic). In towns they entered into numerous contacts with other ethnic groups and adopted new patterns of culture and consumption, thereby exposing themselves to assimilative pressures. One indication of close contacts is exogeneous marriages. Approximately one-third of marriages entered into by the Komi are now inter-ethnic, while about half of the urban Komi marry non-Komis. As for the Mari, 15 per cent of their marriages are with spouses belonging to other nationalities; in the cities the rate is 22 per cent.[7] Inter-ethnic marriages of Udmurts were 10 per cent in 1980 in rural areas and 48 per cent in cities.[8] A significant role in the assimilative process is played by the fact that a considerable part of Finno-Ugric peoples live outside their republics: for the Komi – 13 per cent, Udmurts – 33 per cent, Mari – 52 per cent, Mordva – a substantial majority, Komi-Permiaks – 38 per cent.

Given the increase in inter-ethnic contacts as well as the ideological desideratum about the formation of a new historic community of people (the 'Soviet people'), the influence and significance of the Russian language in the lives of all Finno-Ugric nations has inevitably grown. And indeed, the processes taking place in language use of the Finno-Ugric peoples of Russia show a comparably high level of language assimilation. According to the 1989 census data, 17.8 per cent of Mari identified Russian as their native language. For Komi-Permiak people this indicator came to 28.7 per cent, for Komi – 28.9 per cent, Udmurts – 29.0 per cent, Mordva – 30.9 per cent, Khants – 38.5 per cent and Karelians – 51.2 per cent.

We need to introduce the caveat that census data do not characterise the linguistic situation very accurately. Surveys show that the level of linguistic assimilation of the Finno-Ugric peoples of Russia is significantly greater than the census suggests. These surveys studied linguistic orientations and linguistic skills. The results confirmed that only a small proportion of urban Komi, Komi-Permiaks, Udmurts, Karelians and Mari spoke their native language outside their families; in social life preference was clearly given to Russian. To examine this issue more closely, let us look at the linguistic situation in Komi, in terms of survey results from 1988 and 1992.

Among urban Komi-Permiaks 62.9 per cent speak their native language fluently; among their rural counterparts the figure is 90.1 per cent. As for the Russian language, 94.3 per cent of townspeople of Komi-Permiak nationality and 81.7 per cent of rural people speak this language fluently. Compare these data with those for the Komi Republic: among urban Komi 68.3 per cent speak the native language fluently (a higher proportion, therefore, than Komi-Permiak), and among rural people the figure is 88.7 per cent. What is more, 97 per cent of people from cities and 87.8 per cent of people from rural areas have a complete command of Russian.

Undoubtedly, the most important indicator of linguistic preferences is speaking a language within the family. Among Komi-Permiaks from cities only 11.4 per cent speak only their native language at home; 16.2 per cent mainly speak Komi-Permiak. The rest speak mainly or only Russian. The picture is very different among rural Komi-Permiaks: 58.1 per cent speak exclusively Komi-Permiaks at home, and 8.0 per cent speak mainly this language. Others use either mainly Russian, as in the cities, or only Russian for talking with their families.

We have comparable data for Komi because we used a single method and instrument for the investigation. What does the picture of the Komi-Permiaks' neighbour look like? Among Komi from cities 8.5 per cent speak only Komi at home and 17.0 per cent more use mainly Komi. Others prefer to use the Russian language. In the rural areas fewer Komi (40.2 per cent) than Komi-Permiaks use only Komi at home; 20.3 per cent speak mainly Komi, while the others use Russian exclusively or primarily. We see that the degree of linguistic assimilation of Komi and Komi-Permiaks is approximately the same, but we need to recall that the ethnic conditions on the territory of the Komi-Permiaks is more favourable than the one on the territory of the Komi. As for reading and writing, only one-half of Komi and Komi-Permiaks, whether in cities or rural areas, have enough knowledge to read literature in their native language without difficulty, or to use it in personal and business correspondence. Udmurts, Mari, Mordva, Karelians are in about the same situation. When it comes to preferences, the majority of Komi-Permiaks prefers to use Russian to read or write. Research into the linguistic orientations of Komi showed the same picture. Udmurts, Mari, Mordva and Karelians display a similar preference for written Russian.

During the 1990s serious efforts have been undertaken to raise the prestige and status of titular nationalities in the former Finno-Ugric republics of Russia. Together with greater use of the languages in the mass media and increasing their role in the education system, their legal status has changed. In 1992 in Komi a law entitled 'State languages of the Komi Republic' was passed. According to this law Komi and Russian are now the official languages on the territory of the republic. In 1994 a programme to implement this law, entitled 'Preservation and Development of the Komi Language', was adopted. Similar laws were enacted in Udmurtia and Mari. Regulations on the Komi-Permiak language state that it, too, may be used in official business.

The Russian Federation's law on languages states that every nation has 'linguistic sovereignty'. This is true at present. But if we look at history, we find that in February 1927 in Komi-Permiak district a regulation on the introduction of the Komi language was passed. The first paragraph of the regulation asserted: 'Komi and Russian languages are considered to be official within the Komi-Permiak district.' The second paragraph declared: 'Komi and Russian language have equal rights in all meetings, conferences and congresses.' Similar regulations were in force in the autonomous district of Komi and in a number of other national-territorial units.

The present situation is different and linguistic development is taking place under different ethnic conditions. For this reason the adoption of laws of languages in the republics does not really change linguistic orientations. A survey we conducted in November and December 1993 in Komi, as part of a Russian–American project on the 'Election situation in Russia', showed, for instance, that the majority of the population does not consider that all people living in autonomous administrative units have to know the language of the titular nation. The majority also opposed the introduction of this language in school (even among Komi fewer than half of our respondents spoke in favour of this). Social reality brings stronger pressure upon people's orientation than a series of laws and programmes. Thus practical everyday work is more important than declarations in changing the linguistic situation .

Present-day ethno-linguistic conditions reflect the processes of ethnic erosion taking place among Finno-Ugric peoples. Many domestic ethnologists correctly note that the most important factor promoting ethnic development of any nation is a condition of ethnic (or national) self-awareness. However, research results show that many Finno-Ugric nations have undergone profound changes in the sphere of ethnic self-awareness. For example, national loyalty of ethnic groups living in towns has become seriously weaker. No doubt, these observations are not a revelation, and the national intelligentsia concerned with processes of ethnic erosion in all Finno-Ugric national formations is looking for solutions to this predicament.

This circumstance, when combined with the process of democratisation, led to the emergence (sometimes re-emergence) of modern national cultural and national movements among the Finno-Ugric nations. Their influence and scope varies among the different peoples. The Komi national movement is the most influential among them. In between congresses of the Komi people, the political expression of its ideas is the 'Committee for the Revival of the Komi People'. The *Doryam as'nymos* ('Defend Ourselves') party takes extreme positions. In turn, Komi-Permiaks have the *Yuger* society which is practically completely subordinated to the Komi National Movement. The Mari union *Mari Ushem* is active in Mari El. In Udmurtia there is a Society of Udmurtian Culture, in Mordva there is Mastrova, which has splintered, and in Karelia the 'Union of Karelian People' is the main national movement.

Let us focus on the ideology of these movements, setting aside the question of influence of these societies and movements on the general population. Of primary significance is that 'Idealisation and politisation of ethnic groups is going on at a time of social tension, competition and hostility, when ethnic leaders convince bearers of ethnic cultures to view their destiny in ethnic rather than in personal or class categories, and persuade them that without their ethnic communal solidarity their distinctive values and customs will be under threat and group survival will be exposed to danger.'[9]

It is important to note that the basic principles of ideology in Finno-Ugric national movements were elaborated not inside them but brought in from without. Some principles were borrowed from the General Programme of the People's Front of Estonia. They include the need to 'give all peoples the right of self-determination and to give real sovereignty to national republics on their historic territory. A guarantee of the rights of a native nation is a constitutional acceptance of its language as official, citizenship of the republic legal and national symbols as legitimate.'[10] Incidentally, not only general principles but also specific details on, for example, reforming legislative power bodies, were borrowed by Finno-Ugric movements.

National movements in each republic evolved under different conditions and faced different difficulties, but it is important to observe that these movements began to integrate quickly. A conference of plenipotentiaries of national forums (congresses), and of social-political and national–cultural movements took place in February 1992 in Syktyvkar.

It was convened by the embryonic Committee for the Revival of the Komi People. The conference set up an Association of Finno-Ugric Nations, and stated that the purpose of the association was 'the consolidation of efforts and co-ordination of the actions of the Finno-Ugric nations struggling for survival, and the creation of favourable conditions for the formation of a united Finno-Ugric social-economical, cultural area.'[11] Then, in May, the first congress of Finno-Ugric peoples of Russia was held in Izhevsk. It was declared at this congress that 'The majority of the peoples of the Russian Federation are not recognised by the authorities and do not have the opportunity to express and realise their aspirations and rights.'[12] In December the World Congress of Finno-Ugric nations took place in Syktyvkar. Delegations from Estonia, Hungary, Finland, all Finno-Ugric republics of Russia and a number of districts attended this congress. It adopted a 'Declaration of general principles, purposes and tasks for co-operation of the Finno-Ugric peoples of the world' and it made an 'Appeal to the Parliaments and Governments of the Russian Federation and Finno-Ugric republics included in it'. It also agreed upon 'Regulations of a Consulting Committee of Finno-Ugric peoples'. This Consulting Committee is a co-ordinating body of the World Congress with headquarters in Helsinki. It issues an 'Information bulletin' on a regular basis.

These leaders of the Finno-Ugric movement have co-ordinated their political positions and drafted enabling documents. Securing the status of the languages, reforming the political structures, promoting ethnic self-determination, and regulating citizenship in the republics are the main political objectives. Not all Finno-Ugric republics agree on the methods to be used, however.

Let us discuss political ideas since we have already illuminated the situation with regard to the languages. The first idea concerns ethnic self-determination. Understanding self-determination as requiring national statehood is an example of the politicisation of ethnic groups. First, it is dangerous to elevate the political interest of one national community at the expense of others in the multinational Finno-Ugric republics. '"National state" itself is just an illusion in the modern world', observed political scientist Gudmundar Alfredson.[13] What is more, a number of Western social scientists consider that those whose aim is self-determination in the modern world undermine democratic development in new independent states and imperil citizens' rights.[14]

The effort to reform representative bodies is directly related to the idea of self-determination. During the congress in Izhevsk, all national delegations agreed that the parliaments of the Finno-Ugric republics should consist of two houses, one of which would consist only of persons from the titular nation of the republic (or district). The rationale for this approach was that persons of 'native' nationality would not be represented sufficiently in the parliaments to provide effective defence of their interests. Besides, an admired model was the so-called Saamsky parliaments in Sweden, Finland and Norway.[15] However, Russian practice shows that representatives of titular nationalities included in parliament do not play a decisive role (examples are Tatarstan and Yakutia). In turn, Saamsky parliaments cannot serve as a model because they were created according to 'Saamsky' specifics. Constituting a representative body according to nationality is a rejection of the principle of direct, equal and secret elections. To be sure, we agree with Valery Tishkov's argument that 'the normal democratic principle of one person, one vote is not a universal one for complex societies. It provides only a basis for democracy and is oriented first of all towards individual civil rights.This principle must be complemented by a system of limits, balances and stimulii which ensure the collective rights and interests of culturally differentcommunities.'[16] However, a mistake of these national movements was that they did not look for these 'limits, balances and stimuli', but began to demand extraordinary representations in the parliaments.

The idea of republic citizenship is logically related to the idea of reforming parliaments. Moreover, it originates in the declarations of state sovereignty that were adopted in practically all republics of Russia. These declarations had a political objective: to apply pressure on the federal centre with the purpose of expanding the powers of authorities and territories. It is important to emphasise that the proclamations of sovereignty and adoption of laws on republican citizenship (and the appearance of presidential posts in the republics) were means of distancing themselves from the centre and from Russia. In a country with 82 per cent ethnic Russians who serve as a reference group for other national communities and often dominate life in the republics, the idea of republican citizenship was not realistic. Let us consider data on the identification of respondents found in our December 1993 survey and part of the Russian–American project on the election situation in Russia. The response to the question 'of which state do you consider yourself a representative?' was as follows: only 9.6 per cent in Komi Republic said they considered themselves to be representatives only of their republic (21.6 per cent of Komi, 5.1 per cent of Russians, 3.8 per cent of representatives of other nationalities). The majority considered themselves to be both Russian and representative of the given republic. A minority considered themselves to be more Russians or only Russians.

Approximately the same results were obtained in the other republics. Applying the laws of republic citizenship would in practice mean depriving a part of the population of its civic rights because they include residency and other limitations. In such republics as Komi it could affect the interests of wide strata of the population because the north of the republic was traditionally developed by migrants from other regions of the country and temporary residents.

National conflicts also emerge when there is an accumulation of dividing social markers (native – non-native, citizen – non-citizen, speak the ethnic language – do not speak it, and so on). Under conditions of developing political culture and civil society, the creation of 'internal borders' is simply destructive.

We should also not overestimate the role and influence of the national movements. In Komi Republic less than one-third of the population is familiar with the activities of the Komi movement (among Komi people alone a little more than one-third), in Mordva it is about 40 per cent, and similar proportions apply to the other republics. When it comes to assessing the actions of these movements, opinions differ.

Finally, we agree with the many Western social scientists who assert that nationalism cannot be an ideology because it does not have features of universal significance. Nevertheless there is ethnic mobilisation in the Finno-Ugric republics and it does affect the political process.

To be sure, there are some who oppose the idea that every nation should be free to develop its culture and its social institutions. They add to the fear in society that political extremes may destabilise the nation-building process and lead to the appearance of ethnic conflicts. To avoid these conflicts and optimise relations between ethnic communities, it is critical to establish special procedures for helping co-ordinate the interests of national communities, to stand up for their rights, and to avoid the abuse of power directed at one of them. The American specialist on ethnic conflict, William Yuri, believes that special discussion groups would be helpful in this regard.[17]

Notes

1. G.I. Marchenko, 'Etnopolitika kak nauka', *Vestnik Moskovskogo universiteta*, seriya 12, Sotsial'no-politicheskie issledovaniya, 1994, no.3, p.63.
2. S. Saarinen, 'Problemy formirovaniya i razvitiya finno-ugorskikh literaturnykh yazykov', *Komi-Permyaki i finno-ugorskii mir* (Syktyvkar, 1995), p.75.
3. V.I. Lenin, 'Proyekt Programmy RKP', *Polnoe sobranie sochinenii*, vol.38, p.95.
4. Ronald Wixman, 'Applied Soviet Nationality Policy: A Suggested Rationale', *Passé* –

Turco-Tatar, Présent Soviétique (Paris, 1986), pp.449–68.
5. Peter S. Duncan, 'Ideology and the National Question', in Stephen White and Alex Pravda (eds), *Ideology and Soviet Politics* (Basingstoke: Macmillan, 1988), p.203.
6. *Izvestiya*, 5 July 1995.
7. K. Sanukov, *Mariitsy: proshloe, nastoyashchee, budushchee* (Ioshkar-Ola, 1992), p.14.
8. *Udmurty: istoriko-etnograficheskie ocherki* (Izhevsk, 1993), p.366.
9. Anthony D. Smith, 'Introduction: The Formation of Nationalist Movements', in Anthony D. Smith (ed.), *Nationalist Movements* (London: Macmillan, 1976), p.29.
10. O. Ottenseon (ed.), *Narodnyi kongress: sbornik materialov kongressa fronta* (Tallinn, 1989), p.176.
11. 'Deklaratsiya uchreditelei konferentsii polnomochnykh predstavitelei finno-ugorskikh narodov', *Parma*, 1992, no.1, pp.4–5.
12. *Dokumenty prinyatiya Vserossiiskim s"ezdom finno-ugorskikh narodov* (Izhevsk, 1992), p.2.
13. G. Alfredson, 'Prava menshinstv: ravenstvo i nediskriminatsiya', *Leningradskaya konferentsiya po pravam menshinstv. Doklady i soobshcheniya* (Leningrad, 1991), p.24.
14. A. Utkin, 'Natsionalizm i budushchee mirovogo soobshchestva', *Svobodnaya mysl'*, 1993, no.3, p.83.
15. E. Helander, 'A Saami Strategy for Language Preservation', *Readings in Saami History, Culture and Language*, vol.II (Umeå, 1991), p.145.
16. V. Tishkov, 'Mezhnatsional'nye otnosheniya v Rossiiskoi Federatsii. Doklad na zasedanii Prezidiuma Rossiiskoi Akademii Nauk' (Moscow, 1993), p.40.
17. V. Yuri, 'Ethnicheskie konflikty: chto mozhno sdelat'', *Natsional'naya politika v Rossiiskoi Federatsii* (Moscow, 1993), p.78.

13 Gypsy Nomads in Bulgaria: Traditions and the Contemporary Dimension

Vesselin Popov

One of the primary ethno-cultural characteristics of a given community is its way of life; with the Gypsies, this aspect is closely connected to their professional specialisation. The situation among Gypsies is very specific indeed, as it cannot be established with certainty whether their initial 'traditional' way of life was settled or wandering. The question whether their ancestors in ancient India were sedentary or not, whether the nomadic way of life was adopted during the long journey to Europe or prevailed since the very beginning, still remains open. If the answer is equivocal, so are many other assumptions concerning the origin of Gypsies. Their very origin is linked to rather heterogeneous groups and communities back in ancient India who, in addition, left the country by different routes and in different periods. It is quite probable, therefore, that the dichotomy 'settled–wandering' had already existed at the time of departure, that is, that some parts of the Gypsy community were traditionally bound to one kind of existence while others stuck to the other.

This distinction was observed at the time of the arrival of the Gypsies in the Balkans and in Europe, and it persists until today. Even in countries where a process of forced, mandatory sedentarisation took place in the 1950s and 1960s (mainly in Eastern Europe), the former nomads preserved a marked taste for a life on the move; by contrast, sedentary Gypsies, even when constrained by different circumstances to change their habitat and move into new territories (for example, the migrations from former Yugoslavia into Italy), carry with them a propensity for permanent settlement. Of course, the line distinguishing 'sedentary from wandering' is very fluid and precarious and may often change (for *not occupation but State policy*

example, nomads may settle and adopt the main characteristics of sedentary Gypsies). But it still is identifiable. On the other hand, the congruence between way of life and professional specialisation (traditional occupations) is not absolute, even if certain crafts and occupations definitely entail a nomadic or semi-nomadic way of life. Generally it is difficult to decide which occupations are pertinent to the wanderers and to the sedentary Gypsies respectively, and it is certainly normal that a craft may be practised by the two groups simultaneously.

These preliminary observations can help us understand the ostensibly paradoxical situation that in Bulgaria the most widespread nomadic tradition is carried on by the community which was the latest to arrive in Bulgarian lands, conventionally called by the generic name *Kardarashi – Lovari* (*Zlatara, Grastara, Niculeshi, Dodolania, Zhapleshti, Tasmanari* and other sub-groups), *Layashi* and *Niamtsuri* (*Bakardjii*, 'Avstriiski' [Austrian], 'Nemski' [German], 'Ungarski' [Hungarian] Gypsies and other appellations).[1] Separate groups of this community arrived one after the other sometime after the 'Great Kelderara invasion'. Greater numbers came even later: the last big wave followed the change of the Bulgarian-Romanian frontier in 1940, after the restitution of Dobrudja to Bulgaria. The movements of these communities were not confined to the borders of a state, until 1944, though even after that date they managed to maintain their contacts with relations abroad, mainly in Romania and Yugoslavia. Tihomir Dzordjevich mentions groups of *Layneshchi* who came every year from Bulgaria to Eastern Serbia at the beginning of the century.[2] In the period between the two world wars, different sub-groups of the *Lovari*, such as *Grastara, Zlatara* and *Tasmanari*, wandered through Thracia, Macedonia and especially northeastern Bulgaria and Dobrudja (by this time belonging to Romania) with no regard for existing state borders. These cross-boundary migrations were related to one of the group's stable occupations, horse-dealing, which frequently involved the smuggling of stolen horses across borders.

Professional specialisation among the so-called *Kardarashi* is quite conditional and one traditional occupation is often supplemented by others during the wandering. For example, besides the repair and tinning of copper utensils, the *Layashi* men could make and sell pottery (jugs, whistles, and so on); in turn, some of the *Lovari* men sometimes made combs (hence the name *Grebenari*). The women of this community were mainly engaged in fortune-telling (palm-reading) and different kinds of sorcery (mainly the breaking of spells) and offering remedies, but often they combined them with the selling of medicinal plants, fuller's earth, and the like. In some instances, they all took up seasonal or temporary labour such as construction work, harvesting and so on. They wandered in groups of three to six families, called *katun*, in open horse-drawn carriages, and they used simple tents for camping. In winter, they usually gathered in larger groups in settlements near some village where they had already established contacts with the local population. But they often changed their winter settlement places and their wandering territory as a whole.

The active nomadic season is usually clearly defined: it used to be considered that the *katun* should be out for *Zagovezni* (the beginning of Passover Lent) and be back for *Nikulden* (the Day of St. Nicholas), that is, December 6. The general rule was that they should not stay at the same place for more than a month (in contrast to the rule recorded on the isle of Crete in the fourteenth century and the similar trend existing among the Gadolia *lohara* in India nowadays). Contacts between members of the group were established and maintained chiefly when they encountered each other during wanderings and in the winter settlements, though some of the sub-groups held traditional annual meetings (such as the *Layashi*, who gathered in the region between Botevgrad, Mezdra and Cherven briag every August). Because of the great expanse of territory covered and the lack of a fixed regular gathering for the exchange of matrimonial partners, the system of kinship division among them was especially strongly developed and was often the most certain trait in group identification during encounters between wandering communities.

The nomad traditions of the *Kardarashi* were not lost after the forcible sedentarisation of the 1950s. The *Layashi* and *Niamtsuri* men continued to practise their traditional crafts (making, repairing and tinning copper utensils) in one form or another. They continued to move, too, but over shorter distances and with the family only. In the 1990s, after the restrictions imposed by the communist authorities were lifted, these traditions were resuscitated and expanded and some of the groups returned to their semi-nomadic way of life (seasonal, with permanent domicile). The modifications in the nomadic tradition among the *Lovari* are stronger. In many instances, they adopted new forms of seasonal activities after sedentarisation. For example, a few families worked together in construction or on contract. At the same time, they initiated specific, family wandering of women (the mother-in-law together with one or two of the daughters-in-law going for a few days to the big cities as fortune-tellers or pickpockets). Recently, a tendency has been observed towards an expansion of this modified form of wandering, especially in Greece, Italy and Germany.

The wandering of the *Ursari* (Romanian-speaking bear and monkey trainers) has long been cross-national and of a very specific kind. After their penetration into Bulgarian lands, probably in the second half of the nineteenth century, they settled in a few localities, the most famous among them being the neighbourhood of Galats near Karnobat, where they built permanent houses –'huts covered with straw', according to K. Irechek.[3] They used to live there in the slack season, from Dimitrovden (the day of St. Demetrius, 26 October until the beginning of March and prepared their 'repertory' – the necessary animals, bears and monkeys and paraphernalia. Besides the *Mechkari* and *Maymunari* (bear and monkey trainers), there were in the past *Kuklichari* (puppeteers), probably a specialised sub-group. They wandered in small groups of three or four families (usually father and son or husband and wife) and travelled, in Bulgaria, in small tented wagons. At the same time, travel abroad over greater distances aboard trains and ships was also widely practised. At the end of the nineteenth and the beginning of the twentieth centuries, *Ursari* from Bulgaria toured the Middle East, Northern Africa and all of Europe; they frequently visited Moscow and St. Petersburg, and more than once their names appeared in port documents all over the world, in places such as Liverpool and New York.[4] The scope of their travels is well illustrated by the following case described by Dr Todor Neichev: 'Being a student in France, one day in 1891 in the city of Lyon, I was taking a walk with friends, both Bulgarian and Frenchmen, alongside the river Saone when we saw a multitude of people flocking and watching something with great curiosity. We got nearer and what do you think we saw? We saw a group of Galatenski Gypsies (that is, from the neighbourhood of 'Galats') who led two big bears and carried on their shoulders a playful monkey. When I discovered that they were from my part of the world, I addressed them and they told me proudly that they had toured all of Russia, Germany and France and now were heading for Italy, and afterwards they were returning home across Austro-Hungary and Serbia with purses stuffed with gold.'[5]

The scope of *Ursari* wanderings was scaled down in the course of time, especially markedly after the Second World War. However, they never broke definitely with their traditional occupation, modified as it has been in the new conditions. It is interesting to note that they have preserved their penchant for working with animals and have often been employed as seasonal or permanent workers on animal farms. Performing with bears and monkeys has been transferred to the elderly members of the family. The wanderings usually began in spring. Opening day for those who lived in Thracia was Easter day in the 'Catholic villages' of the Plovdiv district (the town of Rakovski), where their traditional annual gathering took place and where their movements were co-ordinated. Similar spring meetings were convened in other places also; for example, those living in northeastern Bulgaria met in Russe. The wandering groups are small, consisting of family members. Lately, this traditional occupation has, if anything, grown as an alternative to unemployment, and younger participants appear side by side with elderly ones. Most often we can see a change in the way of moving – by train to the big cities and resorts (mostly on the Black Sea coast). Temporary camp-sites with bears and monkeys are built close to rail stations.

The revival of the wandering way of life in present-day conditions is not uncommon among other Gypsy groups, too. This trend is most strongly manifested among the 'Thracian' *Kalaidjii*, whose semi-nomadic (seasonal) way of life, bound to a certain region, is typical of Bulgarian conditions and occurs among other Gypsy groups. They are characterised by a commitment to a certain territory or locality, such as the place of their winter settlements in the past, and of their permanent residence at present, and by regular annual gatherings of the entire group preceded and followed by periodic meetings of the different sub-divisions. These gatherings were held on a fixed date: in the past they convened during the visits to the monastery of Bachkovo on the day of the Assumption of the Virgin Mary in August. It is interesting to note that the *Kelderara* in Romania have their annual meeting in the monastery of Bistriţa on 8 September, the birthday of the Virgin Mary. These meetings were usually held near certain villages of the Plovdiv and Chirpan regions (Belozem being mentioned as 'capital'), where big tents were put up and the month of weddings was inaugurated. These annual gatherings were modified after the mandatory sedentarisation of the 1950s: the annual meeting split in two, the first held in Stara Zagora on Todorovden (the day of St. Theodore), the first Saturday of Lent, the second in Nova Zagora, on Vrabnica (Palm Sunday, the last Sunday before Easter). In addition, regular regional meetings were held – each Monday at the Filipovo station in Plovdiv, each Thursday in the market in Yambol, each Saturday at the bus station in Stara Zagora, and so on. The young girls who were to be married were presented at these gatherings (for this reason called 'brides' fairs' by the surrounding population) and the contacts with the other members of the group were reinforced. Newly-wed couples who had married during the year were also introduced at this general meeting: in other words, the marriages were given practical legitimacy.

The present-day wanderings of these groups are reminiscent of earlier descriptions: they travel by horse-drawn open carriages and sleep in tents. Their preferred routes ramble through the countryside, where they can pick up orders to make and repair copper utensils, and especially through mountainous regions. This way of life at present does not reign absolute among the representatives of the community, of course, but it still can be observed among large groups of them.

Also noteworthy is the fact that traces of the nomadic tradition, preservd today mainly as reminiscences can be found among certain traditional groups belonging to the large community of the conventionally-named *Yerlii*. They were representatives of the first wave of Gypsy migration who settled in Bulgarian lands relatively early in the fourteenth and fifteenth centuries. This nomadic tendency exists among the *Zvanchari* in the district of *Pazardjik*, the *Koshnichari* (Christian) in the district of Lukovit and of Peshtera, the *Koshnichari* (Muslim) from Plovdiv region and in Eastern Bulgaria, and others. Their way of wandering fits the conventional pattern – a few families of relatives travel in open or covered carriages drawn by donkeys. At the same time, their life illustrates the very phenomenon of sedentarisation: initially they rented houses in the villages where they would spend the winter and also prepare materials and goods to be sold during the next season; subsequently they purchased them and then, in the aftermath of the mandatory sedentarisation of the 1950s, they settled in them indefinitely. At present parts of these groups are reverting to the nomadic way of life and the traditional forms of nomadism, for example, the basket-makers from the Lukovit and Peshtera regions. A similar pattern is found among some of the wandering groups belonging to the so-called *Vlakhichki* (*Vlakhove, Vlakhuria, Lakhove,* or *Lakhorii*): the *Koshnichari, Sitari, Grebenari* and others. In a number of cases they travelled without transportation, or only with donkeys which carried the handicraft ware. For them the process of settlement took place earlier, mainly in the period between the two world wars, and it was oriented towards the urban neighbourhoods.

More particular was the situation of two well-defined and preserved groups. The first were the Burgudjii (from the large *Yerlii* community) who were engaged in metal-working. In many places, as in the districts of Pernik, Plovdiv, Sofia and others, they were settled long ago and were often without any memory of the wandering life. On the other hand, in eastern Bulgaria, they are described as nomads and do have some recollection of nomadic life. Their expanded winter settlements in the valley of the river Rusenski Lom have been mentioned more than once in the scholarly literature. Dozens of families stayed there in winter, actively involved in the making of ironware that was sold later in the year during their wanderings, which featured no transportation other than donkeys as pack animals.[6] We are faced with a situation where two different groups had the same name, or where parts of one group had split and settled in urban or village neighbourhoods. There they joined new structures of the Gypsy community, while the nomads stuck together in an integral and distinct group.

A second, similar case involved the *Lingurari*: Romanian-speakers, together with *Ursari* they form a meta-community, with the self-appellation *Rudara*. In many places, as in their large settlements in the Vratsa district, they were sedentary, with no reminiscences of life on the move and their travelling limited to visiting the fairs in order to sell their merchandise (wooden-wares such as spoons, basins and spindles). On the other hand, descriptions and memories have been preserved of their intensive wandering from village to village and from town to town, mostly in eastern Bulgaria, with large covered wagons drawn by buffalo or oxen, in which all their necessary materials and instruments, as well as the ready-made woodenware were stashed.[8] Probably the explanation for these seemingly contradictory reports is that there were two waves of migrating *Lingurari*, an earlier one and a later one, at the end of the nineteenth and the beginning of the twentieth centuries.

In general we can depict a traditional model of nomadic itineraries in Bulgaria, excluding the more specific cross-border travels. This is the movement from the plain to the mountain, that is, from the rich rural agricultural regions with winter settlements to the less developed and poorer mountain and semi-mountain regions requiring permanent no-madic itineraries. The relationship of nomadic economy to agriculture is something normal for Bulgaria where, until the end of the Second World War, more than 80 per cent of the population used to live in villages. Besides, despite the presence of different nomadic Gypsy groups, their specialisations are too narrow and thus there is almost no direct competi-tion between them. This is very important since mutual recognition of the regions of nomadism is possible only within the limits of one Gypsy group, or a meta group community, and there are no mechanisms for overcoming conflicts between different groups. Such conflicts were prac-tically non-existent, even in those instances when different groups had the same occupation (such as Thracean *Kalaidjii* or tinsmiths, *Layashi*, and *Nyamcoria*). In the past the natural boundary for nomadic regions was Stara Planina mountain, which was never crossed by Thracean tin-smiths to the north. However, at present, when a lot of *Layashi* and *Nyamcoria* have withdrawn from their traditional occupations and nomadic way of life, the Thracean *Kalaidjii* have quickly gained new territories.

These basic models of nomadic traditions are manifested after the forced sedentarisation of the 1950s. In Bulgaria this sedentarisation took place – it is not clear whether deliberately or accidentally – in the winter period when the nomads were in their winter settlements and the authorities let them choose their own places of permanent settlement. Thus the separate groups could settle in specific regions without mixing and could choose the manner of sedentarisation within the group: for example, one or two families of Thracean tinsmiths go to one village and cover wide regions; *Kardarashi* are united in local communities (several extended families in nearby villages and small towns, mainly around big towns and highways), and thus they cover greater territories; there is a higher concentration in some villages, and so forth.

One should not conceive of the transition from a nomadic to a sedentary way of life, which in Bulgaria took place in two rounds during the same century – first in the 1920s and 1930s, and secondly and more decisively in the 1950s – as an automatic and radical change in the way of life of Gypsies and a total break from nomadic traditions. On the contrary, a modification and preservation of this tradition in different forms can be observed in the majority of cases. Possessing a proper home and permanent residence opened up new opportunities to develop a stable occupation. Certainly, in many instances these traditional crafts were abandoned, but in other instances they survived, in the past as a source of supplementary income, or nowadays very often as the only possible means of subsistence. Except for the above-mentioned cases of revived wanderings, there are a number of occurrences when traditional crafts organised in the permanent residence are combined with short trips to display the merchandise in the villages, in addition to the fairs in the big cities, as with the *Lingurari, Koshnichari,* makers of different kinds of ironware, and so on. In addition, the practice, popular in the past also, of seasonal family or group wandering connected with lumbering, preparation of charcoal, picking wild berries and medicinal plants, and so forth, continues to proliferate.

It is interesting to observe how these phenomena have caught on among members of groups who have never had a strong tradition of a nomadic way of life, such as the so-called Gradeshki Tsigani from the village of Gradetz in the Kotel region. Most recently, a new type of wandering has emerged and is quickly spreading. It is more like cross-national seasonal (often illegal) work abroad, mainly in Greece, Turkey and some countries of Western Europe. We can observe a differentiation here: *Rudari* are oriented towards seasonal agricultural work in Greece and Italy, whereas a lot of *Yerlii*, mostly *Horahane Roma* (so-called Turkish Muslim Gypsies some of whom speak Turkish and have an appropriate self-consciousness) prefer small crossborder trade with Turkey. *Kardarasha*, in turn, are oriented mainly towards Western Europe. All these variants of Gypsy life clearly indicate that the processes of transition from a nomadic to a settled way of life are not linear and that, depending on the specific social and economic conditions involved, new modifications of traditional nomadism may arise as well as its 'resuscitation' for a second life.

Notes

This article is part of a research project financed by the Open Society Institute Research Support Scheme, Grant No, 2/94.

1. For more information on the Gypsy community in Bulgaria, the classification of its internal subdivisions and territorial distribution see Elena Marushiakova and Vesselin Popov, Циганите в България (The Gypsies in Bulgaria) (Sofia: 'Club 90', 1993).
2. T. Gjorgjevič, *Naš narodni život*, vol. III (Belgrade, 1984), p.315.
3. K. Irechek, *Patuvania po Bulgariya* (Sofia, 1974), p.807.
4. A. Fraser, *The Gypsies* (Oxford, 1992), pp.227-38.
5. S. Ivanova, *Etnografsko izsledvane na kvartal Krasno selo, grad Karnobat* (Sofia, 1942); Rakopisen fond nd katedra po slavyansko ezikoznanie i etnografiya, SU 'Sv. Kliment Ohridski', No.343, pp.34-5.
6. Mui Shuko (Andreas Scott MacFie), *With Gypsies in Bulgaria* (Liverpool, 1916), p.267.
8. Petulengto (B.G. Smith), 'Report on the Gypsy Tribes in North-East Bulgaria', *Journal of the Gypsy Lore Society* **IX** (1915-16).

14 Self-government Among Bulgarian Gypsies

Elena Marushiakova

The existence of potestary institutions (inter-group self-government) and their specific structure is one of the most important traditional character-istics of the Gypsy community, clearly displaying its ethnic specificity. The potestary institutions of the different Gypsy groups represent an idiosyncratic and effective mechanism of ethnosocial organisation. A similar form of social organisation is not observed among other Euro-pean ethnic communities. It has some parallels in the reality of ancient Indian society, namely in the institution of the 'panchayat' (literally 'the council of the five') in the different Jatti.

Besides its direct functions, the Gypsy potestary organisation performs the role of an indicator. It defines and distinguishes the separate sub-structures in the Gypsy ethnic community, since the presence or absence of a similar institution and its form and functions define to a great extent the very character of the Gypsy goup (the main structural unit in the Gypsy community).

This specific pattern of self-government is strictly preserved among all Gypsies, wherever in the world they might live. Belonging to the group called *Kardarashi* in Bulgaria,[1] and *Lovari, Kelderari, Churari, Mach-vaya*, in other countries, all of them were dispersed during the so-called *Great Kelderara invasion*. The term universally accepted as defining the potestary body of these groups is *Romano Kris* (Gypsy court), which, however, is unknown in Bulgaria. In its place the term *Meshare* or *Meshariava* is used, with an etymology obscure even for its bearers.[2]

Problems related to the legal system, to Gypsy self-government as a whole, and to *Romano Kris* in particular are widely discussed in Gypsy studies. There are conflicting arguments about its different aspects.[3] It is often thought that similar institutions do not exist among the other (non-Vlach) Gypsy group, but this is not so. Western scholars often encounter the problems of a lack of comparative material from Eastern Europe. These institutions can be found among various Gypsy groups, especially in the countries of the former Soviet Union (Russia, Ukraine, Latvia, Lithuania, Moldova). Among the so-called *Ruska* (Russian) *Roma* who are widely scattered all over the former Soviet Union, *Romano Kris* is usually called *Send* (from the Polish court), with such variants as *Sondo* in Lithuania where members of this group are called *Polska* (Polish) *Roma*, or *Sjond* in Poland, where they are often called *Haladitka* (that is, Russian) *Roma*. *Send* or *Sjond* exist among *Polska* (Polish) *Roma* in Poland, among *Servs* and *Vlachs* who live mostly in Ukraine, and even among some Ukrainian-speaking Gypsies in Russia who have lost their language and most of their ethno-cultural traditions and who use the Russian appellation *Prodelka* from the so-called *Vorovski* slang.[4] A similar institution is *leige di beaşa* (the Beashi court) among some Rumanian speaking *Beashi* in Croatia and probably also in Hungary.[5] A similar institution exists with the *Sintis* in Austria, Germany and Italy.[6]

Contrary to the opinion of some scientists that the institution *Romano Kris* emerged on the territory of Wallachia and is related to slavery and a sedentary lifestyle accompanied by marriage through elopement,[7] comparative material from groups living and travelling mainly in Eastern Europe shows that the institution of the Gypsy court is popular mostly with travelling Gypsies who arrange their marriages. It is found among non-Vlach Gypsy groups (for example *Ruska* and *Polska Roma*, *Sinti*) on the territories of Wallachia and Moldova who had never been enslaved.

The *Meshare* in Bulgaria is an actively functioning institution among different groups from the so-called *Kardarashi* community – *Lovari* (*Zlatara, Grastara, Niculeshi, Dodolania, Zhapleshti, Tasmanari*, and other sub-groups), *Layashi*, and *Niamtsuri* (*Bakardjii, Avstriiski* [Austrian], *Nemski* [German], *Ungarski* [Hungarian] Gypsies and other appellations). The *Meshare* is composed of people having the highest prestige in the group, and as knowledge and prestige come with age, they are at the same time the oldest members of the community. They are men only, are not elected, and their position is not hereditary; it is acquired through demonstrated wisdom, judiciousness, moderation, impartiality and good knowledge of the traditional norms and rules of the group. Their number is not strictly fixed and may be higher or lower, depending on the complexity of the case, but at all events the number must be odd. When a problem arises inside the group, the concerned sides turn to the *wise people* with a request to help settle it. The members of the *Meshare* should be invited to the meeting *respectfully* (driven in a car). Every sub-group belonging to the Kardarashi community has its own *Meshare* and only in especially complicated cases are respected people from the farthest possible sub-group or region asked to come as 'they are an outside eye, and may decide more fairly'. In other words, if the argument is between two *Zlatara*, the *Meshare* arrive in the morning, and as the hostess lights a fire, they sit around it on a rug or sheepskins, discuss the problem and announce their decision. When the cases are more complicated, the *Meshare* is notified beforehand (orally or in a written form) by both sides to the dispute, and some time for investigation is allowed. In this period the witnesses are questioned and the material evidence collected.

The investigation may continue during the meeting of the *Meshare* with additional interrogation of witnesses. When there is no clarity, the material evidence is lacking, or the collected information is contradictory, the last and most certain means to obtain the truth is applied: the taking of an oath in front of the *Meshare*. The taking of an oath is done in a manner reminiscent of 'God's justice' in the Middle Ages. It takes place in the manner of a ritual, by a river (because *O'Beng*, the Devil, is in the river), and involves swearing an oath over two crossed sticks where two cigarettes are placed (the 'cigarette being a tar, a fire'). After taking the oath the person has to smoke the cigarettes. The centre-piece of the oath-taking ceremony is the enumeration of punishments, each more terrible than the preceding, that will befall the perjurer and his family. It is a deep conviction that every word pronounced during the ritual oath-taking will come to pass in the shortest time. The oath-taking, being an extremely serious instrument of control, is applied only as a last resort. The procedure is normally as follows: first a *small Meshare* composed of other people. The appellation is permitted up to three times, and the third *Meshare* has a larger number of participants, with respected people from the farthest sub-group (or a few sub-groups) being invited who may have recourse to an oath-taking. After the ceremony, the *Meshare* announces its decision and no further appeals are permitted. Disobedience to the decisions of the *Meshare* is unthinkable and would bring 'civil death' to the offender, that is it would deny him the protection of the group.

The *Meshare* decides on problems related to the internal life of the group's members only. It does not have the right to interfere in an argument between a Gypsy and a non-Gypsy, between Gypsies belonging to different groups (such as between a member of the *Kardarashi* community and a person from a different Gypsy group) or between a group's member and the state. Most often, questions from the realm of common law are decided on, pertaining to the observance of inter-group norms, conjugal norms, family relations and family honour. Often economic problems arising inside the groups are discussed. Recently there has been a considerable expansion of this set of economic issues related to the growing presence of *Kardarashi* in the sphere of the legal (or rather the semi-legal) economy. The punishments are usually monetary (fees are imposed and compensations determined), with the withdrawal of group protection from the violator used only as the extreme sanction. The tales and rumours spread in recent times by the mass media about inhuman punishments reigning among Gypsies, such as cutting off nose and ears and even murders, or about the 'Mafia' character of the Gypsy potestary bodies, are more than exaggerated and do not contain any truth. They only display the complete ignorance of the character of this institution.

The presence or absence of a *Meshare* is one of the main dividing criteria in the eyes of the group members from the *Kardarashi* community. It is said: 'They are from ours, they are different, but if they acknowledge the authority of the *Meshare*, they are with us.' The establishment of a potestary institution and the possibility for a few otherwise endogamous groups (though related by origin) to call a general *Meshare* points to a tendency to make a transition to a higher stage in ethnic evolution to the meta-group community of the *Kardarashi* as a whole. In addition, there is an alternative possibility for the expanding group: to split into parts and for each newly created group (or kin) to establish its own *Meshare*, which would legitimise its separation. The recognition of the general *Meshare* as an arbiter in important cases and arguments at the same time unifies all sub-groups, clans and group members in a single community, the *Kardarashi*. From a historical perspective it becomes evident that proper potestary institutions turned out to be the most powerful tool for the preservation of the ethnic specificity of a given community, and an instrument for the peaceful settlement of conflicts. They help to avoid conflicts that might lead to blood vengeance – a phenomenon that has been observed in Bulgaria among groups who lack common potestary bodies, as among the *Parpulii*. The *Meshare* exercises control over the deviant behaviour of certain members and secures the preservation of endogamy. Thanks to the existence of the *Meshare* institution, even Gypsies from the *Kardarashi* community who live dispersed or at great distance remain its fully-fledged members.

Back in the nomadic past of the *Kardarashi* communities, similar bodies of self-government had existed on the same pattern and performed the same functions as today. However, the wandering life required additional power structures and empowered persons to direct the life of each wandering group. At the same time the separate nomadic group needed an influential person to represent it before the official authorities, to obtain permission for sojourn and camping, and to see that no conflicts arose with the local population, or at least to moderate them. Most often, the chieftain in the *Kardarashi* groups was the father of the family (*phuro dad*), but if another individual was more capable and sociable, he might assume these obligations. A nomadic group could be headed by the mother of the family (*phuri dei*), providing that she was capable and old enough to become the leader.[8] This was the case most frequently when she became the former leader's widow. The grandmother (*phuri dei*) in each family was in charge of all questions related to the extended family and dealt with morals, marriages and domestic relationships. The routes of wandering were decided upon after agreement among the leaders of different wandering groups; when arguments in this respect arose, they were settled by the convoked *Meshare*.

Very specific is the situation with the 'Thracian' *Kalaidjii* ('tinsmiths'). They lack a group potestary institution such as the *Meshare* but to a large degree its functions are fulfilled by the institution of the extended clan, represented by the so-called *Svatos*. *Svatos* is an actively functioning general gathering of the clan where the opinions of everyone (including small children) are listened to, agreement is reached and the decision is formally made by the head of the clan (or his widow, if he is deceased). Mainly problems of marital relations and corresponding financial arrangements are discussed at *Svatos*. In cases of conflict between two clans, a general gathering is called in order to come to an agreement. The idea of a third, independent arbiter is not accepted by them, notwithstanding the fact that collective opinion (of the entire group community) is a factor of primary importance. The collective opinion is always taken into account and often proves to be decisive.

The nomadic way of life, traditional for the *Rudara* community in the past, also required adequate leadership, which was especially well pronounced among the *Ursari*. However, in Bulgaria there is no evidence of the existence of institutions resembling the *Meshare* with clearly defined functions and ritualised activity. After the end of the slack season and before the start of the wandering, the *Ursari* would hold (and still hold today) a group meeting where they would announce the composition of the group, choose the leaders, called *glavatari* (chieftains), and decide upon the routes. The leader is responsible for the travel, the gains, and the general success of the wandering season. If the outcome is unsatisfactory he may fail to be elected the following year. In general, it is considered inappropriate to have a female leader. Still, if she happens to be the best suited within the wandering group, her husband is chosen as leader but it is clear that she will make the decisions. The mother of an extended family among the *Rudara* (as in the case with the *Kardarashi*) is in charge of all problems that may emerge, related mainly to conjugal relationships and moral norms. The *glavatar* (chieftain) among the *Ursari* (as in the case with the *Kardarashi*) represents the group before the authorities and the local population. In addition, he is responsible for the celebrations of major holidays and feels obliged to treat his fellow members to a drink on these occasions.

At present, with the new circumstances of nomadic life, the functions of the chieftain have been preserved to a certain extent even though they have been transformed. Most often a group of several *Ursari* families make a temporary camp in the big cities (usually under a bridge or a railway underpass) or resorts. The people living there elect a temporary chieftain whose daily job it is to collect the income of the families who lead bears or monkeys and distribute it according to a complex system. The group as a whole is quite unstable – it can be abandoned by any family, and others can join or separate.

Similar patterns regulated the life of wandering Gypsies, who belong today to the large community of the *Yerlii*. Among the so-called 'non-Vlach' wandering Gypsies (*Burgudjii, Koshnichari* and others) the wandering group was headed by a *cheribashi* (chieftain). He was elected by all adult members of the respective nomadic group and judged according to his abilities and knowledge. If the elected *cheribashi* turned out to be a bad choice, it was possible to replace him. The position was not hereditary. The obligations of the *cheribashi* were restricted mainly to the arrangements and relations with the surrounding population: obtaining permission to camp, work and sell goods. The *cheribashi* was responsible for the behaviour of group members: he had to prevent them from disturbing the peace of the local population, stealing their property, and so forth He was entitled to impose fines on the group's members; when they disobeyed his orders, he had the right (unlike the leaders of other communities) to seek help from the wider society. He also had the right to allow the offenders to be punished by local village authorities. No mechanism for the settlement of possible arguments between two different nomadic groups existed among these groups. When two wandering units (belonging to the same group, of course) came upon each other, they organised feasts and set up their camps next to each other, but the next day they necessarily separated and each pursued their way in a different direction. Questions concerning the different families were decided in this community by the fathers (that is, the oldest men), including those related by marriage. Unlike other communities described above, the patriarchal model is dominant in this group. During the sedentarisation of these communities, the institution of the *cheribashi* gradually died out and it is nothing more than a memory today. A similar situation is found among the wanderers of the so-called 'Vlach' group of *Yerlii* (that is, the group of the *Vlaches, Vlahichki, Vlachove, Vlachuria, Lachove, Lachorii*), where the authority of the *cheribashi* has been much weaker and often adopted under the pressure of surrounding society. During their settlement, these communities frequently accepted the leadership of a prominent chieftain of a neighbouring group. In the long run, this stimulated the process of their integration into the meta-group community of the *Yerlii* or of the *Dassikane Roma*, respectively.[9]

Institutions like the *Meshare* or chieftain are not found among the communities of sedentary Gypsies. As a rule, in the past each settled group had a representative appointed by the authorities of society at large and sometimes also called *cheribashi*; today these functions are performed by the local deputy mayors. Self-government is confined to certain families and clans, headed by the members with the highest prestige, most often men, but women in instances when they happen to be the most prominent persons. The observance of customary law was monitored by the eldest and wisest women who kept an eye on behaviour and morals, offered advice when necessary, presided over the performance of rites and rituals, advised brides and young mothers, and so on. At present, this specific institution has ceased to function, especially in the environment of urban neighbourhoods where social control is delegated mainly to the nuclear family. The mechanism of decision making in conflict situations in the absence of corresponding institutions in the neighbourhoods is reduced to oath-taking. Nowadays, when complicated and contradictory questions mostly concerning family relations arise, or when problems emerge which might jeopardise family cohesion, a ceremonial oath is taken. This ceremony seeks to establish the truth or to induce certain individuals to avoid certain temptations (adultery, drinking, and the like). The oath is taken in front of witnesses at a sacred place and on a 'holy' day – for example, for the Gypsies in Sofia and its surroundings this is the tomb of *Ali baba* (The Muslim saint Bali Effendi) in the churchyard of St. Illia in Knyazhevo.

Other novel forms of social organisation and social life, unknown to the wandering groups, appear in the reality of sedentary living, to a great extent influenced by the wider society, which is a frame of reference for the Gypsy community. The guilds constituted on an ethnic base were institutions of that kind in the past (the so-called 'Gypsy esnafs') which had their own organisation, self-government within certain limits, and their own holidays. The evolution of this tradition nowadays is especially interesting. For example, the specific women's institutions, called *Iondjii* in Sofia, recreate some of the reminiscences and terminology of the ancient guilds and represent a sort of 'mutual aid fund' and the centres of social life for women from the Gypsy neighbourhoods.[10]

The functions of social organisation and self-government can be identified to a certain extent by the 'implantation' in Gypsy milieux of forms from the wider society exemplified in the recent past by different 'neighbourhood chapters'. These were mainly organised by the Fatherland Front, the Communist Youth Union, the Hearths of Socialist Life and Culture and similar bodies, and were constituted on an ethnic basis (that is, organising Gypsies only). At present, this process is acquiring a new dimension through the participation of different Gypsy organisations and movements in the life of society. Some of them even harbour political ambitions. The adoption of new forms of social and political life, and integration into the overall social and political life in the country, reflect the aspirations of ethnic emancipation of a sizeable part of the Gypsy population in Bulgaria. This phenomenon marks a new phase in the general evolution of Gypsies as an ethno-social organism, in the development of the ethnic process among them, and in the transition to a higher ethnic stage. But the processes as a whole are quite contradictory and divergent, and the tendencies and possible outcomes remain hard to foresee.[11]

Notes

This article is part of a research project financed by the Open Society Institute Research Support Scheme, Grant No.3/94.

1. For more information on the Gypsy commuinity in Bulgaria, the classification of its internal subdivisions and territorial distribution see Elena Marushiakova and Vesselin Popov, Циганите в България (The Gypsies in Bulgaria) (Sofia: 'Club 90', 1993).
2. According to some linguists (Birgit Igla and Lev Cherenkov), the word is of Arabic or Persian origin and has entered into Romanes through the Turkish language (personal communication).
3. See, for example, Y. Yoors, *The Gypsies* (London, 1967); A. Sutherland, *Gypsies: The Hidden Americans* (New York, 1975); J. Ficowski, *Cyganie na polskich drogach* (Kraków and Wrocław, 1986); H. von Wlislocki, *Von wandernden Zigeunervolke* (Leipzig, 1890); M.A. Bell, 'Autonomous Lawmaking: The Case of the Gypsies', *Yale Law Journal* **103**, no.2 (1993); W.M. Reisman, 'Autonomy, Interdependence

and Responsibility', *Yale Law Journal* **103**, no.2 (1993); C.R. Gropper, *Gypsies in the City: Culture Patterns and Survival* (Princeton, NJ, 1975).

4. The field research material was collected during the Romani Summer School in Supras, Poland, in 1994.

5. Field research material from Croatia.

6. Based on personal conversations with colleagues (Moses Heinschink, Mirella Karpati, Bruno Nicolini and others).

7. T. Action, S. Caffrey and G. Mundy, 'Theorising Gypsy Law', unpublished manuscript.

8. J. Marushiakova, 'Rodinny život valasskych Ciganov na Slovensky a jeho vyvinove tendencie', *Slovensky Narodopis*, 1986, no.4.

9. T. Kmetova, '"Londja" – specifichna forma na parichna vzaimopomosht sred tsiganite v Sofia', *Balgarski folklor*, 1992, no.4.

10. E. Marushiakova, 'Gruppi ed Organizzazioni zingari in Bulgaria e il loro attegiaamento verso l'impegno politico', *Lacio Drom* **28**, no.1–2 (1992).

15 Ethno-national Orientation Among Lemkos in Poland

Susyn Yvonne Mihalasky

The collapse of communism in East–Central Europe in 1989 created more political space for ethno-national minorities to assert themselves. For these minorities, issues left unresolved since the onset of communism have re-emerged with remarkable speed. The Lemkos of Poland are one such case. Since 1989 this small ethno-cultural group has experienced the swift re-emergence of the ethno-national identity question, namely, who are the Lemko: are they a part of the Ukrainian nation, or of a newly re-emergent Carpatho-Rusyn people?

During the communist era, the Ukrainian identity was the only non-Polish ethno-national identity under which the Lemkos could organise and manifest their cultural and community life. With the fall of communism, however, a Rusyn 'orientation' has re-emerged among the Lemkos, both preceding and inspired by the resurrection of a Carpatho-Rusyn ethnic identity in other former communist countries where they had lived without group recognition: Slovakia, Ukraine and Hungary. The founding of an independent Ukraine in August 1991 has similarly energised the Ukrainian identity option. Thus, the Lemko population has once again come face to face with the vital but unfinished business of establishing its own ethno-national identity.

What does it mean to be a Lemko in Poland today? What role do such ethno-cultural markers as language and geography play in determining the parameters of present-day Lemko ethno-national identity? How do Lemkos understand and define what it is to be 'Lemko', 'Rusyn', and 'Ukrainian'? What impact is the revived ethno-national identity question having on Lemko community life?

In this chapter I will answer these questions by drawing on data collected from a written survey distributed among Lemkos residing in Poland in 1991–92. The survey is part of a larger study on the long-term impact on the Lemko community of their expulsion from their Carpathian homeland in 1947. A brief background section provides a historical and ethnographic profile of the Lemkos. The survey section that follows concerns the questionnaire itself and focuses on the sample and how it was collected. Next comes a discussion of each of the seven questions asked and the tabulation of the responses (where applicable), followed by respondents' illustrative comments. Finally, the cumulative results of the seven questions will be examined to see what they suggest about the ethno-national identity question among Lemkos in present-day Poland.

Historical Background

The Lemkos are, by virtue of culture, language and religion, classified as East Slavs. Before their expulsions in 1944–47 from their Carpathian homeland, Lemkos possessed a rural, agrarian culture; they made their livelihood primarily in farming and shepherding or in the forest-related professions. Lemkos are primarily of Greek Catholic or Orthodox Christian religious background. The Lemko dialect as yet uncodified is considered by most linguists to be most closely related to Ukrainian. Despite the lack of a universally accepted grammatical standard, Lemkos have produced a rich vernacular-language literature, especially remarkable for its poetic expression.

The Lemkos' historical homeland is bounded on the east and west by the rivers Osława and Poprad; on the north by the cities of Nowy Sącz. Gorlice, Jasło, Krosno, Sanok; and on the south by the crests of the Carpathians. Most Lemkos reside at present in Silesia, to which they were resettled in 1947. While the Lemkos' ethnographic origin is the subject of some debate, scholars generally agree that by the fourteenth century their ancestors were already present in the Carpathians.

Lemko ethnographic territory has been under continuous foreign rule and has changed hands frequently throughout its history. As part of the Galician Kingdom, the eastern Lemko region was under the hegemony and cultural influence of Kievan Rus' until 1340, when it joined the western Lemko region under Polish rule. After the first partitioning of Poland in 1772, the Lemko region became part of the Austrian empire's Galician province, where it remained until 1918. From 1918 until the present day, the Lemko region has again been under Polish rule, except for a brief interval during the Second World War (1939–44), when it was ruled by Germany.

In 1945–46 approximately 70,000 Lemkos then residing in Poland were resettled to Soviet Ukraine as part of an international agreement between the two countries on the exchange of minority populations. An estimated 35,000 Lemkos remained in their homeland until 1947 when, in retaliation for acts committed by the Ukrainian Insurgent Army, Lemkos along with the entire Ukrainian population of Poland were resettled *en masse* in the northern and western territories of Poland.[2] During the late 1980s, approximately 10,000 Lemkos have managed to return to their former Carpathian homeland. Since the 1980s, the Lemko community has undergone a resurgence of ethnic pride, which emerged into the open only with the advent of democracy in Poland. An estimated 60,000 Lemkos now live in Poland.[3] The survey below was conducted among this group of people.

The Survey

The questions on the survey raised several issues, including the ethno-national question, the situation of Lemkos in Poland and respondents' expectations about their community's future within Poland. At the start of the questionnaire, respondents were asked to provide basic information for the purpose of generating a statistical profile of the sample, including age, educational level, profession, religious persuasion and place of residence (province). Inasmuch as respondents were anonymous, only these classification data, along with a randomly assigned number, are used to identify them.

No statistical records on Lemkos have been kept since the Second World War. Without the benefit of such a statistical guide, the author chose to generate a stratified random sample by distributing surveys at Lemko cultural festivals and religious holidays. Lemkos of all ages from various parts of Poland attend these annual events, providing a concentrated yet mixed population of both traditional faiths (Greek Catholic and Orthodox) and ethno-national 'orientations' (Ukrainian and Rusyn). Surveys were distributed at the *Rusalia* (held in the Lemko village of Zyndranowa), the Lemko Vatra 'in the Homeland' (held in the Lemko village of Zdynia), and the Vatra 'in Exile' (held in the Silesian resettlement village of Michałów).

All Lemko organisations in existence at the time of the survey received multiple mailings with requests to distribute them among their members. These included the Стоваришыня Лемків (Lemko Association); Об'єднання Лемків (Union of Lemkos); Русинскій

Демократичний Круг Лемків "Господар" в Польщи ('Hospodar' Rusyn Democratic Circle of Lemkos in Poland); Руска Бурса (Ruska Bursa); and the ad-hoc organisational committee of the annual Zdynia Vatra Folk Festival.
Of 250 questionnaires distributed, fifty-two were returned. The sample breaks down as follows:

Age	*Percentage*
Born before 1947 resettlement	44
First Post-resettlement generation	54
Second Post-resettlement generation	2

Level of education	
College Diploma	52
High School Diploma	44
Grammar School	4

Religious conviction	
Orthodox	50
Greek Catholic	38
Pentecostal	4
'Atheist'	4
Roman Catholic	2
'Christian'	2

Returns by province are divided into three categories: the historical territory of Lemko settlement (the Lemko region); the territory to which Lemkos were relocated in the 1947 population resettlement; and lastly, all other parts of Poland to which Lemkos have migrated from one of the first two regions. In terms of location, the breakdown appears as follows:

Location	*Percentage*
Historical Lemko region	50
Resettlement territories	44
Territories of new settlement	6

In terms of profession, the skilled trades predominated, followed by the professions and educators. Respondents described themselves variously as accountants, electricians, technicians, engineers, economists, schoolteachers, teaching assistants, doctors, farmers or homemakers.

Individually represented were a woodsman, a choir director, a cleric, a veterinarian, a university student, a high school pupil, a philologist–translator and ethnographer.

The Questions

Question 1. This question sought to define the outer limits of Lemko identity by asking respondents to think about what in the post-1947 Lemko community is a common phenomenon: a Lemko extensively assimilated into the Polish, Roman Catholic mainstream. Is he in the respondent's view 'still' a Lemko? If so, what makes him so? If not, why not? The question appeared as follows:

Is it possible for someone who does not speak Lemko, does not live in the Lemko region, is married to a non-Lemko and of a non-traditional religious faith, to be regarded as a Lemko?

Response	Percentage
a. Yes	53
b. No	35
c. Difficult to say	12

A small majority was willing without reservation to accept the hypothetical assimilated Lemko as one of their own. Forty-seven per cent (the 35 per cent answering 'no' and the 12 per cent answering 'Difficult to say') either rejected the possibility or at least did not look favourably on the hypothetical Lemko's chances of maintaining his or her Lemko identity.

Most of those respondents who accepted the possibility that the assimilated Lemko could still be considered a Lemko based their determination of Lemko identity on one of two characteristics: the individual's parental heritage and the presence (or absence) in the individual of an emotional attachment to his or her Lemko heritage.

'It is sufficient merely that he [the hypothetical Lemko in the question] is of Lemko parentage', suggested respondent 2, a 65-year-old Lemko of Roman Catholic background. 'Lemkos typically set great store by their family roots', suggested respondent 11, a 49-year-old Greek Catholic. Respondent 36, a 33-year-old Greek Catholic teacher, wrote that 'One becomes a Lemko only once – by being born as one'.

Respondent 8, a 50-year-old Lemko of Orthodox background, wrote that 'It depends on him [the hypothetical Lemko]. A feeling of belonging is born and lives in the heart.' Respondent 15, a 52-year-old economist from Wrocław, also based her understanding of who is and who is not a Lemko on an individual's emotional attachment to his or her heritage. She wrote that one is a Lemko 'when one's heart beats faster at hearing the mere word "Lemko".' From that initial emotional attachment, 'everything else will follow', wrote respondent 25, a 44-year-old factory worker from Zielona Góra.

Representative of those who questioned whether the hypothetical Lemko could truly be considered Lemko was respondent 22, a 40-year-old Orthodox cleric. He remarked that 'A Lemko who does not meet the listed requirements [language, religion, Lemko home life, area of residence] would be a pretty strange, contrived Lemko'. Some respondents felt that a Lemko so far removed from Lemko traditions would simply be unable to resist the forces of assimilation. Respondent 35, a 33-year-old Greek Catholic veterinarian, wrote, 'If he doesn't speak Lemko, is not an eastern rite Christian ... with time he, and definitely his children, will lose connection with the Lemko community'. 'Lack of Lemko language skills', argued 26-year-old Orthodox respondent 44, 'is a barrier to interacting with other Lemkos and to understanding Lemko culture.' Respondent 12, a 51-year-old farmer from Nowy Sącz, concluded 'He'd be a renegade.'

Respondent 14, a 49-year-old Greek Catholic from Tarnów, offered a brief history lesson tracing the political and social climate which brought about many examples of the hypothetical Lemko in the question:

Poles undertaking the illegal [1947 Operation Vistula] population resettlement induced a psychosis of fear and de-nationalisation. People [Lemkos] hid their ethno-national identity.

Question 2. The second question asked:

How can one return to one's Lemko roots?

Respondents' answers emphasised the need to become reacquainted with Lemko culture, history and language. Respondent 15, a 52-year-old economist, wrote that one must 'grow to love [Lemko] culture, customs, traditions – and above all love the mountainous Lemko homeland'. Respondent 47, a 27-year-old ethnographer of Greek Catholic background, wrote that a Lemko seeking to rediscover his roots must 'make contact with other Lemkos, learn to recognise Lemko things and maintain distance from non-Lemko things.' Respondent 31, a 40-year-old electrician from Legnica province, wrote that it is necessary to 'use the Lemko language on a daily basis'.

'It comes with age – a return of interest in the culture, longings ... recharging one's batteries in the mountains', wrote respondent 16, a 47-year-old doctor. 'Don't be ashamed of your people and your religious faith', advised respondent 33, a 33-year-old woman of Orthodox background. Respondent 27, a 44-year-old technician from Legnica province, wrote that one way to return to one's Lemko roots is 'to work for the growth of the Lemko community'.

Seven respondents doubted whether an assimilated Lemko could ever return to his roots. Respondent 44, a 26-year-old farmer, wrote that 'It's difficult to count on a miraculous conversion'. Respondent 22, a 40-year-old Orthodox cleric, noted wryly that: 'There aren't many ways [to return to one's Lemko roots], none of them is ideal; there is no set recipe. It's hard to "become" someone. It's better simply to "be" him.

Question 3. Language plays a key role both in shaping and reflecting a group's culture and identity. Question 3 inquires into the status of the Lemko vernacular, seeking insight into the state of the Lemko ethno-national identity debate. This question asked:

Can Lemkos have or do they have a distinct language and literature?

Response	Percentage
a. Yes	78
b. No	14
c. No opinion	8

The tabulated results suggest that, for a large majority, Lemkos either already do or could have a distinct language. A smaller component of 14 per cent indicated that Lemkos either cannot or do not have their own language.

A survey of the comments of the 78 per cent who feel that Lemkos can or do possess a distinct language suggests that they base their opinions on one of two lines of reasoning: personal familiarity with an already extant body of Lemko vernacular writings, or belief in a theoretical 'right' of Lemkos to aspire to having their own language. The comments of the 'no' group base their opinion on the belief that establishment of a distinct Lemko language undermines the unity of the Ukrainian community. Others in the 'no' group saw what they felt to be the simple impossibility of formulating a distinct Lemko language.

Most respondents' comments, whether in opposition to the idea that Lemkos can have their own language or whether in support, reveal a strong sense of the practical problems in codifying a vernacular. Respondent 9, a 50-year-old woman from Nowy Sącz province, answers that in her opinion Lemkos do have their own language, 'because the Lemko language, in contrast to the prototypical village dialect, has for a long time functioned in many spheres of contemporary life.' Yet respondent 3, a Greek Catholic electrician from Legnica, used the same practical reasoning to answer in the negative: If a resident of Tylicz village has difficulties understanding someone from Dubne village ... twenty kilometres away, how can one speak of a unified language? Given the present scattered settlement, it is not likely and probably impossible.

Other respondents considered the question in the light of concerns about unity within the Lemko community. Respondent 44, a 26-year-old farmer, argued that 'It is important at the present time to create a language and literature, in order to strengthen and unite our community.' Respondent 10, a Greek Catholic teacher from Zielona Góra, saw forces of division to be so strong as to prevent the codification of a Lemko language: 'The intelligentsia is too small and the clergy – I mean both Greek Catholic and Orthodox – work to divide people.' Respondent 22, an Orthodox priest from Nowy Sącz, like respondent 10, felt that divisions within the Lemko community would prevent codification of a Lemko language: 'Lemkos have both a distinct language and literature, but detractors diminish their value. As a result, it's very difficult to raise them to a higher level.'

Respondent 19, a 46-year-old chemist of Orthodox faith, expressing the Lemko Ukrainian perspective, wrote: 'Lemko is a dialect of Ukrainian in much the same way that Silesian speech is a dialect of Polish language.' 'You can't build a language out of a dialect,' maintained respondent 5, an economist from Gorzów.

The comments of respondents 13 and 26 merit special attention inasmuch as they reveal how some Lemkos view the language codification process now being undertaken by Lemko Rusyns. Respondent 13, a 48-year-old Orthodox schoolteacher, comments briefly that it is possible for Lemkos to have their own language, 'on the basis of the Yugoslav [Vojvodin] Rusyn model'. Respondent 26, a 36-year-old schoolteacher from Nowy Sącz, wrote:

Yes [Lemkos can have their own distinct language], but it won't be the language created by [Lemko vernacular poet Petro] Trochanovskii, [Lemko vernacular poet Olena] Duć-Fajfer and [author of Lemko grammer Myroslava] Chomyak, which is a bizarre creation. Nor will it be the Rusnak language created by that Slovak KGB agent [American historian Paul Robert] Magocsi, which contains strange words Lemkos never used. Really, while they are still so divided, Lemkos will never have their own language.

Question 4. Lemko folk culture has been inspired by and celebrates their mountainous Carpathian homeland. As with other agrarian cultures, the connection between land and identity was for Lemkos a strong one. During the years 1944–47, Lemkos were resettled away from their homeland. Those who have since returned found that depopulation of the region, coupled with directed in-migration of ethnic Poles, has changed the ethno-cultural landscape of their homeland. How has the traditional tie between the Lemko region and Lemko cultural identity been altered since the resettlements? Question 4 asked:

Is living in the Lemko homeland necessary in order to preserve the connection with one's Lemko heritage?

Response	Percentage
a. Yes	22
b. No	78
c. No opinion	–

The overwhelming majority of respondents thus feel that living in their homeland is not necessary to preserve the conection with their Lemko heritage, whereas a smaller number feel that residence in the homeland is necessary.

The answer of respondent 36, a 33-year-old Greek Catholic teacher living in Nowy Sącz province, was representative of the 78 per cent 'no' group:

It probably depends on the individual character of a given Lemko. One may need to feel the mountains all around him; another might be able to live in a foreign land flat as a board.

Respondent 39, a 24-year-old student from Legnica province, suggested that

For someone who feels himself to be a Lemko, a return trip to the mountains, even if only for a short time, is a powerful emotional experience that strengthens feelings of belonging. It is of course possible to be a Lemko and partake of Lemko culture outside the Beskid mountain region, but the greater concentration of Lemkos in the mountains provides more opportunities.

Respondent 30, a 40-year-old accountant of Orthodox religious background, lamented: 'Where you live doesn't always depend on your desires. It depends on the past political environment and the present political and economic conditions,' which was seconded by respondent 1, who did not return owing to 'a simple lack of funds'. Respondent 24 found comfort in the thought that 'there are many distinct nationalities without their own countries – one day their dreams may be fulfilled.

The 22 per cent of respondents who felt it necessary to live in the Lemko region did so for two reasons. A strong fear of assimilation was foremost. Secondly, these respondents found that they felt 'at home' only in their own ethno-cultural community and homeland.

Respondent 22, a 40-year-old Orthodox cleric residing in the Lemko region, was representative of those fearing assimilation. He argued that 'no nationality living outside its homeland is able to completely preserve its ethno-national identity or culture.' Respondent 33, a 33-year-old also residing in the Lemko region, agreed: 'Every nationality ought to have its own homeland and the majority of that nationality should live there.'

The remarks of respondent 13, a 48-year-old Orthodox teacher living in the Lemko region, eloquently reflected the views of those who could feel at home only in the Lemko region:

> only in Lemkovyna can I feel like a native son. Here every stone, every roadside chapel and cross is a witness to the existence of our people, who have suffered so cruelly, yet persevered. Returning to our roots may restore to us the dignity of a people in possession of their own lands, where every stretch of meadow is a part of our history. After exactly 30 years in exile, I have at last returned with my family to my beloved mountains.

Questions 5 and 6. Questions 5 and 6 together ask the respondent to define three ethnonyms which recur frequently in the discussion of Lemko ethno-national identity: 'Ukrainian', 'Rusyn' and 'Lemko'. Inasmuch as ethonyms are shorthand for broader identities and world-views, respondents' interpretation and use of these terms offers hints as to the evolution of Lemko ethno-national consciousness, and insight into what issues comprise the discussion. Question 5 asked:

Is there any real difference between Lemkos and Ukrainians?

Response	*Percentage*
a. Yes	67
b. No	27
c. No opinion	6

As indicated above, 67 per cent of respondents did differentiate between Lemkos and Ukrainians, while 27 per cent felt that these were terms of reference for the same population. The respondents' accompanying comments suggest that both groups' views were frequently grounded in historical mythology and stereotypes. To a lesser extent, respondents mentioned material cultural traits (for example, musical traditions, geographic location) as evidence for the correctness of their beliefs.

Thus, respondent 50, a 29-year-old economist from Nowy Sącz, drawing on stereotypes widespread in the Lemko community, wrote: 'Lemkos – hardworking, gentle, peaceful. Ukrainians – hardworking, assertive, stubborn.' Respondent 28, a 41-year-old electrical engineer from Wrocław province, wrote:

> I sense a genetic difference between them: Lemkos are good-tempered, co-operative, tolerant. Lemkos don't want to assimilate into the Ukrainian community. Ukrainians from the very first wanted to absorb Lemkos.

Respondent 22, a 40-year-old Orthodox priest, likewise felt that Lemkos and Ukrainians are distinguished by what he termed 'separate mentalities.' Respondent 39, a 27-year-old student from Legnica, seconded this opinion: 'We can attend the same church, sing the same songs, but often cannot speak the same language. This is because we have different ways of looking at fundamental matters.'

A minority of the respondents couched their opinions in a historical discussion of Lemko ethnogenesis. Respondent 12, a 51-year-old farmer, sees no difference between Lemkos and Ukrainians because 'Ukrainians and Lemkos descend from the same root: *Kievan Rus'*.' Respondent 37, a 45-year-old physician of Orthodox faith, seconded this in a frequently encountered analogy: 'we are children of the same parentage'. Respondent 3, a 64-year-old electrician from Zielona Góra, argued that

> It is sufficient simply to compare the styles of church architecture in the region of Kiev and the Lemko region. They are one and the same. Also worth mentioning is the thirteenth-century poem *Slovo o polku Ihorevi*.

Respondent 5, a 67-year-old economist from Gorzów, considering the matter of ethnonyms, wrote: 'Lemkos are a part of the Ukrainian people.

At one time they called themselves and were called by others *Rusyns*.' Respondent 32, a 33-year-old engineer from Nowy Sącz, viewing Kievan Rus' and Lemko ethnogenesis from the Rusyn viewpoint, wrote: 'Lemkos descend from the Carpathians and the Ukrainians from Kievan Rus'.'

Respondent 45, a 29-year-old Greek Catholic from Wrocław province, cited more recent historical occurrences among his reasons:

> Different language, accent, folk costume, consciousness (only up until immediately after the First World War did Lemkos feel themselves to be Ukrainian), the Operation Vistula population resettlement (when viewed as an undeserved punishment resulting from the activities of the Ukrainian Partisan Army). As Ukrainians do not descend from Rusyns, they treat Rusyns as an inferior ethnic group.

Respondent 43, an unemployed 21-year-old of Greek Catholic background, noted that 'Lemkos have had much contact with Poles and Slovaks. None the less, they have tried to maintain their distinctiveness.' In this vein, several respondents referred to the role of Poland in accounting for any difference between Lemkos and Ukrainians. Respondent 25, a 44-year-old farmer from Nowy Sącz, wrote: 'Contemporary Lemko culture is closely tied in with Poland.'

In accounting for how Lemkos and Ukrainians differ, the comments of respondent 16, a 47-year-old Greek Catholic veterinarian, reveal the historical lack of group pride among Lemkos that, some Rusyns feel, propels troubled Lemkos into accepting a Ukrainian orientation:

> Ukrainians are a mighty nation, mistreated and stepped on by history (albeit themselves not wholly innocent in these matters). Lemkos are just an ethnic group – neglected, forgotten and superfluous.

Respondent 36, a 33-year-old Greek Catholic technician, attributed any difference between Lemkos and Ukrainians to inconsequential regional particularities: 'There are no real differences [between Lemkos and Ukrainians]. If there are, these would be similar to the types of differences found between Silesians, Kashubians and Poles.'

Respondent 4, a 60-year-old technician from Koszalin province, also sees no difference between Lemkos and Ukrainians, but attributes this not to inherent unity between the two, but to '... artificial domination of Lemkos by Ukrainians and Ukrainian nationalism. This is not in the best interest of Lemkos.'

These comments suggest that the matter of Lemko identity – whether Ukrainian or non-Ukrainian – is still very much undecided. How do respondents view the matter of Lemko identity relative to a Carpatho-Rusyn identity? Question 6 asked:

Is there any real difference between Lemkos and Rusyns?

Response	Percentage
a. Yes	6
b. No	82
c. No opinion	12

The overwhelming majority felt that the terms Lemko and Rusyn are synonyms for the same population, suggesting at first glance a high degree of unity among respondents. In fact, this apparent unity hides substantial divisions over respondents' understanding of the idea of what it means to be 'Rusyn'. Some of the respondents of the 82 per cent group regarded the term Rusyn in the above-mentioned historical sense – as an earlier historical name for the Ukrainian nationality. Others in the same group interpreted Rusyn as the name of a contemporary distinct Carpatho-Rusyn people, of which Lemkos are seen to be a part.

The two most succinct and representative statements of the Lemko Ukrainian ideological perspective were provided by respondents 5 and 19, both of whom argue that any Lemko and Rusyn distinctiveness resulted from the deliberate manipulation of Lemko identity by local powers. Respondent 19, a 46-year-old chemist from Legnica, wrote: 'The word 'Rusyn' was invented by Poles (and maybe the Czechs) ... it is a historical concept which incorporates the peoples of Eastern Europe: Russians, Belorusans, Ukrainians, and others.' Respondent 5, a 67-year-old Greek Catholic economist, continues:

> Up until the Second World War, Lemkos called themselves 'Rusnaks', or 'Rusyns'. The ethnonym Lemko was pushed on Lemkos by the Polish government after 1930 ...' in order to replace the ethnonyms 'Rusyn' and 'Rusnak'.

Other respondents offered a different explanation. Respondent 45, a 29-year-old Greek Catholic from Wrocław province, wrote that

> Lemkos themselves use the term 'Rusnak.' The term 'Rusin' only recently began to spread and is slowly being embraced by Lemkos. This is a result of the Ukrainians' strong push for the world (mainly Poland and Lemkos themselves) to recognise 'Rusnaks' as a Ukrainian ethnic group.

The respondents who interpreted Rusyn not as a historical term, but as a distinct modern nationality, answered by arguing that if there are differences between the terms 'Lemko' and 'Rusyn', this is due only to contemporary political boundaries which have divided Lemkos from their Rusyn cousins residing in Slovakia and Ukraine. Respondent 23, a 32-year-old Greek Catholic graduate student, wrote that

> There is a historical difference [between Lemkos and Rusyns]. Under their present circumstances living in separate countries, the external cultural forms and manner of speech have taken on a kind of distinctiveness. Nevertheless, the deeper cultural and psychological layers remain the same.

Respondent 21, a 45-year-old religion teacher in the Orthodox Church, likewise cited geopolitical differences, but 'spiritual' unity, between Lemkos and Rusyns:

> The mentality and spiritual culture are the same. There are minor differences in speech, stemming from 1918, when the border between the countries [Poland and former Czechoslovakia] was hermetically sealed, and from the pacification of the Lemko Rusyns.

Respondent 9, a 50-year-old retired school teacher from Nowy Sącz, wrote that Lemkos and Rusyns differ,

> but not substantially. These differences result from the fact that [Lemkos and Rusyns] live in different countries. Of course, they share the same White Croatian ancestors.

Likewise, respondent 39, a 27-year-old student of Orthodox background, looked at historical and present geopolitical circumstances as the source of only superficial differences between Lemkos and Rusyns:

> Lemkos were always separated from other Rusyns by the borders; the natural geographical centres of their [Lemko] culture were Przemyśl and Lviv.' The situation was better during Austro-Hungarian rule, when the border was porous. The twentieth century was a period of continuous isolation. Many differences arose, although the basic unity remained the same.

Question 7. Born out of the nineteenth- and twentieth-century ethno-national question, Lemko secular organisations have in their worst moments inspired indifference or distrust in the common folk. Secular organisations have often been perceived as vehicles for self-interested and ambitious individuals, or as promoters of political 'agendas' far removed from local, everyday life. The post-1989 resurgence of the

orientation question among Lemkos has again led to the establishment of
new Lemko organisations (mentioned above). What are Lemkos' current
attitudes towards these organisations? Question 7 asked:

*Are you a member of any Lemko community organisation? If so, which
one(s)? If not, why not?*

Response	*Percentage*
a. Not a member of any organisation	57
b. Member	43

Respondents' comments revealed the presence of a profound distrust of
Lemko community organisations and of the motivations of these organisations' leaders. Attitudes towards and participation in Lemko secular
organisations were strongly influenced by a respondent's own ethno-
national orientation or religious background. Respondent 26, a 35-year-
old teacher living in Nowy Sącz province, did not participate in any
Lemko organisation because

> every organisation now in existence limits membership according to its particular ideol-
> ogy, so that the Lemko Association is mainly Orthodox and Rusyn-oriented, and the
> Union of Lemkos is mainly Ukrainian Catholic and favours the Ukrainian orientation.

Respondent 29, a 31-year-old electrician who is a Pentecostal, likewise
sees reason to condemn a perceived selective membership policy among
Lemko organisations: 'Lemko organisations mobilise people according to
religious background – Orthodox or Greek Catholic. People of different
religious backgrounds are not accepted.'

A specifically Rusyn ideological perspective on Lemko organisations
comes from respondent 38, a 31-year-old Orthodox accountant:

> I don't trust the people who are members of those organisations. There are no real
> Lemkos in those organisations – only Ukrainians, who harass our village and constantly
> provoke our people.

Respondents' reactions were equally strong on the subject of the leaders
of Lemko organisations: 'Political opportunists', charged respondent 3, a
64-year-old Greek Catholic electrician; 'intolerant and short-sighted',
inveighed respondent 45, a 29-year-old Greek Catholic residing in
Wrocław province. Respondent 13, a 48-year-old teacher, observed
broadly that the leadership of Lemko organisations possesses the

'powers' formerly exercised by the leaders of Lemko organisations in the communist ' ... bad old days'.

Apart from mistrust of Lemko secular organisations, other reasons for non-participation in Lemko organisations included the fact that none were available in the vicinity of the respondent (28 per cent) or simple lack of interest (7 per cent). Respondent 46, a 25-year-old philologist from Gorzów province, wrote 'Where I went to school ... there was no Lemko organisation; I don't care to travel a long distance for a meeting just because it's a Lemko organistion.' Eighteen-year-old respondent 41, a high school pupil in Nowy Sącz province, wrote with youthful direct-ness: 'I can't find any reasonable [Lemko] organisation; they're all made up either of old fogies or praying bigots.' Ten per cent of respondents indicated that they simply had no time. Respondent 22, an Orthodox priest, indicated that his profession required neutrality, obliging him to refrain from joining any Lemko organisation.

Of those 44 per cent who did report participation in Lemko organisa-tions, the one most often named was the Lemko Association, followed by the Union of Lemkos, the Ruska Bursa and the Union of Ukrainians in Poland.

Conclusions

The survey results suggest the following about the present-day under-standing of what it means to be a Lemko in Poland:

(1) the minimal determinants of Lemko identity today are having Lemko parental heritage and an emotional attachment to one's Lemko family, heritage and homeland. The more 'concrete', material manifesta-tions of Lemko identity, such as language or religious faith, while also very important for maintaining Lemko identity, are not absolutely neces-sary.

This degree of tolerance suggests that Lemko identity has as a result of the post-war dislocations and associated loss of Lemko cultural inven-tory, been artificially separated from Lemkos' traditional material and spiritual culture. This is seen in the respondents' high degree of tolerance on the matters of who is a Lemko (Question 1) and the possibility of reverse assimilation (Question 2). With their churches destroyed, their customs and culture made irrelevant in a new, foreign environment, Lemkos for many years had only family and 'feelings' to define them-selves in their own minds and to one another. In this context, cultural tolerance becomes a necessary cultural survival strategy.

(2) The Lemko homeland still serves as a reservoir of past and present Lemko identity. Confronted by the harsh reality of resettlement, however, the way in which the homeland fulfils this function has of necessity changed. Short vacations to the Carpathians have become 'pilgrimages to Lemkovyna', during which the Lemko 'pilgrim' may reestablish contact with an almost lost ancestral past (Question 4).

(3) What it means to be Lemko in Poland is increasingly torn between the Ukrainian and Carpatho-Rusyn orientations. This is suggested by the fact that respondents, asked to define the terms 'Lemko', 'Rusyn' and 'Ukrainian', displayed a significant disagreement over the meaning of the key term 'Rusyn' (Questions 5 and 6). Some respondents saw it as a historical term for Ukrainian and hence regarded Lemkos as Ukrainian; others regarded the term as a name of a contemporary, distinct Carpatho-Rusyn people. This divergence of opinion is not based merely on ignorance or stereotype (many of the respondents are well educated), but on clear and well-developed world-views.

Inasmuch as a people's growing desire for their own distinct language might suggest the presence of a developing national consciousness, then a Carpatho-Rusyn consciousness has reasserted itself to some degree in the Lemko population. Respondents' comments exposed a strong conviction that Lemkos 'could' or 'should' have their own codified language, rather than simply adopting the Ukrainian language as their own (Question 3). The comments further suggest that the possibility of codifying a Lemko language is far from reality and faced with numerous obstacles, not least of which is division within the Lemko community itself.

(4) The stresses of the Ukrainian–Rusyn ethno-national identity question manifest themselves to detrimental effect in Lemko community life (Question 7). Lemko secular organisations were viewed by most respondents as divisive on both ideological (ethno-national) and sectarian grounds, causing more than half of the respondents to refrain from participation. However, the respondents' own prejudicial rejection of one organisation or another suggests that, while Lemko secular organisations to some degree perpetuate division within the community, they also reflect divisions which ultimately originate with Lemkos themselves.

Index

OPEN
Regionalism
and TRADE
Liberalization

The **Institute of Southeast Asian Studies (ISEAS)** was established as an autonomous organization in 1968. It is a regional research centre for scholars and other specialists concerned with modern Southeast Asia, particularly the many-faceted problems of stability and security, economic development, and political and social change.

The Institute's research programmes are the Regional Economic Studies Programme (RES), Regional Strategic and Political Studies Programme (RSPS), Regional Social and Cultural Studies Programme (RSCS), and the Indochina Programme (ICP).

The Institute is governed by a twenty-two-member Board of Trustees comprising nominees from the Singapore Government, the National University of Singapore, the various Chambers of Commerce, and professional and civic organizations. A ten-man Executive Committee oversees day-to-day operations; it is chaired by the Director, the Institute's chief academic and administrative officer.

The **ASEAN Economic Research Unit**, within the RES, is an integral part of the Institute, coming under the overall supervision of the Director, who is also the Chairperson of its Management Committee. The Unit was formed in 1979 in response to the need to deepen understanding of economic change and political developments in ASEAN. A Regional Advisory Committee, consisting of a senior economist from each of the ASEAN countries, guides the work of the Unit.

ISEAS Current Economic Affairs Series

OPEN
Regionalism
and
TRADE
Liberalization

An Asia-Pacific Contribution to the World Trade System

ROSS GARNAUT

INSTITUTE OF SOUTHEAST ASIAN STUDIES
Singapore
and
ALLEN & UNWIN
Sydney

First published in 1996 by
Institute of Southeast Asian Studies
Heng Mui Keng Terrace
Pasir Panjang Road
Singapore 119596
Internet e-mail: publish@iseas.ac.sg
World Wide Web: http://www.iseas.ss/pub.html

and

Allen & Unwin
9 Atchison Street
St Leonards NSW 2065
Australia
Phone: (61-2) 9901-4088
Fax: (61-2) 9906-2218
E-mail: frontdesk@allen-unwin.com.au
URL: http://www.allen-unwin.com.au
(for distribution in Australia and New Zealand)

**National Library of Australia
Cataloguing-in-Publication entry:**

Garnaut, Ross.
Open regionalism and trade liberalization: an Asia-Pacific contribution to the world trade system.

Bibliography.
ISBN 1 86448 395 4.

1. Free trade. 2. Asia - Commerce. 3. Pacific Area - Commerce. 4. Asia - Economic
integration. 5. Pacific Area - Economic integration. I. Title

382.71

Typeset in 11/15 pts ITC Century Book by Superskill Graphics Pte Ltd
Printed and bound in Singapore by Prime Packaging Industries Pte Ltd
10 9 8 7 6 5 4 3 2 1